Alvah Bradish

Memoir of Douglass Houghton

Alvah Bradish

Memoir of Douglass Houghton

ISBN/EAN: 9783337186456

Printed in Europe, USA, Canada, Australia, Japan

Cover: Foto ©ninafisch / pixelio.de

More available books at **www.hansebooks.com**

Original Portrait by Alva Bradish.

DOUGLASS HOUGHTON,
GEOLOGIST, LAKE SUPERIOR.

MEMOIR
—OF—
DOUGLASS HOUGHTON,

FIRST

STATE GEOLOGIST OF MICHIGAN.

WITH AN APPENDIX, CONTAINING REPORTS, OR ABSTRACTS OF THE FIRST GEOLOGICAL SURVEY, AND A CHRONOLOGICAL STATEMENT OF THE PROGRESS OF GEOLOGICAL EXPLORATION IN MICHIGAN,

BY

ALVAH BRADISH, A. M.,

CORRESPONDING MEMBER OF THE HISTORICAL SOCIETY, BUFFALO, N. Y.; CORRESPONDING MEMBER OF THE ALBANY SCIENTIFIC INSTITUTE; HONORARY MEMBER OF THE HISTORICAL SOCIETY OF WISCONSIN; ACADEMICIAN AND MEMBER OF COUNCIL OF THE CHICAGO ACADEMY OF DESIGN, BEFORE THE GREAT FIRE OF 1871, AND PROFESSOR OF THE FINE ARTS IN THE UNIVERSITY OF MICHIGAN, DURING THE PRESIDENCY OF HENRY P. TAPPAN.

"Wading the streams by day, tortured by swarms of mosquitos at night—often short of provisions, and often drenched by rain—were it not that courage is uplifted by the love of science, both for its own sake and the good it is to accomplish, the task of the pioneer explorer would be hard indeed."—*Houghton.*

"The life of a man of science belongs to his country and his age."—?

DETROIT:
RAYNOR & TAYLOR, PRINTERS AND BINDERS,
96, 98 and 100 Bates St.
1889.

gifted men who had been associated with him. It is due to the science that he loved and advanced, and not less to the citizens of Michigan, who watched his progress and stood by him, and who have instructed their Representatives at Lansing, to honor his memory and secure memorials of his person. It is due also to those younger citizens, who have known of Dr. Houghton only by vague reports, or by his name so familiar to their eyes on the map of the State, that his memory should not be a name only, but an heritage to be appreciated and enjoyed down to the latest generation.

I should have been well pleased if some one more competent than myself could have gathered these materials, arranged and traced his career from his earliest school-boy life, in a way to have explained his studies and labors and illustrated his character.

I cannot omit to mention in this connection, my obligation to Hon. Bela Hubbard, whose brief memoir of Dr. Houghton, published in the "*Journal of Science*," in 1847, and whose intimate personal acquaintance with its subject, have proved of valuable aid to me, in the preparation of this larger work.

In the meantime, materials and reminiscences, though still meagre, have been gathered, until by insensible degrees they have assumed an importance that would seem to justify this attempt to arrange them for publication, and to present to the public a connected narrative of his brilliant career.

The close intimacy of the author with Dr. Houghton—with his father, mother and brothers—would naturally furnish information that could be derived from no other sources.

I am also persuaded that a re-print of his Geological Reports, or a portion of them, will be deemed a welcome contribution to scientific literature—not alone from their intrinsic merits, but from their being to some extent a record of the labors of these earlier Geologists of the State. It should be remarked that these reports are now so entirely out of print, that it is doubtful if a complete copy can be found in the public libraries at Detroit, at Lansing, or at Ann Arbor.

In the Appendix will be found a summary of such reports as it is thought not advisable to include in full; also a general statement of the works that have been published since the death of Dr. Houghton, pertaining to the Geology of Michigan. It is believed that this portion of the volume will be especially acceptable to all intelligent readers who wish to be informed of what has been accomplished by the pioneers of the Geological Survey of the State.

The full-length portrait of Dr. Houghton—of which the frontispiece will give some idea—has awakened such a wide spread interest in the State, and the petitions for its purchase have been so numerous and urgent, that it is thought only just to his memory to include in the appendix, a few of these testimonials to the very great excellence of the memorial portrait, coming as they do from the highest authority in the State of Michigan.

After no little hesitation, it has seemed to me that I could not well ignore the suggestions and demands of a plain duty. What I have said must serve to interpret the motives and explain the appearance of this volume.

It may be stated that these Memoirs are intended for the *unscientific* as well as for the learned, and for all readers who can sympathize with the labors and achievements of the pioneer geologists of Michigan.

Experts in the natural sciences will no doubt find in this volume mistakes and short comings; but as the author had not been trained in any special school of science, he begs that his readers who have been more fortunate will exercise a liberal and magnanimous spirit towards these memorials of Douglass Houghton.

ALVAH BRADISH.

"If I have awakened any one here and there to think seriously of the complexity, the antiquity, the grandeur, the true poetry of the things around them—even the stones beneath the feet, if I shall have suggested to them the solemn thoughts that all these things, and they themselves still more are ordered by laws utterly independent of man's will about them, man's belief in them; if I shall at all have helped to open their eyes that they may see, and their ears that they may hear the great book that is free to all alike, to the peasant and peer; to men of business as to men of science, even that great book of nature, which, as Lord Bacon, says: 'of old the word of God revealed in facts,' then I shall have fresh reason for loving the science of geology, which has been my favorite study since I was a boy."

—*Rev. Charles Kingsley.*

"A physical fact is as sacred as a moral principle— Our own nature demands from us their double allegiance."

—*L. Agassiz.*

CONTENTS.

MEMOIR OF DOUGLASS HOUGHTON.

	PAGES.
CHAPTER I.	1–14

    Houghton Ancestry—Judge Houghton, 1—Parentage—Boyhood —Family, 8—Education, 10—Invitation to Detroit, 13.

CHAPTER II. - - - - - - - - - - 15–29

    Success in Detroit—Professional Career in Michigan, 15—Schoolcraft Expedition, 17—Scientific Pursuits, 19—Inception of a Natural History Survey of Michigan, 25—State Legislators and Geology—Diplomacy, 26.

CHAPTER III. - - - - - - - - - - 30–43

    Appointed State Geologist, 30—Plan of the Survey—Its Character and Results, 31—Annual Reports—Novel Conclusions, 33—Methods—Hardships—Incidents, 34—Suspension of State Survey, 39—Plan for Connecting the Geological with the Linear Surveys of the Public Domain—Its Acceptance, 40—Professorship in the University, 43.

CHAPTER IV. - - - - - - - - - - 44–75

    Honors, 44—Society—Personnel—Home and Family, 45—Popularity—Mayor of Detroit, 48—Anecdotes, 49—Materials for Final Report on the Geology, Topography and Natural History of the State, 51—Social Intercourse—The Detroit of that day—Anecdotes, 54—Association of Geologists, 60— The Storm on Lake Superior—Duty—Death, 64—The News at Detroit—Public Manifestations, 67—General Remarks, 69.

APPENDIX.

PART I. - - - - - - - - - - - 76–87

    Pen Portraits of some of the early friends of Dr. Houghton at Detroit—Gen. Lewis Cass, 77—Gov. Stevens T. Mason, 78—Gen. Sylvester Larned, 79—Dr. Zina Pitcher, 80—Henry N. Walker, 81—Henry R. Schoolcraft, 82—Col. Henry Whiting, U. S. A., 83—Charles C. Trowbridge, 84—Young Men's Literary Society, 85.

PART II. - - - - - - - - - - - 88–97

    Statements Regarding the Death of Dr. Houghton, 88—Letter of Hon. E. H. Thompson, 90—Statements of his two surviving Voyageurs, 92—Resolutions of Common Council of Detroit, 96—Cenotaph at Ann Arbor, 97.

PART III. - - - - - - - - - - - 98–112

    The Houghton Portrait, 98—The Proposed Monument, 99—Testimonials, 103—William A. Burt and his Solar Compass, 105—Discovery of Gold by Dr. Houghton—Recollections of Samuel W. Hill, 107—A Memorial Window, 108.

PART IV. - - - - - - - - - - - 113–132

    Letters of Dr. Houghton—To Hon. Augustus Porter, (1840), 113—To Richard Houghton, (Feb, 1832), 117—To same, (June, 1832). 118—To Hon Jacob Houghton, (Dec., 1834), 121—To same, (April, 1836), 125—To same, (Jan., 1841), 126—To same, (March, 1841), 128—To same, (Nov., 1841), 130.

APPENDIX. IX

PART V.—GENERAL SUMMARY AND SYNOPSIS OF THE WORK
DONE UNDER THE FIRST GEOLOGICAL SURVEY OF MICHIGAN, 133–286

First Organization, (1837), 134—*Re-organization and Report,—*
Official Corps, (1838), - - - - - - - 135

Second Annual Report, (1839), - - - - - - 136–140
Northern Portion of Lower Peninsula, 136—Change in
Elevation of the Waters of the Lakes, 137—*Documents*—
Report of A. Sager, Zoologist, 138—Report of John Wright,
Botanist, 139—Report of S. W. Higgins, Topographer, 139
Reports of C. C. Douglass and Bela Hubbard, Assistant
Geologists, 140.

Third Annual Report, (1840), - - - - - - 141–153
Southern Slope of Upper Peninsula—Suspension of
Departments of Zoology and Botany, 142—*Documents*—
Report of Topographer, 142–152—Procuring Copies of
Patents—Progress of Maps of the Counties, 143—Roads and
Highways—Chicago Turnpike or Trail, 143—Natural Woods
of Michigan, 145—Variation of the Magnetic Needle, 147
—Decrease in Elevation of the Waters of the Lakes, 152—
Report of C. C. Douglass—Details of the Coal-bearing Rocks
—Report of B. Hubbard—Southern Range of Counties—
Ancient Lake Ridge, 153.

Report of State Geologist relative to the Salt Springs, (Jan., 1840) 155

Fourth Annual Report, (Jan., 1841), - - - - - 156–278
General Description and Features of the Upper Peninsula,
157—General Geology of the same, 165—Section, Order of
Superposition of the Rocks of the Upper Peninsula, 173—
Primary Rocks, 173—Trap Rocks, 176—Metamorphic
Rocks, 182—Conglomerate Rock, 184—Mixed Conglomerate
and Sand Rock, 186—Red Sandstone and Shales, 188—
Upper or Gray Sandrock, 192—Tertiary Clay and Sands, 193
—Mineral and Mineral Veins, 196—Progress and Condition
of the Survey, 229—*Documents,* Report of Frederick Hub-
bard, Special Assistant, (1840),— Variations, Latitudes,
Survey of Harbors, - - - - - - - - 230

APPENDIX.

Fourth Annual Report, (Jan., 1841)—Continued.

Report of C. C. Douglass, (1841)—General Character and Geology of Northern part of Lower Peninsula, - - 231

Report of B. Hubbard, (1841), with Geological Section, - 233-260 General Geology of the Organized Counties of Michigan —Rocks of Michigan South of Saginaw Bay, 234—Diluvial or Erratic Group, 235—Ancient and Recent Alluvions, 240 —Tertiary Clays, 242—Coal Measures, 244—Section of Coal Basin of Michigan, 249—Slates and Flags of Lake Huron, 251—Section of Rocks Below the Coal Basin, 255—Dip of Rocks, 256—Diagram of Strata passed through at the Salt Well, Grand Rapids, 257—Summary of the Results of the Survey in Lower Peninsula, 260.

Report of S. W. Higgins, Topographer, (1841), - - - 265-278 Magnetic variation in Michigan, 265—The Magnetic Meridian traced, 269—Burt's Solar Compass, 272—Elevation and Depression of the Waters in the Great Lakes, 274—Table of same compared with June 1819, 278.

Report of the Geologist relative to the *State Salt Springs*, (Jan., 1842), - - - - - - - - - 279

Fifth Annual Report of State Geologist, (Jan., 1842)—Limits of the Copper and Lead Districts—Condition and Wants of the Department, - - - - - - - - 280-282

Report of the Condition of the Work at the *State Salt Springs*, (Jan., 1843), - - - - - - - - 282

Sixth Annual Report of State Geologist, (Feb., 1843)—Progress towards Completion—Publication of the State and County Maps, - - - - - - - - - 283-284

Seventh Annual Report of the Geologist, (Feb., 1884), - - 285-287 Arranging of Materials for the Final Report—Completion of Maps—Figuring and Engraving of Sections, Fossils, etc., 285—Opportunity for Perfecting the Work in the Upper Peninsula through the U. S. Linear Surveys, 286.

Remarks of Judge Campbell relative to the materials amassed by Dr. Houghton, for his Final Report, - - - - 287

APPENDIX. XI

PART VI.—SUMMARY OF GEOLOGICAL EXPLORATIONS IN MICHIGAN, SINCE THE DEATH OF DR. HOUGHTON, - - - 289–298

Pamphlet, with Map of the Mineral Region of Lake Superior, by Jacob Houghton, Jr., and T. W. Bristol, (1847), - · 289

Reports by Wm. A. Burt and Bela Hubbard, from the field notes of Dr. Houghton, on the portions of the South Shore of Lake Superior being surveyed by him at the time of his death, - - - - - - - - - - 290–292

General Geology and Topography of the coast from Chocolate to Carp Rivers, 291—The Granite and Metamorphic Rocks—Argillaceous and Micaceous Oxides of Iron—First published accounts of the Iron Ore beds of Michigan, 291—General character of the Keweenaw Point district—The new system of Dr. Houghton for uniting Geological with the Linear Surveys, 292.

Second pamphlet (July, 1846) by Jacob Houghton, Jr. - 293

Joint Resolution of the Legislature of Michigan, relative to the Notes, Specimens, Maps, Engravings, etc., made and preserved for the State by Dr. Houghton, and in reference to the completion of his Final Report, - - - - 293

Act of Legislature of Michigan, approved Feb., 1859, "To finish the Geological Survey of the State," - - - 294

Appointment of Prof. Alex'r Winchell State Geologist—His first Biennial Report, (Dec., 1860), - - - - - 294–295

Observations on the Geology, Zoology and Botany of the Lower Peninsula—Refers to Act of Congress of 1847, for the Geological Exploration of the Lake Superior district, and Appointment of Dr. C. T. Jackson, 294—Continuance of the Survey by Foster and Whitney, U. S. Geologists, - - - - - - - - - 295

Their Report on "The Copper Lands," (1850), and on "The Iron Region," (1851)—Including Reports on the Fossils, by Prof. James Hall, and on the Zoology of Wisconsin, by Dr. Lapham and Charles Whittlesey, with observations by the latter on the fluctuation of the Lake Surfaces, 295.

Commission to B. Hubbard, in 1846, to report upon the Geology of the districts on Lake Superior being subdivided by the U. S. Linear Surveyors, - - - - - 296

PART VI.—Continued.

Inauguration of new State Geological Survey, by Act of March, 1869—Establishing a "Geological Board,"   -   - 296-298

Vols. 1 and 2 published with Atlas, 1873 (Upper Peninsula) by T. B. Brooks, R. Pompelly and Dr. Rominger, 297—Vol. 3 published, 1876, with Geological Maps, (Lower Peninsula) —Vol. 4, 1881, Iron Region, (Upper Peninsula), by C. Rominger, 298.

Lecture by Prof. Bradish—"Biographical Sketch of Dr. Houghton"—Correspondence (1867),   -   -   -   298

Description of the Full Length Portrait of Dr. Houghton, (Engraved in Frontispiece),   -   -   -   -   -   -   300

MEMOIR OF DR. DOUGLASS HOUGHTON.

CHAPTER I.

PARENTAGE—BOYHOOD—EDUCATION—CALL TO DETROIT.

THE American branch of the Houghton family was settled in the town of Bolton, Mass., near Boston. The ancestors of Jacob Houghton, the father of the subject of this memoir, came over from England about the year 1658. Bolton, Lancaster, in England, has been the home of this family from the time of the conquest. The name was spelled De'Houton; it was a Norman race. The old castle or tower of Houton, a plain venerable structure, still stands, and has been until recently, occupied by the present representative of the family.

Mr. Houghton, of Fredonia, was a lawyer by profession; a gentleman of culture and acquainted with books. He had kept up some correspondence with his namesake in England, and he would very naturally feel some interest in the records and traditions of his early ancestors. If he felt some pride in keeping alive this sentiment, it was at least without ostentation; for this pride—if we must give it a name of reputable connections—was never obtruded on others. With him it was an amiable sentiment, not a passion, and it would be a misapprehension of his character to suppose he entertained any special reverence for titles unless they were deserved, and had been won by great and heroic deeds. This feeling of reverence for olden times and old country ways, was, however, a deep sentiment, though in no way offensive. In all his intercourse with neighbors, socially and in business, of all men that I have ever known, Judge Houghton was the most free from all assumption or arrogance; the most frank, guileless and even childlike. He was a great favorite with young people; the girls delighted to have him as an escort or a companion. The children loved him. Mr. Houghton was thoughtful for the welfare of his neighbors; very tender and delicate in bestowing favors on his friends and on the needy. His reverence for woman was great; it had the flavor of the old days of chivalry, without its extravagance. It was deep, pure and artless. In money matters he was too liberal, and he gave friends his time and his counsel. His memory was singularly retentive, and he would entertain with anecdotes and narratives. The hospitalities of his house were cordial and without stint; and it would be only the want of ample means that should prevent him from following more closely the example of some of the old titled barons of the Houghton family in England. For some years Mr. Houghton had kept up some correspondence with the head of the family in England; Sir Henry had sent him his portrait, and this has long hung in the parlor of the old Houghton mansion in Fredonia. It is a cabinet sized, engraved, half-length, seated portrait. The countenance is one of much benevolence,—a type of the independent country gentleman of England, not unaccustomed to fox hunting in his younger days, a staunch lover of king and church, not over abstemious of wine, and not unacquainted with touches of the gout.

A few years since there had been a rumor widely spread through New England and other States, that a large fortune had been left in some way to the American branch of this family, now only waiting for the claimants to come forward and receive their own. A meeting of relatives was held in Boston to take the necessary measures to secure this treasure. They organized for this purpose, and raised funds to meet expenses. A Mr. Rice, a young lawyer, had married a Houghton, and he was deputized to carry out the wishes of the society. It was soon discovered that Judge Jacob Houghton, of Fredonia, New York, was the only one of this name who was acquainted with the older branch in England, and must be considered very naturally as the head of the family in this country. Mr. Rice, the young attorney, made a visit to Fredonia, full of this promising enterprise,—but Judge Houghton placed little confidence in the existence of any such fund in England. He was too good a lawyer to be carried away with any such plausible rumor. He declined to subscribe to the association, but he gave Mr. Rice a cordial letter of introduction to the head of the house in England—now the present Sir Henry Bold Houghton, and member of parliament. This secured to Mr. Rice a courteous reception, though it is not to be presumed that he revealed the object of his visit. But after examining the records carefully in London, he satisfied himself that no such fortune could be found. In the meantime, during his stay, he accepted the hospitalities extended to him by the member of parliament, to whom his letter was addressed. The reader will readily recall similar rumors as to other American families of English origin, who it had been supposed would be made rich by these long unclaimed fortunes. A pleasing result of this Houghton organization and Mr. Rice's mission—especially pleasing to the Fredonia branch of the family—was a superb gold snuff box sent through Mr. Rice to Judge Houghton, as a gift from his relative and namesake, Sir Henry Bold Houghton. The old fable of the division of the oyster among disputants, and its shell, came as a natural suggestion, perhaps, to the members of the association; but no one, bearing the name of Houghton in America, would doubt for a moment that the precious memorial gift had gone into the right hands.

Judge Houghton had married early in life a lady of New London, Connecticut,—a Miss Mary Lydia Douglass—who survived her husband eight years and died at the old residence in Fredonia, in 1875, at the great age of ninety-two, retaining her faculties to the last moment of life. Her parents lived in New London during the war of the revolution, and she remembered well the burning of the city by Benedict Arnold, then in command of an English marauding flotilla, when she, with father and mother, fled into the country for safety.

This Jacob Houghton, came to Fredonia, New York, in 1812. He came with his young family when Chautauqua county embraced a large extent of country, and all that region was a wilderness. The journey from Troy to this remote region was performed by horse teams, a distance of about four hundred miles, and Rochester, a small village, was the frontier town, still in the wilderness looking west from the Hudson. His family were several weeks on their journey before they reached their destination—a long tedious journey, not free from peril and suffering. But these hardships were encountered with resolution and a firm purpose. They were young, not easily discouraged; virtually, it was the beginning of a new life with them, and they were animated with a noble passion for securing a home in the new region of the west for themselves and their children.

They would be surrounded by almost an unbroken wilderness; it would be a long period before they could be reached by the comforts and amenities of eastern life. Mr. Houghton had been a student at law and was already admitted to practice at the bar. He immediately opened his office in Fredonia, a rude structure no doubt. It was in the midst of the woods; noble chestnut and oak trees, maple and white-wood, surrounded him on all sides. The village as yet did not exist, save a few rude cottages. But the services of a lawyer were soon in demand, and it was not long ere his practice became extensive; and he was able, very early, to begin building a home for his family. This was a two-story frame house, with ample room for his growing family, his library and his law office. It was no doubt the best and most imposing private residence that had been built west of Rochester. From time to time through these early years Mr. Houghton had been solicited to occupy such offices as were in the gift of his fellow citizens. He was appointed one of the judges of the county; was elected justice of the peace, and was at one time postmaster. But in truth he had no love for the trammels of office, and would shrink from all those usual arts of the politician to secure favor. He loved his independence, nor could he afford to sacrifice his law business for the small compensation and loss of time incident to holding office in a small village still in the woods, and in a county hardly organized. Very early he was admitted to practice in the higher courts of the State. In subsequent years many of the leading lawyers of that part of the State, became students in the office of Judge Houghton. Among those will be remembered the names of Chauncy Tucker, Hanson Risley, Cutler, Brown, Hazelton, and James Mullet; and others well known, and some eminent members of the bar, of western New York.

Mr. Houghton's reputation for ability in his profession, for scrupulous attention to the interests of clients, for sound advice and probity of conduct was not excelled by any man, either in the profession of the law or in any other calling. These qualities gave him a large practice, which might, or might not lead to fortune. Judge Houghton was of a companionable temper; he would never deny himself to those who needed help. His yielding nature sympathized with the hardships of new settlers and laborers, who were making homes in the wilderness around him. These sought his counsel and his aid. If his law practice was large, his good nature and benevolence kept pace with his business, and often went in advance.

If a new country like that now being settled in Chautauqua county offered great opportunities for shrewd men to accumulate property, as it undoubtedly did, so the deprivation to which the poor are exposed is a perpetual appeal to the better feelings of the kind and benevolent spirits who are able to give their assistance. Both Judge Houghton and his wife were widely known for unobtrusive charities, for thoughtful care of the sick and poor, far and near. But it must be admitted that this spirit was not the spirit of money making. Such a talent Jacob Houghton did not possess. He had, to be sure, all the application and the ability that might be essential to success, but while his professional business was large, this show of success would be rather seen on his ledger than on his bank account; for it was too true if the debt of a client was on his books for one hundred dollars, and the client in the meantime should be in need, Judge Houghton would lend him fifty dollars and forgive him the balance!

Mr. Houghton was a great lover of books; his reading had been extensive, especially in English and early American history. His library was well supplied with such works, and it was rare that a day would pass without a reference to this storehouse of ideas. This love for solid reading was imbibed by his children; and this passion for learning, thus early inculcated has been a marked trait through life of all members of his family. These circumstances and conditions of the family of Houghton, have been, perhaps, rather unduly dwelt on; but it seemed rather called for to enable us to realize the influences that surrounded the childhood and earliest days of Douglass Houghton, the subject of this memoir. The development of young Douglass's mental powers and his studies was greatly influenced by the character of his parents, as well as by the peculiar circumstances of place and opportunity. It should be observed that Mrs. Houghton not only sympathized warmly in the studies and advancement of her children, but like other noble mothers was ready at all times to make every sacrifice that would be necessary to their education.

The family now was a large one,—five sons and two daughters. The highest ambition of the father was a thorough education for his children. It is true, this desire for culture, would, no doubt, interfere somewhat with that early discipline and initiation into business of a more practical kind—farming or trade—that a new, wild country would seem to demand. Even the limited means of the family would seem rather to suggest some trade or pursuit that would bring quick returns. In fact, it is usually difficult to restrain boys from entering on a career of business long before they have mastered even the rudiments of education.

But the Houghton boys sympathized with the ambition of their parents, and their studies began very early in life. It may be said the first passion of these brothers was for distinction in scholarship. Alured, the eldest, pursued his studies at the new college at Meadville, Penn., then just opened for the reception of students. His collegiate course was completed at Geneva, New York.

Mr. Horace Webster, Prof. of mathematics at Geneva, has said to the writer that Alured Houghton was an accomplished scholar, already deeply read in the classics, and that his future eminence was certain if he had lived. At this date, Alured Houghton, the oldest of the family, as will be seen by the following letters, was at college, Meadville, Pa. He was eleven years old, and his younger brother Douglass, the subject of our memoir, was nine years old. We insert these few letters to show to the curious reader the spirit that prevailed among the members of the Houghton family—it is not often that boys are studying Latin and Greek at college at the age of eleven years, or that they write letters in these languages to brothers of nine years. Douglass Houghton was born September 21, 1809; he was the fourth child born to his parents; he was feeble in body and diminutive in size. His mother has said she had fears that she could not raise him. But his intellect was sound and bright, quick in apprehension, of a joyous nature, sympathetic and sensitive. As he grew to boyhood his strength and health were assured; he was no recluse or dreamer in boyhood. He mixed readily and heartily with those of his age, and was distinguished for bold enterprise among his companions at the age of six years. But for close intimacy he was singularly fastidious; not every boy that trained with him would secure his confidence. He seemed to have at this early period that instinctive estimate of character that ever distinguished him through life. His figure, even for a boy, was small, but it was instinct with nerve and activity. In temper he was quick and resolute, a little obstinate, perhaps; his decisions were prompt, like those of a commander, and his boyish plans were matured without much consulting others. In 1824 the Fredonia Academy was organized and established. Douglass, with his younger brother Richard, were among its earlier pupils. He had now at home for his companions his two sisters Lydia and Sarah, and his brothers Alexander and Richard. Jacob, the youngest of the family, was not old enough to join in these studies. Alured, the eldest, had completed his studies at Geneva College and had been called to Baton Rouge, Louisiana, to take charge of an academy which had been recently opened there. Soon after his arrival there he was taken sick and fell a victim to the fever that prevailed. The death of this son who had been admirably educated, and whose life with every bright prospect, had, as it were just commenced—that is the life of manhood—was a severe blow to his parents, a profound sorrow to all members of his family.

After the lapse of so many years, we must not expect to recover many traits or incidents of the early boyhood career of Douglass Houghton. All his faculties were developed early; in the midst of play he was a student, not always, perhaps, according to academy rules; no doubt he often vexed his teachers. In truth the traditions of the old Academy at Fredonia tell us of sundry pranks and exploits not laid down in the list of allowable pastimes. Sometimes it would be a pumpkin mask, lit up with a candle to frighten obnoxious students; again he would be leading his trained company of boys around the academy walls, uttering groans to disturb the school or to express disapproval of the master's discipline. Such outbursts of temper are not very serious and they do not last. They come less from any vicious traits of character than from the buoyant outflow of spirits and that irrepressible disposition of the young to do something heroic. Douglass had ways of his own to master his lessons and gain time for other studies not connected with the academy course. The eldest brother, as has been mentioned, was at college at an age that might appear premature, as he was already a good Latin and Greek scholar. Alexander had mastered his Latin and Greek and had shown all through life a strong taste for classical literature. Richard had a gentle and amiable nature, beloved of his sisters with more than usual affection, was strongly inclined to scholarship. Soon after Douglass settled in Detroit Richard commenced his studies as a medical student in his office. But during the season of the cholera of

1834, Richard, who was of a delicate constitution, fell a victim to its ravages.

Douglass, not behindhand in the usual studies of the new academy, and sufficiently skilled in Latin, showed a strong bent towards the natural sciences. It will soon be seen how strong was this tendency of his mind, and how admirably fitted he was to grapple with these subjects and to master them.

The Houghton homestead that had been built or finished in 1813, continued to be the home of this family; it was in fact a home and school house, the academy and college, for these brothers and sisters. They were indeed more than usually united by natural affections, by a community of studies and by a profound love of parents and home. An orchard, still in bearing, (1888) was planted early; it extends some rods on the slope back of the house and embraces two or three acres. A row of noble locust trees extends along the whole front of the premises for four or five hundred feet. These were brought from Mayville, as slender cuttings that Judge Houghton secured within the leg of his boot, traversing the woods on horseback. The Houghton house occupies the highest ground in the vicinity of Fredonia, overlooking the beautiful village embosomed among trees. At the west and north the eye takes in a stretch of farm land that slopes gently to lake Erie; the lake itself is seen through copse and over groups of the elm and sycamore. The Canadaway stream of considerable volume traverses the village. From the house it is seen at the foot of the hill; its beautiful and rapid waters sparkle as they find their way between high banks and through open glades to the lake, two miles distant, while on the south the hills of Chautauqua, rising into elevations of from six to eight hundred feet, yield the scenery that is often bold and always picturesque; and these trending to the west, skirting the lake shore, offer to the eye a noble range, softened by the haze or purple of distance, and diversified by cultivated farms, by orchards and vineyards, by embossed dells, by groves and by virgin forests.

A few rods from the house, just back of the orchard where the ground slopes suddenly, the boys had excavated a room or cellar in the bank, and this, with a roof extending over the doorway and covered with turf, gave the Houghton boys a study large enough to admit three or four persons. This primitive school room was devoted exclusively to hard study; no play, no cards or amusement of any kind were permitted here. It was a sort of close-communion troglodyte college. It was here that these earnest students would retreat to master all their severe studies without interruption; it was here, as much as in the academy, that they perfected that self discipline which prepared them for their after career in life. None of the boys of the village, rarely even their companions in school, were ever admitted here, none but the two sisters, whose studies received the aid that loving brothers could give. It may be considered by some that such slight incidents as these should hardly be deemed important, but it must be remembered how much these earlier habits enable us to see the influences that strengthen character and give the assurance of success in life's struggles. The writer of this memoir remembers well visiting this rustic study of the Houghton boys as early as 1838. It was then somewhat dilapidated, but still sufficiently intact to admit a visitor and to show him the seats and crude shelves that were wont to accommodate these youthful Greeks. Since that period the scythe and plow, time and the elements, have levelled the slope and obliterated all traces of this rustic sanctum of Douglass Houghton.

At a very youthful period Douglass had been recommended as a candidate to the Van Renssaeler scientific school at Troy, New York. This polytechnic school was founded by the Patroon Van Renssaeler, and at this time was under the charge of Prof. Eaton, so well known as a distinguished educator. Here Douglass graduated and received his diploma of Bachelor of Arts, in 1828. Within a few months after this well earned honor he accepted the appointment of assistant professor in the branches of chemistry and natural history in this same institution, conferred on him by Prof. Eaton. At this time he was nineteen years old. In 1830 some friends of science in Detroit, including such men as Gen. Cass, then Governor of the Territory of Michigan, Maj. John Biddle, Col. Henry Whiting, E. P. Hastings, Shubal Conant, Rev. Dr. Berry, and others, applied to Prof. Eaton to recommend to them a person to deliver a course of public lectures on the sciences of chemistry, botany and geology. The Hon. Lucius Lyon, then a delegate in Congress from the Territory of Michigan, on his return from Washington, called on Prof. Eaton at Troy, as the leading scientific educator in this country, to make the proper inquiries; for it should be remembered that lecturers were not so easily found then as at present, nor was it an easy or inexpensive experiment to traverse new states by stage for this purpose. Prof. Eaton listened to Mr. Lyon's request, then arose, opened the door of the little labratory adjoining, and calling him by his familiar name of Douglass, introduced the young philosopher to the member of congress;—for he was but a boy in appearance, as indeed almost so in age. Mr. Lyon, a gentleman reserved in manner and of much dignity, was not a little surprised at such a presentation. He could hardly believe Prof. Eaton to be in earnest. Could he propose to send a mere pupil, a boy student, still in his teens, to discourse on subjects of science, and to address men of mature culture, conversant with the great outlines of the natural sciences, for such as these he would certainly encounter in Detroit!

But Mr. Lyon was soon convinced that young Houghton was competent to fill such a mission; nor did the youthful professor hesitate for a moment. Prof. Eaton had implicit confidence in his ability to acquit himself with credit and honor, and while retaining his professorship in the Van Renssaeler institute, at the special request of his friend, he gathered up his simple apparatus to serve for illustration and experiment, visited his parents for a few days at Fredonia, then departed by stage and boat for that small but ancient settlement on the Detroit river—that future city of the straits and beautiful metropolis of a great and wealthy State. At that time it was known only as an old French town, a border military post touching the Indian country. Houghton brought letters to several prominent citizens, and warmed by the prospect of success, confident in his knowledge and capacity, with these lectures and thus invited, commenced the career of Douglass Houghton in the State of his adoption.

CHAPTER II.

Success in Detroit — Schoolcraft Expedition — Scientific Studies — Scheme for Natural History Survey of Michigan.

Douglass Houghton's subsequent advancement to positions of trust, honor and responsibility was a matter of pride to the citizens of Detroit, for they had assurance that every office he should occupy would be raised and honored by his genius and integrity. Even before leaving Fredonia for the institute at Troy, before he was seventeen years old, he had found the time to study medicine under the direction of his father's friend, Dr. White, and was admitted to practice by the medical society of Chautauqua county, in the spring of 1831.

No man who has ever entered into business or in a professional career in the State of Michigan so speedily won to himself such a body of able, enthusiastic friends as Douglass Houghton. These friends were not confined to the city of Detroit, where the charm of a daily intercourse might to some extent account for this popularity; they could be counted by scores all through the State. Even now, after a lapse of more than forty years since his death, his memory is cherished with enthusiasm, mingled with a tenderness that can only be explained by those who were intimate with the man. A stranger looking over the map of Michigan will observe that a township, a county, a lake, a city, each bears the name of Houghton; one of the union free schools of Detroit carries this name, and his labors and gifts at Ann Arbor make it certain that the honored name of Houghton will long be cherished at the seat of the University.

It seems due the memory of such a man that we inquire into the cause and origin of these unusual honors and homage bestowed on one so young, at first without friends and without money. The leading men of Michigan now were boys, or were unborn, when the name of Houghton was the most familiar name spoken in all her borders. The generation that knew Douglass Houghton is rapidly passing away, but his name should not pass out of the memory of men. Houghton's life was a brief one, but it was full of purpose and activity, of energy and achievement. We will try to gather the records of his labors, his intercourse with public men, his explorations and discoveries; and these will reveal to us the secret of his power and will illustrate the rare traits of his character.

When he landed in Detroit his resources were but slight; but he had courage, and that indomitable energy which insures success. He was struggling, indeed, to earn the means to carry on his studies and lectures. He was not yet twenty years old, a total stranger save through the letters that made him known. To be sure, he had money left in his wallet—it was just one dime! He commenced his lectures in the old Council House on Jefferson avenue. His enthusiasm, the thorough knowledge of his subject, the precision of his thoughts, the artless manner of the young scientist, carried his audience with him, and soon rendered larger rooms neccessary. His talents secured the confidence of the leading men of the city and brought friends. These friends stood by him; his success as a lecturer was assured. And though impediments might for a moment discourage him, they were but slight, for he speedily triumphed over all. These new scenes, the friends he made, these lectures, the crowd that pressed in to secure seats, are all modestly related in filial letters to his parents. It was only a few months after his arrival in Detroit that he received the appointment of surgeon and botanist to the expedition for the discovery of the sources of the Mississippi, organized under the direction of Henry R. Schoolcraft, whose distinguished career was then just opening, and whose subsequent labors have conferred honor on his country. The Hon. Bela Hubbard, so well known in this state, and long attached to the Geological Survey of Michigan, as Assistant Geologist, says that "Houghton's report on the botany of that then remote and unexplored region displayed not only an extensive acquaintance with that science, but his researches did much to extend our knowledge of the flora of the Northwest." When we consider that at this time he had hardly reached his majority, it is impossible to withhold our admiration of that firmness of temper and that vigor of genius that enabled him to achieve success so early. From 1832 to 1836 he practiced as physician and surgeon in Detroit; he united also the skill of a dentist, in which he was considered an adept. But in the midst of an extensive practice he never relaxed his studies in natural science.

(2)

It is to the credit of the citizens of Detroit, and should be remembered, that Dr. Houghton was not only welcomed with confidence and with open hearts, but he was warmly and efficiently sustained. The friends he made then he never lost, and these were among the best men of the state, and not a few of historical interest. Here were Governor Cass, Dr. Zina Pitcher, Lucius Lyon, Judge Campbell, father of the present Chief Justice, C. C. Trowbridge, Dr. Rice, the two Hubbards—Henry and Bela—Chancellor Farnsworth, Henry S. Cole, Edmund Brush, Col. Whiting, John Owen, and a little later Stephens T. Mason, the youthful and gifted Governor of the State. These, with many others, were warm, stable friends of young Houghton.

It was in the summer of 1834 that the writer of this memoir first formed his acquaintance. During that season, when the cholera visited Detroit with such fearful and fatal results, no one could be more devoted or make greater sacrifices to solace the sick and dying than young Houghton; and it is known that in the perilous exercise of his profession, in the midst of suffering and panic, amid the appalling progress of a mysterious and terrific scourge, he stood firm and self-possessed. Much of these labors would be gratuitous. He hastened to the bedside of the poor and deserted, as well as to the rich, and like others of his profession thought only of duty and humanity. If not always in money, the reward would come, the most acceptable to a true physician, the grateful remembrance of those who had recovered under his faithful attendance.

There are certain tendencies to special pursuits, which if we could always trace to their origin, would explain why one man has devoted his life to law, another to theology, one to science and one to art. In some families this diversity of pursuit is as great as though there had been no common influences acting at once on all members of the same family. No doubt the cause of this diversity of development would be found if we were able to carry our investigations far back into the first impressions of childhood. While the boy Houghton was a student in the Fredonia academy from its foundation, yet long before his serious studies here, the common school had offered its advantages; and his mind had received the loving discipline of a home culture. A few hours of the day served for the mastery of his lesson, the balance might find him boating down the Canadaway Creek, or setting traps for the muskrat; or while threading streams on fishing excursions, or hunting in the neighboring woods for the black squirrel, his taste for natural science would be nourished. Every bird he shot, every chipmunk he brought down from its hiding place, the spotted trout from the hill streams, the wild flowers, the stately tulip trees with their imperial blossoms, the rocks that cropped out from the sides of gorges—each and all of these were his teachers. They offered lessons pregnant with meaning to a mind so quick, so curious and so independent.

After he entered the academy he showed some aversion to classical studies—especially to Latin, and perhaps in a less degree, to arithmetic. We can see causes for this, and may remember what new and improved methods attract and beguile the reluctant student in these unsavory studies. An eminent English author, himself an Oxford man, has said "That any one who has passed through the regular graduation of a classical education and is not made a fool of by it, may consider himself as having had a very narrow escape;" while on the contrary, Sir Walter Scott has remarked, that he would have given half his fame could he have been well grounded in the Latin language! We must not give too much weight to the opinions of those who feel that they have lost time in classical studies. The knowledge they bring is very precious. We would sympathize more cordially with McCauley's words, expressing his disgust and horror of mathematics. Douglass's father never relaxed his interest in the thorough education of his children. His reverence for scholarship was great; he was indulgent in most matters affecting his boys, but he desired them to be faithful and earnest in all their studies in the academy. But indeed, Douglass seemed to have lost his interest in the study of Latin, which gave his father much uneasiness. A friend of the family, Dr. Walworth, a gentleman of liberal education, advised Mr. Houghton to have his son drop these classical studies for the present, and to allow Douglass to pursue botany and other kindred sciences, to which he seemed strongly inclined. This judicious advice was accepted, and no doubt the after career of young Houghton was shaped in no inconsiderable degree by these well timed and friendly suggestions. With his ardent temperament, he will be found within a few brief years, ready to aid in every liberal enterprise that appeals to him in the growing city of his adoption. He had quick sympathies and a clear judgment. The Young Men's Literary Society of Detroit, was organized in 1832; he was elected its first vice-president. He would be among the active teachers of the Sunday school of the church in which he was nurtured.

But as it has been seen, long before he came to Detroit, before he had been appointed assistant professor in the institute at Troy, while yet in Fredonia, his mind had been strongly bent toward the natural sciences. A remarkable phenomonen near the homestead awakened his inquisitive spirit. Even at the age of ten years, he was attracted by the presence of a gas observed to rise spontaneously in the bed of the Canadaway Creek; older men, of course, were not ignorant of this;—long before the white man had penetrated these forests, the Indians had noticed its presence. But the boy Houghton began to investigate it. Mr. Hanson Risley informs the writer that he remembers Douglass Houghton gathering the light fluid in a bottle, and afterwards setting fire to it,—and Mrs. Risley recalled, when a girl at school, being alarmed one day by the rumor that Douglass, in some wanton freak, threatened to burn up the Canadaway stream, and she and her companions hastened to get out of the way!

His mother, living to the great age of ninety-two, has told the writer, that Douglass, one day, brought up to the house some gas in his hat, and there lit it in her presence to convince her that it was a burning fluid. He thus commenced his philosophical investigations while a student; almost a school boy and before he entered the academy. Even at this early day he was looking into the mystery of the things about him. In the boy we see the man. His mind would be analytic; too bold and active to feel at ease in the pursuit of classical studies. Even mathematics would have but a partial hold on him, except as they might promote the more practical investigations of science. He was the observer of nature thus early and throughout his brief life. Not so much the artist, who studies the harmonies of color, and the significance of form and expression, as the naturalist or chemist, who seeing changes going on in nature, is compelled to investigate the causes of such changes, or the means by which they may be reproduced. His younger brother, Richard, constructed an orrery to aid the classes in astronomy, and this was long used in the academy. Douglass, in the meantime, grappled with the subject of electricity, and the garret of the old Houghton house may still offer evidences of these labors in the form of sundry jars, glass tubes and circles, by which the young philosopher tried his hand at these nice manipulations. He repeated the experiment of the Italian savant on a frog, with success. The family dog, old Prince, so called, was often aroused from his day's slumber by an electric spark cautiously applied to his nose. It must have been as early as 1825 or 1826, when Douglass engaged in the enterprise of making an explosive powder, for we still have to notice his active energies before leaving Fredonia for Troy.

A young man, a school companion, by the name of Wm. Hart, discovered, jointly with Houghton perhaps, a method of making a coarse grained powder, to be used on the panlock of the gun—the cap had not then been invented. Hart would need a chemist and a knowledge of detail, which he did not possess himself. These boys entered into a sort of partnership, Houghton furnishing his portion of brains and purpose, with some money. Just back of the orchard on the Houghton premises, some twenty rods from the house, is a branch of the Canadaway creek that, crossing the field through a gorge, and falling from a ledge of rocks five or six feet in height, gives a water power of considerable force. The quick eye of young

Houghton saw that he could obtain the power necessary to carry on his machinery, and very soon the young philosopher was seen busy fitting up suitable structures to receive the various materials and the apparatus necessary to carry on the enterprise of manufacturing powder. We do not know how long these labors were continued, but not long, perhaps a year. It was not without some success, as the powder was offered and sold readily in a limited market. But for some reason that cannot be known now, it did not prove profitable. At all events the powder mill met with a sudden and disastrous termination. Douglass Houghton was alone in the mill at this time; he was carrying a pan of powder from one room to another; in passing a stove perhaps, a spark, it is thought, fell on the contents of the pan, which instantly exploded; the shock threw Douglass through the door, a sudden rebound carried him back again, prostrating him to the floor. He rose to his feet, not realizing for the moment the amount or the nature of the injuries he had received. He had the presence of mind to close the door, and plunging his head and arms into the floom to subdue the pain he suffered; then with dimmed vision, and ignorant as yet of the extent of the disaster, he made his darkened way through the orchard to the house. His mother has described his appearance on that fearful occasion. We do not know, he hardly knew, how he reached the house. His face was blackened with powder, his hair was nearly burnt off, his eyebrows singed, the skin of his face, hands and arms burnt and crisped, but he staggered to the arms of his mother bewildered with suffering. A beautiful instance of his tenderness even in this dark moment shall be mentioned here. On first reaching the well he attempted to draw water to render his appearance to his mother less shocking; but at this moment she first caught a glimpse of him, hardly knowing her own son. "Don't be alarmed, dear mother; I am not much hurt." These were his first words. His mother describes him to the writer as the most dreadful sight she ever beheld. In a few hours he was totally blind. It was long before he recovered from these injuries. But the vigor of youth, the faithful attention of his father's friend, Dr. Walworth, with those tender cares that come from a mother's love, ere long restored the youthful philosopher to health and vision.

The science of botany had early engaged his attention. Geology, less attractive to the young, soon divided his interest, and these studies became a passion with him. He could not pick up a pebble but his mind would dispose of its geological relations or its mineral qualities.

In crossing a fence you might see him seize the shield or cocoon of a moth, hidden to ordinary eyes, place it carefully in his pocket, and on his return to the house put it in a safe place where he could detect its final exit. But he was never a mere collector of specimens, an amateur in science. He would master the principles that must underlie all scientific studies. He was a great reader, and before he became so absorbed by his various duties in Michigan, he had found the time to read history, especially English and American. The example of his father had quickened his taste. A friend and companion, Judge Samuel Douglass, tells the writer that while young Houghton was recovering from the powder explosion, and after he could use his eyes with safety, he beguiled his time in reading Homer's Iliad. But his reading outside of special science could not be extensive. He had not the time for the cultivation of a literary taste, and no time would in the future offer to him the leisure for these more elegant studies, such as had won and distinguished his older brother Alured. But he loved music, and often beguiled a few moments by taking his flute. Indeed he performed on this instrument with great taste and feeling. He would leave the drudgery of office labors now and then, come up stairs to the parlor, and join his sisters in a brief concert.

His memory was tenacious, what he read he retained, and this not in a loose, desultory way. Even after his professional and scientific studies had entirely absorbed every hour of the day, he would still find a moment to indulge in this earlier taste. A new history or biography would arrest his attention. It is remembered when Botta's excellent history of the United States first appeared, the Doctor could hardly lay down the volume till its pages were devoured.

He had an excellent judgment and a taste for didactic and epic poetry, and would select the best reading for his sisters. He had read the Iliad of Homer, and Virgil was not a stranger to him.

But all these studies and indulgences must now be postponed. Already the professional demands on his time, and the scheme of the Geological Survey of the State were occupying all his powers and filling that active brain with plans for its achievement.

It was in the year 1837 that Dr. Houghton matured the scheme of the Geological Survey of the State of Michigan. There were few, if any persons in the State at that period whose acquirements fitted them to give council even in a plan of this nature, and in consequence the labor and responsibility of projecting and maturing such a survey would devolve almost wholly on him. Since that time so many Geological Surveys of States have been organized that such a labor would now be greatly lessened. But Dr. Houghton had no example or model applicable to the state of Michigan to guide him. He proposed to himself a system that should comprise four departments or divisions, geology, zoology, botany and topography, each having its official head, and all united under the general guidance of the State Geologist.

It would be necessary that this plan should be brought before the Legislature, and it must be approved by that body. The members of the Legislature were assuredly not familiar with the facts or the value of geology, in any sense, either as an economic or as a theoretic science. The departments of zoology and botany might appear to them even of very little practical or public importance. Michigan had just entered into the great family of States; she was as yet inexperienced in public works of all kinds. She was poor, her people were sparsely scattered over a wide field of dense forests, prairies or oak openings. The members of the Legislature were mainly farmers or merchants, hard-working, practical men, timid from inexperience, and economical from habit and necessity. They made no pretense to a knowledge of science, they would be jealous of all attempts at unnecessary expenditures of money, they knew well how hard it was to pay taxes. But it was necessary that these plain, practical men should be convinced that geology was not only a noble, true science, that its development would redound to the honor of the new State of Michigan, but that the State Survey would be accomplished within a reasonable period of time, and above all that it would pay. It is honorable alike to Houghton and to the State of Michigan, that at the early period of her independent existence she was willing to appropriate some eight or ten thousand dollars for this noble object. On his part, it had required a thorough knowledge of the science of geology, its prospective bearing on the polity of the commonwealth, confidence in himself, knowledge of men, tact, vigilance, courage and labor. He, indeed, possessed all these qualities, and he accomplished his purpose. It is true he would meet with active, honest opposition. Under such circumstances there will be always found some narrow minded, some ignorant, some obstinate and in opposition, from constitutional meanness, or habitual pugnacity. Some would try their hand at satire or ridicule, but all the arrows of ridicule directed against himself or his pursuits, or insinuations of his boyish inexperience and incompetency, he met with good humor, a sagacious knowledge of the men who opposed, with wit and with unshaken good temper. All these a man can afford to wield when he is sure to win. And in fact over every impediment thrown in his path he triumphed.

A State Legislature is a good school in which to study diplomacy, and Dr. Houghton found plenty of occasion for the study of this new art, and for its efficient practice.

Though Dr. Houghton had many friends in the Legislature of the newly organized State, which then met at Detroit, there were many also who could not or would not realize the importance of a scientific exploration of the State; nor was this at all strange. Scientific studies, and especially geology, had up to this time received but little consideration in

America. Excepting the institute at Troy, there was no school of science in the country, no chair of science in any university or college. Practically in the western country it was a subject so new and unknown as to be received with suspicion and indifference.

It became the custom of the more intelligent members to bring to Dr. Houghton's studio the less friendly and intelligent ones, who were there so instructed in the subject nearest to the Doctor's heart as to enable them to form independent judgments.

Among the members of the Legislature of 1837 was a worthy farmer from Macomb county, a man of commanding presence, genial, and a general favorite, but totally ignorant of the first principles of science. Naturally he looked down upon the little Doctor with some contempt, nor would he be persuaded by his best friends to visit the Doctor in his studio, examine his collection and listen to his expositions. He could find on his own farm quite as good specimens of stones, sticks and dry herbs, and he poured ridicule over the whole matter. At last he was induced by a few boon companions to accompany them to Dr. Houghton's house for an evening. They were met by the Doctor—as boon a comrade as the best of them—in his parlor, and all sat down to cards. Dr. Houghton entertained them with stories brim-full of jollity and fun, and it was late when they were ready to leave. Not a word had been uttered on the subject of the survey, or any matter pertaining to science. The Macomb member was delighted. He swore that the little Doctor was a right good fellow, and had more in him than many a man of twice his size. The friendship thus begun never wavered. The member from Macomb voted for the appropriation, specimens and all, and he remained a firm friend ever afterwards.

Will not even the most exacting find excuse for such finesse in consideration of the end in view? At all events the story will serve to illustrate the versatility of the hero of it, and the ease with which he won the hearts of all.

CHAPTER III.

STATE GEOLOGIST — CHARACTER AND RESULTS OF THE SURVEY — METHODS — HARDSHIPS — INCIDENTS — PLAN FOR CONNECTING THE LINEAR AND GEOLOGICAL SURVEYS OF THE PUBLIC DOMAIN.

Dr. Houghton had a warm, efficient friend and coadjutor in the young Governor, Stevens T. Mason, and on the passing of the law establishing this scientific department of the State, Houghton was immediately appointed geologist.

After a rapid reconnoissance of the State under a small appropriation in 1837, an act was proposed by the Legislature in March, 1838, contemplating a full organization of the geological department.

The seasons of 1838 and '39 were spent in explorations of the lower peninsula and the portion of the upper peninsula bordering on Lakes Huron and Michigan. The reader is referred to the Appendix for a summary and review of the annual reports of the Geological department from its first inception.

In a brief memoir by Mr. Hubbard published in the American Journal of Science, soon after the death of Dr. Houghton, the scheme matured by the State Geologist is thus alluded to:

"The plan upon which this survey was organized reflected great credit upon the enlarged scientific views and enterprise of Dr. Houghton, and may be considered as a model. It comprehended four departments, namely, geology and mineralogy proper, zoology, botany and topography, each having its official head and assistants, and all united under the general direction and surveilance of the State Geologist. Thus, while all were expected to work in concert, by a division of labor the results would necessarily be more extended and accurate. One of the duties connected with the topographical department may be considered as novel to a geological survey, and could at least be but ill accomplished in any of the older States. Like all the States northwest of the Ohio, the system of rectillinear surveys had been applied to Michigan, by which the State is divided into towns and ranges of six miles square, which again are subdivided into thirty-six square miles or sections. The topographer was directed to furnish the geologist and his two assistants in geology with skeleton plats of these townships, copied from the returns of the Deputy United States Surveyors, on a scale of two inches to the mile, these serving the latter as a basis for laying down with more than ordinary accuracy and facility as well the geological as the topographical and civil features of the country. These being returned to the topographer, were reduced by him to the scale adopted for a series of State and county maps, the publication of which was projected as a part of the results of the survey.

The condition of the State finances permitted the issuing of a few only of the maps thus prepared, rather as specimens, but they sufficed to show that for comprehensiveness, minuteness and fidelity of detail, these maps of the counties of Michigan far exceed anything of the kind ever attempted in this country."

They would have accomplished, had the scheme, for which abundant material was collected, been carried out in the liberal spirit with which it was conceived, and with far more accuracy, what the State and general government have since attempted by triangulations, at a vastly enhanced cost. We shall see that the same idea entered into and formed a part of the plans for connected linear and geological surveys which the comprehensive and practical mind of Dr. Houghton subsequently applied to the linear surveys in progress in the Lake Superior region.

The scheme for the survey of Michigan which Dr. Houghton had entertained, and which he now proceeded to mature, showed evidences of that large comprehensive spirit which, reaching out beyond the present aspect of things, grasps the future demands of science. It showed, in fact, a good deal of creative organizing genius, for which the Doctor was not undistinguished. Unfortunately the financial calamities of the country, which fell on the western States with unparalleled severity, proved fatal to a portion of this plan and greatly crippled the efficiency of the Geological Survey proper.

Before the close of the second year he was obliged to abandon the departments of zoology and botany, so that the State lost the great advantage of a prosecution of these kindred sciences, hand in hand with its geology. This was to be regretted, because in the virgin state of the country there would be found many plants and animals which with the progress of settlement would become either wholly extinct or dispersed.

His report for this second year, notwithstanding, comprised very copious and valuable reports by the State Zoologist and the Botanist, of the animals and plants so far made known. A reference to these will be found in the Appendix.

The season of 1840 was passed by the geological corps in an exploration of the southern coast of Lake Superior, and the general results were reported by Dr. Houghton to the Legislature the following February. In regard to the mineral wealth of that region, the State Geologist saw very clearly its future importance, but he was extremely cautious in his statements. He knew how easily the public pulse might be excited and speculators induced to rush in and appropriate extensive tracts of mineral land. But the time would soon come when these evidences would be too plain and patent to allow him, from conscientious motives, or any politic scruples, to withhold such information from the public.

His reports sent in to the Legislature, brief but comprehensive, offered such an array of facts bearing on the mineral wealth of the upper peninsula, so philosophically deduced, and carrying such order and system into what all previous observers has regarded as unintelligible confusion, that public attention was speedily attracted to that region, and thousands of the bold or inquisitive residents of States further south and east were soon wending their way to the Lake Superior mineral region.

With few exceptions, all the vast region touching the great lake of the Northwest was an uninhabited wilderness; dense, tangled unbroken forests. These exceptions were the hunting and fishing communities, half Indian, half French, that had found a lodgment under the cliffs of a bleak coast.

The novelty of the geological positions taken by Dr. Houghton, and their non-conformity in many particulars with the state of facts existing in other well known mining districts, created a profound incredulity in the minds of those who had received their teachings in other schools of science. In truth, so bold and unlooked for were some of the statements made by the young Geologist of Michigan, that he was at this time called by some of the solons of the east "the backwoods geologist," or "the boy who had a good deal yet to learn," and in these phrases, no doubt, there was implied both incredulity and derision.

Perhaps even the accomplished and learned editor of "Silliman's Journal of Science" may be suspected at this time of a want of that catholic spirit of liberality that should always characterize a scientist.

But Dr. Houghton was a courageous and independent observer, and it should be observed here that the lapse of years and the progress of discoveries under more favorable circumstances have absolutely redeemed the sagacious suggestions, and confirmed the almost intuitive accuracy of his observations. Indeed, his conclusions, apparently founded on a limited examination, have proven singularly prophetic. This is the more remarkable from the limited means he had at command, the brevity of time he had to complete the exploration, the vastness of the areas to be examined, as well as the extreme difficulties of traversing an unbroken wilderness. But we may repeat and emphasize the fact that all subsequent explorations of this mineral region, so far from discrediting a single fact stated or any position taken at that time by the State Geologist, have confirmed, with singular minuteness, all the theories propounded and every prediction he made. Nor have later observations been able to add much that did not flow mainly from Houghton's acute and cautious examinations.

His fourth and last report of the geology of the upper peninsula, Prof. Winchell speaks of as "a masterly description of the mineral veins of the trap, conglomerate and other rocks." He says: "Dr. Houghton's report, published in 1841, furnished the world with the first definite information relative to the occurrences of native copper in place on Lake Superior, and the mining interest now rapidly growing up in that region has been to great extent created by the attention directed to it by the report of my late predecessor."

This report of Dr. Houghton's, with others of special interest to the public, that were laid before the legislature, will be found in a subsequent portion of this volume. But the arduous labors which Dr. Houghton imposed upon himself in developing the geology and mineral wealth of Michigan, can hardly be realized. They have not been told. He was no egotist, and his assistants, taking example from their leader, thought only of duty and success. Now and then we get slight intimations of their labors through reports and letters. By day they were often wading unknown streams, threading a trackless forest, making their observations, securing specimens of rocks, fossils or minerals. The nights often made sleepless by swarms of mosquitoes, drenching storms and the howling of wild beasts. They would eke out the scanty provisions they could carry by such game as they might by chance meet.

Exposed thus to cold and wet, to storm and perils of many kinds, it is not surprising that Dr. Houghton's health should have suffered severely. He mentions this in one of his reports, a rare instance of any allusion made by him to the hardships he encountered. To the legislature he says:

Feb., 1841.

"It is a matter of regret to me that the sufferings and hardships to which I have been exposed in conducting the field work over this wilderness portions of our State, have so far impaired my health, as to render it impossible for me to enter into so minute details as had been anticipated. I regret this the more since it leaves many wide spaces in portions of the present report which are of much consequence to a proper understanding of the whole. But since the annual reports are intended to refer rather to the progress of the work, than to its results, and since the whole will be embraced in a more perfect form hereafter, this defect is of less importance than it otherwise would be."

To realize these hardships one must have the experience of living exiled for two or three months in the midst of unknown forests, and being obliged to strip the bark from trees and creep under their shelter to escape the fierce storms by night, satisfied with a few hours of rest, but always in good cheer. Houghton says in one of his letters, "the darkest moments are rendered comparatively light and cheerful from the grand scenes that surround us, and that sense of duty in our pursuits which gives nerve and courage to meet every peril."

It was in the season of 1840 that an incident happened, related to the author by one of the men present, which vividly illustrates the dangers he was destined to encounter. It is mentioned here, because at the time Dr. Houghton lost his life there were persons ready to censure him for needless exposure; they felt perhaps that he had been careless of a life so valuable to science, and so important to his own fame; but this idea would be absurdly unjust. Life to Dr. Houghton must have been as precious as to anyone. It is true he was without fear in danger, and would never spare himself to accomplish a great purpose. In the course of his explorations amid the wilderness, or on the unfrequented waters of the upper lakes, he had often encountered perils of a frightful nature. He had faced these and overcome them. He was indeed fearless to heroism in danger. But he was never reckless at any time,—rather was he deliberate and cautious by nature.

On this occasion he was making his way along the rock-bound coast of Lake Superior. He was in his "Mackinaw" row-and sail boat, the same that was subsequently dashed to pieces in a storm. Night was approaching, black clouds suddenly overcast the heavens, and the darkness of midnight seemed in a few moments to overshadow them. He was approaching the celebrated Pictured Rocks, well out to sea. But he had some fourteen miles still to reach his destination. His men, obedient to his will, tried hard to keep off from the shore, but the wind blew a gale. Thunder and flashes of lightning added their horrors to the scene. With all their effort to keep out to sea, the storm was taking them directly on the rocks, against which the fierce waves were heard to dash. Houghton saw there was hardly a chance to escape, for their frail bark was speedily sweeping them to inevitable destruction. He knew that at wide intervals along these perpendicular ledges there were narrow breaks or rifts cut away by rivulets. Such a break might possibly, if reached in time, admit of shelter; these were in truth but narrow crevices as it were, sloping rapidly up, and in a storm hardly to be seen. But this was their only hope. While the wind whistled and moaned, and the waves broke in thunder, leaping high up the cliff, the geologist stood firm at the helm, guiding the tossing boat to avoid the threatened wave that might swamp them, his eagle eye taking in the long range of sandstone cliffs, watching with intense eagerness, in the midst of this terrific tempest to discover, if possible, one of those slight breaks in the rocky walls that threatened any moment to receive them, to crush and grind them to pieces. The boat now almost touching the dreaded rocks, he might only discover a possible haven of safety by the lurid flashes of lightning. Suddenly amid breathless silence and the pallid faces of those faithful assistants, save the roar of the elements, that imperfect narrow opening appeared, and the frail bark with its precious freight was whirled in and shot up the slope, safe on the narrow gravelled beach; and here these storm-beaten toilers of the sea remained until daylight.

It will be seen that Dr. Houghton in the prosecution of his favorite studies, and to achieve his great mission, was no mere theoretic, parlor geologist. He loved to study the operations of nature in the midst of her wildest scenes. He would not trust to the speculations of others, however plausible. His mind could only be satisfied when he had put everything into the crucible of observation and experiment, and tested each for himself. Other men have been smitten with this impassioned love of science, this profound desire for new discoveries, but they are not so numerous that we can afford to forget them.

Dr. Houghton had early attached to him several of the young men of Detroit, who became afterwards closely associated with him in his scientific survey of the State; others were drawn to him from sympathy, some were connected with him in business, while others again pursued the study of the natural sciences under his instructions. These associates constituted a kind of club, called sometimes "the Houghton boys." His influence on the deportment and habits, on the intellectual discipline of these associates was admirable and lasting. How many names of high, hopeful and ardent young friends and co-laborers come up to me as I write this.

As he had been the leader when but a child among his little associates, so the same trait was conspicuous now that he had to deal with men. And why should he fear danger? Among these wild and stormy scenes he was in his chosen element. He never hesitated to face the snow storm, or the sleet of hail; if capsized in an open boat, as often happened, he and his men could swim or wade ashore. In truth he was well fitted for these encounters. He brought to bear his experience, a deep steady enthusiasm, indomitable courage, and heroic self-sacrifice. He had the entire confidence of his boatmen and associates, who were bound to him like children to a parent; and they were inspired by a common danger, they were enthralled by the example of purpose, decision and energy, by confiding counsel and, in fine, by the unfailing resources of genius.

The report of 1841 was the last one made by the State Geologist to the legislature; the poverty of resources of the young State having compelled a suspension of the survey, but Dr. Houghton had other resources within himself.

The linear survey of the public domain had been early projected by the United States government; and these surveys had been in progress in the State of Michigan, as in other portions of the nation's property not yet deeded to settlers. Dr. Houghton had found from time to time great advantage in his explorations by enlisting the intelligent minds of the public surveyors in the cause of geology and the related sciences. In fact the doctor saw in this union a rare chance to carry forward his own scientific examinations on a large and permanent scale. It was indeed at that moment an enterprise opened up to him, novel in its character, quite original, and full of promise in the promotion of his special studies. This idea was nothing less than to achieve a thorough geological, mineralogical, topographical and magnetic survey of the new wild lands of the United States, contemporaneously and in connection with the government survey.

As the law making provision for the State geological survey proper would very soon expire, leaving still a large territory in the upper peninsula unexplored, Dr. Houghton set about the perfecting of this double and more complete survey of the public domain. At one of the annual meetings of the American Geologists, held at Albany, New York, Dr. Houghton explained his views in regard to the new methods by which he proposed to carry on the public survey of the national domain. This idea was well received by the members of the association, and as chairman of the committee appointed, Houghton proceeded to Washington. This was in 1844, during the session of the 45th congress, that the doctor laid his scheme before the Secretary of the Interior. It was carefully considered, and its objects were approved. Its feasibility, however, was but cautiously admitted. . To be sure its great value to these natural sciences was seen and acknowledged. But there were difficulties that seemed to block the way— some indifference and some "red tape," perhaps. Doubts were expressed if deputy surveyors could be found sufficiently versed in these sciences to undertake such a work with any reliable prospect of success. In this dilemma, Dr. Houghton did not hesitate; he offered at once to take the contract himself, a contract to complete the survey of the upper peninsula, making upwards of four thousand square miles, at a price but little in excess of the sum that would be paid for the single survey—such as it had been under the established system. This prompt action on the part of Dr. Houghton showed the authorities his entire confidence in the plan he had devised, and inspired confidence on the part of the government to adopt it. Dr. Houghton had already submitted this scheme of survey to the Hon. Lucius Lyon, U. S. Surveyor General, who heartily approved it. It was also endorsed by a joint committee of the State Legislature of Michigan. The Doctor had a corps of surveyors early in the field, and his plan was fully tested before his untimely death. Its success was even beyond his expectations, and prominent scientists, we understand, have expressed regret that this new and enlarged mode of survey of the public lands has not been continued.

The Hon. Lucius Lyon, Senator in Congress, and afterwards Surveyor General, says, in his reports to the Commissioner of the General Land Office, in 1845, speaking of this survey, "that enough has been done to show clearly the great value "of such accurate geological and topographical surveys as the "one in which he was engaged, and to demonstrate the practi- "bility of carrying them on in connection with the leading "surveys of the public realms, without increasing the ex- "penditures of the government for surveying more than one- "half a cent per acre over a rough and thickly wooded "country like that on Lake Superior. And further, the "additional information which such a survey would give if "finally adopted, would certainly be worth to the purchaser "of the public land far more than the small extra cost. In a "mining region its value and importance would be greatly "increased. It would enable the government to know at once "the exact location and probable value of every section and "quarter section of the mineral lands."

The reasons for this abandonment have not been given. It will always require some personal enthusiasm and independence to carry forward schemes of improvement in which the public is not immediately aggrandized or benefited. In this more thorough survey of the national domain, the deputy surveyors had been instructed to make notes of soils, forest growth, running streams, coal, and minerals of all kinds, geological appearances, etc., and to make collections of rock specimens and fossils; all these would be received at the General Land Office at Washington. Indeed, Houghton's scheme contemplated a scientific bureau at the seat of government, where would be gathered not only all the information embodied in the field notes, such as must speedily accumulate in this enlarged system of organized labor and observation, extending from the great lakes to the Pacific, but, in addition, there should be found at this bureau duplicate specimens of everything pertaining to the individual States, as these should advance in their more detailed and scientific explorations.

Such were some of the ambitious plans which the young savant of Michigan had formed—which, indeed, he matured and tested with every promise of success. It was his ambition and his hope to carry this large enterprise to a complete success.

But the sudden and calamitous death of Dr. Houghton prevented even the final report of the geology of the State, as well as the more complete work, including the several departments originally comprised in the survey. But it is due to his memory to state here that the amount of materials in the form of maps, notes, charts, drawings, specimens of the geology, botany, mineralogy and zoology, which now enrich the cabinet at Ann Arbor, perhaps surpass those of any other State in the Union excepting New York. It is needless to say that to the students in these various departments, as well as to the more advanced scientists, their value is not easily overestimated. It is true that since his death large and important additions have been made to the State Cabinet by purchase. His widow has bestowed on the university an extensive and most precious Herbarium, Dr. Houghton's private collection, gathered and preserved through many years. Soon after Houghton's appointment as geologist of the State, the Regents of the University appointed him Professor of Geology and kindred sciences in that institution. He held this chair at the time of his death. The university, which has expanded to such dimensions in the last forty years, was at that time in its infancy, and needed, as it received, the fostering care of enlightened citizens, who were often obliged to give time and labor with slight compensation.

The disinterested sacrifices of men of letters and science during the probationary struggles of liberal institutions are not always remembered after their maturity and success has been assured. Houghton's duties in the meanwhile in the field and wilderness had been too numerous and too pressing to admit of a continuous attention to the special work of a Professor at Ann Arbor. But he found time to give lectures now and then, and his counsel was constantly sought in the administration of its affairs at that time. His influence, indeed, was felt as a magnetic vital power in the embryonic struggles, as in the more mature growth of this favorite institution of Michigan.

CHAPTER IV.

HONORS — SOCIETY — HOME AND FAMILY — THE ANNUAL REPORTS — STORM ON LAKE SUPERIOR — SCIENCE AND DUTY — DEATH.

It was an honor for a young man not yet thirty years old to be offered the Presidency of the State University, but his reply is equally honorable to him, that he "could be of more service, perhaps, outside, for the present."

During his brief career up to 1844 he had been the recipient of honors at home and abroad, unsought and rare for one so young. And he had organized and conducted a geological survey of the State with singular energy and success.

Let us now go back a few years. Before he was nineteen years old he had been appointed assistant professor at the Scientific School at Troy, N. Y. Yielding to the invitation at Detroit, he had hardly opened his office in the spring of 1830, when he was appointed surgeon and botanist to the expedition for the discovery of the sources of the Mississippi, organized by Henry R. Schoolcraft. As President of the Young Men's Society, he succeeded Franklin Sawyer, who was afterwards so favorably known as Superintendent of Public Instruction. Within a few years, (1842,) he had been elected Mayor of Detroit for two years in succession. He was made an honorary member of the Academy of Sciences, Philadelphia; a member of the College of Natural History, Vermont; a member of the Hartford Natural History Society, Connecticut; a member of the Literary and Historical Society of Quebec; a member of the Boston Society of Natural History. He was appointed State Geologist of Michigan in 1837; a member of the Geological and Historical Society, Newark Seminary, State of Ohio; an honorary member of the Antiquarian Society, Copenhagen, Denmark; a member of the National Institute of Washington; and Professor of Geology, Mineralogy and Chemistry in the University of Michigan.

Regarding a man so young, the recipient of so many unsolicited honors, and who has left so deep and lasting an impression upon the popular thought and sympathy, it is natural and proper that we should wish to form some definite idea of his personal appearance.

Dr. Houghton's height was about five feet five inches, a little less, perhaps. His father, Judge Houghton, of Fredonia, New York, was small in person, about the size of the Hon. Alvah Walker, of St. Johns, of this State. All the members of his family were of the medium size. His hands and feet were small and delicately formed; his head was large, well developed and well balanced; his nose was prominent like his father's, a little Roman in aspect, and of generous proportions; his eyes were blue, verging towards hazel; they were well sheltered underneath light but rather massive brows, and were bright and merry at times, and expressed his feelings without disguise. His ears had been scarred by that powder explosion, and his nostrils and mouth had retained some marks of that disaster. In early boyhood, he had suffered long and severely from a hip disease, and this had left one leg a little short, not enough to give him a limp, but it had produced a slight inclination to one side, with a swing or roll of the body as he walked; the head somewhat inclined. He was not aware of this himself; these blemishes were instinctively disguised, and so completely that not even his intimate friends would be likely to notice them.

His temperament was warm and nervous; his movements were quick and earnest. His voice rang out with the melody of unaffected enjoyment, or the gayety of social and confiding intimacy. But he had command of all his faculties; he could in a moment control his language and his feelings. His sensibilities were feminine in delicacy; a tale of suffering would suffuse his eyes with tears, an appeal to his kindness or to his purse brought a quick response.

Like most men of ability engaged in the pursuit of science or letters in the new States of the west, Dr. Houghton saw the importance of making friends of the political leaders of parties, and to associate in their minds the cause of good government and wholesome laws with the progress of scientific discoveries. He had, indeed, the faculty of inspiring others with a portion of his enthusiasm, and to awaken a profound respect for his pursuits. He was young, ardent, and generous to a fault. His intercourse with all who had claims on him was the ideal of frankness and cordiality. Was it strange, then, that he should win all? But while he maintained the dignity of science as a pursuit in itself worthy of all devotion and every sacrifice, he did not disdain to point out and insist on the economical features of a liberal cultivation of the natural sciences. It may be stated with entire truth, that all the leading men of the State were his friends, most of these warm, efficient, personal friends. They saw in their midst a young man of singular activity, full of knowledge, ready to impart it, and one so earnest, impetuous and generous, that they could not help being drawn to him by a strong sympathy. This admiration, this confidence, came in part, too, from his liberal conduct towards the young men engaged in kindred pursuits, by the high tone and balance of his character, by the fidelity of his attachments; in fine, by the transparent probity of his mind.

But Dr. Houghton would not confine himself exclusively to the study of science; far from this. He was a man—young as he was—of disciplined habits of business. Had he lived, his fortune was assured. He felt every pulsation of the growth and prosperity of the city and State. His credit was excellent, his word was good as a bond. No one had better judgment of the value of real estate in a new commonwealth, and his investments were good. He understood the tactics of political parties, and would not hesitate to bend them to the cause of the sciences he loved. He was himself a fair, temperate thinker and speaker on all the great questions of national and municipal significance—most catholic and liberal towards all who differed with him, and tolerant of opinions and creeds not his own. But no one knew better than Dr. Houghton that there are times when a man can have but one side, and must stand by the integrity of his principles and of his faith.

As Mayor of the city of Detroit, we are informed that he often took very decided ground, quite above and outside of party politics. Mr. Silas Farmer, of Detroit, mentions a scene he witnessed at a meeting of the common council. In some discussion the members were excited and loud in their talk, and with evidence of some violence. The doctor bore this for a time, but after a little rebuked them and tried to bring them to order. But after repeated efforts in vain to command silence, he arose from his chair, told them that as Mayor and their presiding officer unless they ceased their wrangling and came to order at once he would vacate the chair and decline to preside over them. This was sufficient; order was instantly restored. It takes a man of nerve and independence to do this. But it was in this way that Houghton won the esteem of all parties and all classes of men. They respected his energetic business habits, and his impartial administration of the municipal government of the city.

For several years before his death, Dr. Houghton, beyond doubt, was the most prominent and most popular man in the State. Everywhere his ability and energy were acknowledged. No name throughout the distant and rural districts was so often uttered. His bold daring, his generous acts, his good humor, his racy stories, were repeated everywhere. There were certain peculiar qualities in this widespread popularity that can hardly be defined or appreciated. Every man seemed to feel a pride in the growing celebrity of Houghton. His long practice as physician had rendered his person familiar and dear to all. His gentle and sweet nature was better than medicine; his skill in his profession was not surpassed. After the necessity of withdrawing from practice, many families refused to give him up. All classes, and especially the poor, looked upon him as a personal friend. His stories were always fresh. His small, active figure, his almost boyish manners, the utter absence of all-put-on dignity, were characteristic. But notwithstanding this unstudied and impulsive manner, it must be said that no man would ever think of treating him with undue familiarity. His intimacies were well chosen, and he was scrupulous in his respect shown towards others. It was from this sort of hearty cordiality, and from a nature that was not afraid to be open and frank, came those familiar epithets, "the little Doctor," "our Dr. Houghton," "the boy geologist of Michigan;" these were common throughout the State. His name had become a household word. The young and the old everywhere were eager to serve him. No doubt Dr. Houghton was conscious of this general homage, but he never sought and most certainly never encouraged it.

How much importance he attached to a respectful demeanor in his intercourse with people, the following incident may illustrate. Traveling once with a younger friend, they had occasion to inquire their road, when his companion called to a lad whom they had met, addressing him as "boy." When they had passed on the doctor mildly corrected him by saying, "Always address such a person as 'young man.' It appeals to his self respect."

At one time he was traversing the woods some hundreds of miles northwest of Detroit, when he came to a farm house. He enquired about the rocks, the sources of streams, coal, iron ore, and the kind of trees in that neighborhood. The farmer was somewhat annoyed by his curiosity—a stranger in a rough torn dress and showing such ignorance was offensive, so he cut him short by telling him "he had better go and see old Dr. Houghton, of Detroit; he knew all about such things and had more time to spare than he had!"

As a specimen of humor, we recall his visit to the studio, then on Jefferson avenue, Detroit, near his house, to announce that he had just come into possession of ten thousand dollars! This would not surprise anyone in those bright days of speculation in corner lots. Some of his young friends present were but too happy to congratulate the Doctor on his good fortune. Nor were they less so when they discovered it to be, not in a land sale, but in the birth of a daughter. This precious gift of fortune was Hattie Houghton, now the wife of the Hon. Morgan, of Coldwater, Michigan, the beautiful mother of sons and daughters.

With such elements of strength and popularity, it should not be surprising to learn that enthusiastic and eager friends were only too ready to bring his name forward as candidate for the highest office in the gift of the people of Michigan. They knew how faithful he had been to public trusts, that he had ripe judgment, and could govern men. It was near the approach of a political convention of 1844 that would select a candidate for governor. At this time the Geologist, with his assistants, were engaged with their work in the woods in the northern parts of the lower peninsula; they were exploring the wilderness by day, and camping by night under strips of bark torn from the trees for shelter. He would be clothed in a forest suit less fitted perhaps for the governor of the state than for an out door geologist; and so disguised and roughened would Dr. Houghton appear—with unshaved beard, iron-stained boots, torn and dilapidated clothes, that had his fellow citizens caught a glimpse of him at that moment they might have hooted him from their doors. But while thus engaged and thus adorned, and distant from his constituents, he ran the narrowest chance of being made candidate for governor of Michigan, as we learn, almost by acclamation. But in his absence, some judicious friends interfered and very firmly resisted this unsought, and, at that time, undesirable honor. They insisted that the geological survey to which he had pledged himself should take precedence of all other claims. And this, no doubt, would be in accordance with the deliberate views of the Geologist himself. Political honors could wait.

It may be remembered that when Dr. Houghton had been elected mayor of Detroit he was far in the woods pursuing his scientific investigations, and he knew nothing of his being a candidate till his return to the city. See his letter in Appendix.

The Reports on the Geology of Michigan, commencing in 1838, were sent to the Legislature from session to session, through a period of four or five years. These reports, with one exception, are brief, but they are drawn up with care; they are full of valuable information, evidences of labor and thought, often betraying an acute forethought touching certain geological phenomena, that will not be overlooked by the reader. A phrase will indicate a principle; a few words will often comprise the result of many days of patient and perilous examinations. But they were always clear, and expressed with singular felicity. These reports were not intended to present a full exhibit of his labors in the field through the preceding year; far from this. They were made brief as possible, that the members of the Legislature should have a general idea of the progress of the work.

But a more complete account of the whole geological system of the state would be reserved for the indoor work, where he could command the time to arrange his materials for the final report. Such a work was not only in contemplation, but had already made great progress. See the remarkable unfinished volume in manuscript at Ann Arbor.

This large folio volume is very fully and beautifully illustrated by outline maps of the coast touching Lake Huron, the Straits of Mackinac, Lake Michigan and islands, showing the outcropping of rocks, forest growth, soil, mountain ranges, sand-dunes, head-lands, gulfs and bays. Besides these, and the collection of rocks and minerals, varied specimens of soils, etc., etc., deposited in the University, are many drawings, beautifully executed on wood by the State Topographer, of fossils, geological sections, views, etc., designed for the final volumes.

Such is the work that was being prepared for the citizens of Michigan and for the scientific world. Though incomplete it is still a monument of labor, design and method. It may be observed that this manuscript volume has been open and free for the inspection and study of all students in natural science, either in Michigan or in other states. No man ever had more faithful or more disinterested aid than Dr. Houghton.

It may be remembered that these young men, his assistants, who had been his faithful co-workers had not been trained in any school or branch of science; and for this reason the 'care and exactness by which the reports of Mr. Bela

Hubbard and Mr. C. C. Douglass and others have been drawn up, is the more remarkable. It is another striking instance of that trait in Houghton's character, the skill of choosing his men. They were very young men, including the Doctor himself, they made no pretense to being experts in natural science, they had to educate themselves to become good observers, and this is no small matter. It requires vigilance and practice to discriminate the various kinds of rock and minerals, of bog ore, coal and soils, and no inconsiderable amount of study to master even the nomenclature of a science.

In regard to certain problems involved in the discussion of the question of the presence of minerals in the upper peninsula, the upheaval of rocks, the origin of mineral veins, and their deposition in rocks apparently not conformable to other regions, in portions of the globe corresponding to Lake Superior geology; these and related questions would engage Houghton's earnest attention. They had never been solved by others—hardly had they been intelligently entertained. Houghton would form his opinions as he went forward and got light. He was in no haste to proclaim them. In the progress of his careful examinations, his theories would become certainties, and after his convictions were thus sustained by hard facts that had come under his own eyes, from personal inspection, he had the courage to proclaim them.

A meeting of the American Geological Society met in Albany, N. Y. Young man as he was, coming from a far western state, a new name in the galaxy of bright stars that shone in the eastern firmament, he had claims to be heard; he arose to his feet in his place to address the learned assembly. He had studied the subject of the Lake Superior mining region. His opinions founded on his own experience were presented to the association in a modest but clear manner, and he sustained these views with his usual earnestness and ability. It should be remembered that the association was composed of such men as Prof. Hall, the Rogers brothers, of Pennsylvania, Dana, Silliman, Torry, and many others, many of whom were among the most distinguished of living geologists. They would naturally be somewhat incredulous of these new and dubious theories of the "backwoods geologist of Michigan." This quality of independent thought and action on the part of Dr. Houghton has not been surpassed. It was very conspicuously shown in his views on the subject now under discussion.

He was, indeed, little disposed to be led by other men; he would reject the authority of names. He was not afraid of new paths if they would lead him to truth. Houghton was willing to see and accept of facts with his own eyes, and to apply them with his own honest convictions. Still the Doctor was shy of new theories or mere speculations in science. This feeling might even reach to over-caution or dread. He was by nature cautious, and his hesitation to accept speculative views in science will be remembered as a marked trait in his whole career. His letters and reports attest this.

As may be inferred, the social qualities of Dr. Houghton were among the elements that drew friends to him. On all subjects connected with the natural sciences his information was very full and his conversation entertaining. His descriptions of the characters he had met on the water or in the woods were graphic and racy. He was well read in books pertaining to the sciences he was pursuing, and kept up an extensive correspondence. He could hardly drop into a store or office without being surrounded by a group of admirers. He was quick and cordial to make friends.

As an instance of tact, we remember a little occurrence at his house one day on Wayne street. The Doctor, looking through the window, saw or supposed he saw a gentleman passing whom he wished to see on some special business, and called to him or tapped on the window; but he discovered his mistake when the tall form of Bishop McCoskry walked into his sanctum. They were not at that time personally acquainted. The Doctor, however, instead of being embarrassed or ready to apologize, received him with cordiality. He at once began some inquiries as to certain features of the country northwest, where he knew the Bishop had been visiting some missionary station, I think, among a small tribe of Indians. It was not necessary that the Bishop should know that Dr. Houghton had made a little mistake. The acquaintance thus commenced was a very cordial one and often of service.

The cause of temperance in these primitive days had not made much progress in Detroit. Good old Jamaica rum, apple toddy, and the sparkling champagne, were as free as water, and many citizens were better acquainted with their seductive qualities than with the natural beverage of their wells.

Houghton was brought into close intercourse with all classes, and no one would enter more heartily into social life, and it is saying a good deal when we declare that he was absolutely temperate. This resolute abstemiousness was based on conviction and principle, and will be sufficiently appreciated by those whose memories can go back to the period of 1829 to '40. Houghton united with a few other friends of the cause to form the first temperance society of Detroit, and was its first president.

At that period Detroit was famous for the elegance and refinement of its inhabitants; at the same time society was marked by a charming simplicity. It had been a military post for many years. The governor of the territory was a gentleman of noble presence and of high attainments. It was the residence of a major-general of the United States army. It was often visited by Major-Gen. McComb, commanding general of the national forces. Several families connected with the military had become fixed residents. All these were persons of pleasing manners. The Whitings, the Hunts, the Casses, the Biddles, the Farnsworths, the Trowbridges, the Hastings, the Masons, and other conspicuous families, were abounding in hospitalities and entertainments. Nor was it all dissipation; far from this. There was beauty and gayety, but not a spark yet of shoddy and pretense. The night might be given up to champagne and some "noise and confusion," but there was the balance wheel of culture, love of order, and love of ideas. There was a ready and prompt appreciation of merit. Good manners and good intentions then had their due weight. But for accurate knowledge, for a quick sagacity, for a genial temperament, young Houghton was equal to the foremost. His education had been thorough. No man in the territory could stand before him. This was not classical, for reasons that have been seen. It was scientific rather than literary. His manners were open, direct and confiding. His mind had been well disciplined by the habit of writing and by lectures. It was prompt and accurate by a responsible intercourse with men of affairs, even before he was twenty years old. Dr. Houghton embodied in the character of his mind the Baconian maxim that "Reading makes a full man, talking makes him ready, and writing makes him accurate."

Houghton had the instincts of a gentleman; he was quick to consider the feelings of others. His patience would be often tried by careless or impertinent callers, frequently speculators in disguise, who would draw from the Doctor information touching the mineral land or the salt springs, but we have no remembrance of any show of irritation under severe trials.

To escape interruption he often commenced his hard studies late at night, and they were prolonged into the small hours of the morning. Houghton was a bright example of the students of a liberal science; no one can recall on his part a single act of narrow jealousy, though he himself did not always escape the concealed weapons of the envious and the illiberal.

To escape the possible imputation of taking advantages of his opportunities, Dr. Houghton avoided while in the employ of the state all speculations, though his chances for such were peculiar and abundant.

The writer was in Canada when Mr. Wm. Logan, afterwards Sir William, and so well known as an eminent geologist, first reached the upper province. Kingston was temporarily the seat of government. Mr. Logan had just been appointed geologist of Upper Canada. Before he commenced the examination of Canadian rocks it was important that he should know what had been done on the opposite shore. Mr. Logan was in great perplexity. He was not familiar with the labors of the New York geologists nor those of Ohio. He entertained some doubt how his inquiries would be received. It will be remembered that he was an Englishman and we were "Yankees;" that in Canada a good deal of ill-suppressed irritation still existed among all classes, growing out of what has been termed the "Patriot War." Mr. Logan was an accomplished amateur artist as well as a scientist, and he had called several times on the writer. Learning his anxiety and hesitation, we wrote Dr. Houghton, then in Detroit, but without the knowledge of Logan. In a few days Mr. Logan received a letter from Dr. Houghton full of generous expressions of welcome, and the offer of every assistance he could give, proffering access to all sources of information his department could furnish. This was very agreeable to a stranger, and the Canadian geologist called immediately to express his thanks and gratification.

It was said of Charles Fox, the great orator and liberal statesman of English history—this was the language of Edmund Burke—that it was impossible to know him and not love him. There was a charm in the deportment and manners of Houghton that one could not resist. His quick sympathy and hearty appreciation drew friends to him and secured their co-operation. His devotion to science, his profound insight into principles obscure often to others, the dangers he encountered, the wilderness he explored, the coasts he traversed, these had made his name associated with that of Humboldt. The nerve, the courage, incessant toil and splendid achievements of the late French savant, Victor Jaquemont, strongly remind us of the bright but brief career of the Michigan geologist.

The readers of this memoir of Dr. Houghton will pardon the author if he shall dwell at some length on such traits and anecdotes as will tend to illustrate his character. It will be remembered that after a lapse of more than forty years, there will not be found many incidents of his life that can be recalled. It is incidental to a new country that its pioneers shall give their services and their lives to build up and develop the resources of the country, whose population at the time will be but little impressed with the value of such labors. At a later day, when a succeeding generation may desire to do honor and raise monuments to their memory, it will be found that much of the detail of life, many acts and many incidents that would throw light on a career, have passed away forever. No instance can be recalled of his taking credit for generous acts. The following occurrence is here mentioned, and will be remembered by some of the old friends :

An uncle of Dr. Houghton had bought a farm in Wisconsin, and had moved his family from Chautauqua county, N. Y., to his new home. The financial cyclone of '38 overtook him there, and the mortgage on his farm would soon be foreclosed unless paid. In fact, he was in peril of losing his homestead and his family reduced to poverty. He had no resources in Wisconsin. He must seek Dr. Houghton, in the hope that he would be able to relieve him. To do this, he would have to "foot it" a good many miles even to reach a stage coach, and it would take a full week to reach Detroit. In twenty days his day of grace would run out. At that time there were no railroads and no telegraphs. Mr. Douglass could not know the fact, but Dr. Houghton himself was deeply embarrassed and hardly knew how it would be possible for him to get through the panic. Perhaps no city in the Union suffered more from the utter prostration of business and collapse of credit than did Detroit.

But the Doctor, when his uncle reached him, worn with anxiety and wearied with travel, cheered him with hope. $700 was necessary to be raised. A good many old professional debts were still outstanding. Houghton resolved that he would raise this amount. He did not write notes and send out bills,—but with bills in his hands he started out determined to collect the amount. In forty-eight hours the amount was raised, some of it borrowed, and his uncle started for his home rejoicing, reaching his home just in time to save it.

Those who knew Dr. Houghton will remember that such an act as this was not exceptional with him.

The following is related by a friend who was with him traveling east by stage from Toledo along the lake shore—this was before the days of railroads. Houghton was on his way to Albany to a meeting of the Association of Geologists. The roads on the low ground by the lake shore in the autumn season were usually bad. Progress was slow; the coach was full of passengers all impatient of delay and mostly disposed to be in bad humor. This friend, an eminent lawyer of Buffalo, the Hon. Henry W. Rogers, a great story teller himself, says that Dr. Houghton's resources were marvelous and inexhaustible. A coach full of total strangers, cramped and confined, shy of too much confidence, like most American travelers, would resist these attacks on their reticent dignity. But long before they reached Albany, Houghton's versatility, his winning ways, his good humor, had captivated everyone. There was one exception, however; an elderly gentleman, who would not yield to these noisy seductions, but wrapped himself in his dignity and reserve. He was also a geologist on his way to Albany, but the two gentlemen were strangers. On his reaching Albany, this stranger and member of the association soon found the hall where his associates were to meet. His surprise may be imagined, when he saw his recent companion of the stage coach, rise to his feet to address the Association!

But we are a little in advance of our journey. The stage was to pass through Fredonia, the residence of his parents; it would pass through about twelve at night. The Houghton mansion stands on the edge of the village. A half mile, perhaps, before they reached the house, Houghton got out of the stage, and ran ahead through rain and mud, to have an interview with his mother. He would not ask the passengers to wait for him. This tender affection for his mother was a living flame of his soul; a tap on the window would bring them again face to face; a few cheering words, a promise to come and make a visit, some advice left for the family, an embrace and a blessing, and the eager, resolute young savant was off and again striding through the mud to overtake the coach. Nothing but death could cool or abate that profound love and devotion he felt for his parents. It is impossible to do justice to Houghton without a reference to these traits of his character; his brothers and sisters he held as dear as his own life.

Mrs. Houghton, the Doctor's young wife, was the daughter of a Mr. Stevens, of Fredonia, New York; they had known each other from childhood. She was a young lady of culture and refined sympathies. As soon as the Doctor's business would allow it they were married, and the young couple commenced their house-keeping. Doctor Houghton bought the substantial frame house on or near the corner of Wayne and Larned streets, where the family continued to reside up to Houghton's death.

Mrs. Houghton was well known to all the leading families of Detroit,—a devout Christian, a devoted wife and mother. Her goodness and her charities were the natural offspring of a most tender sympathizing nature and sound Christian principles. She made her home a welcome resort of her husband's friends, and her own winning and sincere manners contributed largely to the social popularity of the Houghton house. She was the mother of two daughters, Hattie and Mary, both now living; the eldest is the wife of the Hon. Mr. Morgan, of Coldwater, of this State. Mary is married to Dr. Haroun, who settled in Chicago; both these gentlemen are graduates of the Michigan University.

Long before and during the first years of the geological survey, the Doctor's house had virtually become a museum of natural history. His private collection was large; he had already accumulated a valuable library, both miscellaneous and scientific. All the lower rooms were given up to these and to the increasing volume of specimens in all branches of natural history. They were constantly accumulating from many sources, and he was finally forced to seek larger rooms for his accommodation. These he found on the corner of Jefferson and Woodward avenues, where the Young Men's Library was until recently located.

Dr. Houghton had now, in the fall of '45, brought his great labors so far to a close, and so near the time when he would be able to devote his mind to the methodizing his materials, as really to offer him some prospect of comparative rest. He could look back on these struggles with some satisfaction Although his health had suffered severely, he might hope for a restoration, and for a completion of that fame, the foundation of which had been laid in a fervid devotion to the great mission of his life.

In these pages we have traced his career in the State of his adoption almost from boyhood. The practice of his profession as physician and surgeon in Detroit, with a high reputation, seemed to him only a means. His mind was bent upon the study of the sciences. He saw that this State offered a field for new and important discoveries. He had no fortune to spend, that he might carry on these explorations and labors without assistance; he must educate people up to this great theme; and that wealth which would be the outcome of the scientific examination of the resources of the State of Michigan, could only be made a certainty by the united action of the Legislature and the enlightened friends of culture. It was his resolute and persistent mind that would unite these various conflicting elements and fuse them into a power that he could wield. In truth, such was his hopeful nature and the faith he had in his own power, that he never had a doubt of success. All along, his progress was upward and onward. He never halted;—even from the moment he landed from the steamer at Detroit, we might believe almost, that a premonition of a brief life had admonished and impelled him to incessant toil. A Christian philosopher has said, that "he who is cut off in the execution of a noble enterprise has at least the honor of falling in his ranks, and has fought his battle, though he missed the victory."

It was on the 13th day of October, 1845, that Dr. Houghton was lost on Lake Superior. He had left Eagle River in the morning in an open sail boat, making his way along the shore west some eight or ten miles. The Doctor wished to reach the camping ground of his surveying company under the superintendence of a Mr. Hill; as this corps of men were to remain through the long winter in this region, Dr. Houghton desired to give them his final instruction, as he would soon return to Detroit. It was late before he reached these men, and the interview was necessarily prolonged into the night. Mr. Hill then advised the Doctor to wait till morning, but Houghton had important despatches that should go to Eagle River, and down the lake by schooner. As the vessel would leave in the morning, it was really important that he should be there, as these opportunities at that season would be very rare, and his anxiety was the greater, therefore, not to fail to be at Eagle River that night. A storm threatened, but it would take only a few hours to get back, and the night was not dark. They were in an open boat propelled both by sail and oars. The wind was rising; a snow storm had set in. The Doctor was at the helm, as was his custom. They were obliged to take in sail and depend on the oars. There were five men in the boat. The weather was cold; October on Lake Superior is a late season. They put out about nine o'clock at night. At this time the wind was blowing hard from the north. They had not gone many miles when they discovered that the boat was making but slow progress, though the men were bending well to their work. A storm of snow sharpened by a northern blast beat in the faces of the weather-hardened mariners. It was now necessary to put well out to sea to get around a point of rocks, a low, broken promontory that shelved to a considerable distance seaward. Dr. Houghton's anxiety to reach Eagle River no doubt betrayed him here; but he was not daunted, he encouraged his men to brave the storm. The waves had increased in violence and were running high. We must remember that this was an open boat with five men, his faithful dog—a black and white spaniel, Meemee by name, who was always with the Doctor, and often of service—his specimens, valuable field book, instruments, notes, etc., such as must accompany him at all times. The frail bark could only be propelled now by oars in the midst of this whirl of wind and wave. The Doctor was accustomed to steer his own boat, especially when there might be danger. They had now rounded the point, and at intervals could see the light through the haze of the storm, at the mouth of Eagle River. Houghton knew the coast well. He was familiar with such storms, and within sight of land did not fear the result. It is easy for us now to say that he ought to have paid more heed to the signs of the coming tempest. But who can blame him for trusting to his own judgment, to his own skill and good fortune? Heretofore these had never deserted him. By courage and intrepidity he had often escaped destruction. No man under such circumstances can determine the extent of danger, or the moment when he must not venture another chance. His men even now proposed to go ashore, which in itself would be perilous, but the Doctor encouraged them to proceed. "We are not far from Eagle River," he said; "pull away, my boys, we shall soon be there—pull steady and hard." Did he imperil the lives of his men, so did he his own life. No danger that they could be exposed to would he shrink from. But amidst the increased violence of the gale the boat encountered the surf and was instantly capsized. They all went under for a moment; Dr. Houghton was raised from the water by his trusty companion and friend, Peter McFarland. He told the Doctor to cling to the keel, then uppermost. "Never mind me," cried Houghton; "you go ashore if you can. Be sure I'll get ashore without aid." Everything in the boat was now lost, scattered on the tossing waves; but the men were all good swimmers, and very soon the boat was righted, the water bailed out, and these devoted heroes all again at their oars obedient to command. But this bright interval was of brief duration. In a moment after, a wave struck her with such force, that the vessel receiving the blow at the stern was dashed high in the air, the boat going over endways, and everyone thrown again into the tumultuous sea. Even at this moment they were not over two hundred yards from the shore. Two of these hardy mariners with exhausted bodies, reached the rocky beach, or rather were thrown with violence on the stones in a helpless condition. But the leader of that devoted band, in spite of Peter's heroic efforts and his own unshaken courage, went down not again to rise. It was in this way and at that moment that Douglass Houghton perished.

It would be impossible to describe the mournful disappointment and grief that touched all hearts when the news of this calamity reached Detroit. It was, indeed, a sincere and profound sorrow. The citizens of Michigan who had watched his progress with so much pride felt now that the most gifted man in the state had been suddenly and mysteriously cut off at the very moment when he was to achieve victory. A light, luminous and expanding had been extinguished. Every man grieved as for the loss of a relative. The city in truth was in mourning. Some outward expression of these overpowering feelings would find utterance. The common council was convened for this purpose by the mayor of Detroit. Tender resolutions of appreciation and sympathy were passed, affecting allusion being made to the Doctor as so recently presiding over their deliberations. But this action of the common council was thought to be insufficient to express the popular and widespread sentiment of distress. A public meeting was therefore called at the city hall, that the citizens at large might be able in this way to give a wider and more emphatic expression of this universal sorrow. At this meeting resolutions offered by the Hon. Zina Pitcher, his early and fast friend, were passed, that embodied the utterance of the most tender sentiments of love, admiration and condolence. In the streets you would hear these words: "Is it true that Douglass Houghton is dead?" "Is it possible that we shall see our friend no more?" Such were the exclamations everywhere heard. His fellow citizens could not give him up. No affection, no sorrow could equal this, unless some precious member of one's family had been snatched suddenly from a mother's arms. His whole life so far had been an honor to the state. In science he was distinguished abroad; at home his friends expected to crown him with a special honor. They would place him in the highest position in their power to bestow.

He had, indeed, so identified himself with the best interests and the future of Michigan, was so replete with intellectual and progressive life, so intrepid in action, so faithful to the highest duty. In the course of Houghton's labors through the wilderness or on the bleak coast of the north, how few of his friends in the southern part of the state could realize the dangers that surrounded him ! These perils were constant and far more imminent than could be realized except by those who had shared his hardships. The citizens of Detroit watched his return from these explorations with increasing interest. The story of wreck, of passing down foaming cataracts, of crossing swollen rivers, of wet powder, of short rations, of storm without shelter; these were told everywhere. But no one ever thought that Dr. Houghton might at last fall a sacrifice to these exposures. This sort of confidence in his star, in his future, was shared by the whole community.

The entire coast east and west of Michigan, and the shores of Lake Superior had been traversed. The vast wilderness, from the extreme eastern shores of the upper peninsula to the banks of the Mississippi, on three widely separated but approximately parallel lines, had been threaded in person by Dr. Houghton. His assistants were able and efficient; they were devoted to their chief—all glowing with confidence in him and faith in the future. So far the very elements had shielded him. The glory of new discoveries in science, a generous ambition, lifted him above the thoughts of rest or fear. Though broken in health, neither storm nor the wilderness had any terrors for him. He was often in the presence of sublime scenes of nature; the forest growth of untold centuries, or the shattered masses of rock, evidences of irresistible and sudden disturbance. He had but few words to express his emotions, but he had all the sensibility to appreciate the grandeur of such scenes. These he felt to be the work of a power beyond that of man, and he loved to contemplate them. This communion with nature removed from his mind the clouds of doubt that might gather there. The deep forests, the rocky coasts, the moaning winds, all spoke to him in a voice which he could understand.

These aspects of nature he loved; long intimacy with such had made them, as it were, his companions. With all his gayety of manner and social impulses, there was in the constitution of Houghton a deep sentiment of reverence for the mysteries of nature,—not the systems of man. He did not discuss religious themes, but his convictions were deep and sincere. He respected the creed and services of the church in which he was nurtured, but he did not attempt to solve the mysteries of faith or God's providence. But amidst his labors, surrounded by the visible marvels of the greatest of architects, he saw, "God's temples not made with hands." If indeed he was not bound to any sect, if he was shy of mere forms of worship, he might yet see Deity in the clouds and hear His voice in the winds;—nor could it well be otherwise, but that these studies, these associations, should lead him to reverence; and science, the dream of his life, did not undermine his faith.

It was amid this tumult of the wild elements of nature, amid forces that no skill and no courage could master, in the good cause of science, truth and duty, bravely and tenderly he yielded up his spirit.

The upper peninsula of Michigan had not been explored in any systematic manner before the time of Houghton. The large masses of pure copper that had been seen from time to time by adventurous travelers in that region, and especially that unique mass on the banks of the Ontonogon, had excited great curiosity. But all these strange, loose pieces of copper were but bowlders out of place. They had no relation necessarily to the rocks in the immediate neighborhood. Although an English company in former years had had the faith or the temerity to sink a shaft on the spot with "great expectations," the scientific truth could only be determined by the careful examinations of a geologist. These outlying bowlders of copper had been known for a century, but they had missled everyone. Years before Dr. Houghton had been appointed geologist of the State, he had traversed that pathless region, first by the northern shores of the peninsula, and afterwards more centrally and mostly through a dense wilderness. These earlier explorations were extended to the banks of the Missisippi. It was these labors that gave the Doctor intimations of the true relation of the rocks to each other, so that when he entered on the survey to which he had been appointed, he was not without definite views and strong convictions touching the mineral wealth of the upper peninsula; and his subsequent official studies of this little known region resulted in a confirmation of these earlier conclusions to which his mind was advancing.

In science, as in letters and art, there must be enthusiasm; nor can we ignore the force of the imagination. It is by this divine gift that the mind can achieve great discoveries and great triumphs. Houghton's enthusiasm sustained him amid all these past hardships and sufferings; nothing else could have carried him through. These labors, this enthusiasm, will remind one of the great Scotch geologist, the word-painter of the old "Red-sand Stone Memory," whose works awakened such profound interest throughout England and America, forty years ago. But Hugh Miller had one advantage over the Michigan geologist; his rocks were more recent, and were alive, so to say, with the fossil remains of a remote and mysterious vitality. The reconciliation of these discoveries with certain questions, or axioms of his theology, perhaps disturbed the serenity of an intellect of admirable force; and possibly, at last, shrouded in clouds a life that had been devoted with extraordinary zeal to the cause of science. But there must be a charm beyond language to express, to be delving among rocks that at any moment may open to the eyes some embodied silhouette or skeleton of a fish or reptile—some embryonic form that shall point to a connection or an evolution of extinct races of being.

This promise of fossil existence among the granite and trap rocks of the upper peninsula was not offered as a stimulus to Dr. Houghton; he knew they must be barren of this interest.

One of the greatest of students in science, especially in geology and rock literature, was Louis Agassiz. A careful examination of the deep canons of the Swiss Alps had occupied him for several years. The mysterious moraines of these valleys and the striated surfaces of shales and granite, the cutting along the sides of mountain declivities, were phenomena of a mysterious and unexplained nature. They had been noticed by all observers, and they had puzzled and confounded all. But Agassiz saw in these strange but uniform phenomena the stupendous action of the land ice-bergs, and the grand system of the glacial degradation of mountain ranges of granite was thus evolved Fortunate was Agassiz beyond most men that he not only lived long enough to see his views fully confirmed and accepted by the savants of the world, but that his lot had been chosen among a people that could appreciate and reward his genius.

The northern portion of Michigan presented a geographical area of great extent; not less than three hundred miles, touching Lake Superior, stretching west and northward, and from fifty to seventy-five miles in width. It was almost wholly a dense wilderness. The few fishing and trading posts along the coast would be considered hardly an exception. Before Houghton's time no one had pretended to solve the mysteries that hung over these deep forests, these rugged upheavals of granite, trap, sand and metamorphic rocks. There had been intimations of the presence of minerals of great value. But as no one had been able to determine the relation of these rocks to time and place, so no definite knowledge as to their contents could be possessed by any one, for those portions of the rock that were visible along the coast, or within gorges that had been opened by disruption, or cut by water courses, presented in fact so much of confusion and complexity, that all observers heretofore had been baffled in every conjecture about them. To examine these with the eyes of an outdoor scientist, to bring the labor, the patience, the power of endurance to bear on these problems, would demand rare qualifications on the part of a geologist and a close inspection of scattered and isolated facts. Their value when applied to theories and results, required a cool head and acute powers of reasoning. In these discussions important principles were involved, and his standing before the world of science would be tested. It required, indeed, a remarkable grasp of thought to be able to arrange and methodize these wide spread and often obscure facts, and so fuse them as to display the genuine metal of truth. That Dr. Houghton possessed these essential qualities no one can doubt who will study the record of labors he has left behind, his letters herein published, and his masterly reports to the legislature. Some of these reports and letters are now for the first time placed before the citizens of Michigan in a connected popular form.

It has been undertaken to give in an Appendix a careful summary of all the reports which emanated from the departments, while under the surveillance of the first state geologist. These constituted the basis of all the explorations that have since followed, and though much has been published by other men of science, covering the same ground fully and well, the earlier reports can never be superceded in interest and importance to the people of Michigan. It has been the aim of this summary to note the more important points and conclusions, free from the cumbrous array of facts.

As the report of 1841 upon the geology of the Lake Superior district has long been entirely out of print, no apology seems to be needed for its republication here in full.

The summary is followed by a review or general statement of all that has been published on the geology of Michigan since the death of Dr. Houghton.

Prof. Alexander Winchell, of the Michigan University, has in generous words repeatedly given Dr. Houghton that meed of praise and honor which he had so well earned. Prof. Winchell was appointed State Geologist in 1859.

Speaking of the labors of Houghton, he says: "Though the work was unavoidably arduous for the Geologist, and expensive for the State, it served to acquaint us at an early day with many of the sources of our mineral wealth, and to awaken and maintain a lively desire for more full and definite information relative to the coal, salt, gypsum, copper and iron, of which the published reports of progress had afforded hasty glimpses. Dr. Houghton's report, published in 1841, furnished the world with the first definite information relative to native copper in place on Lake Superior, and the promise of wealth now so rapidly growing up in that region, has been, to a great extent, created by the attention drawn in that direction by the report of my lamented predecessor."

The sudden death of Dr. Houghton arrested the progress of the Geological Survey of the State. The final report so often alluded to in his brief papers to the legislature, and which must so much depend on Houghton's faithful performance, has never been given to the public. In the meantime, the labors and sacrifices of the great Geologist are passing out of the memory of men. The notes left by Dr. Houghton, or a compilation of them, together with such materials as could be collected intended for his final report, would have been published, it is stated, but for the refusal of the Executive to act on the resolutions of the Legislature empowering the Government to cause such publication to be made.

There is hardly a sketch of his life to be found in any of our public libraries. His able reports are entirely out of print; it is difficult if not impossible to find a copy, while every season gives us new evidence of the value of his explorations. All his discoveries and his convictions are being confirmed by subsequent observers, and while the State is being enriched by his unpaid labors, his fellow citizens who enjoy the honor he conferred on the State, are to a great extent ignorant of the life and labor of Douglass Houghton.

A discourse by Prof. Alvah Bradish, giving some more full account of Houghton's earlier life, and tracing somewhat his earlier career, has been read by invitation before several scientific and literary societies. It was read before the Young Men's Society, of Detroit. The invitation in this case seemed particularly appropriate, as both Dr. Houghton and Mr. Bradish were among the first members and founders of that literary society. It was read before the members of the Audubon Club. Once before the Pioneer Society of this State. The Historical Society of Buffalo had invited its reading before its members; and in 1879, Prof. Bradish read his discourse by invitation before the Senate and House of Representatives at Lansing.

APPENDIX I.

PEN PORTRAITS OF SOME EARLY FRIENDS OF DR. HOUGHTON, AT DETROIT.

At the period when Dr. Houghton came to Detroit to give a course of lectures on the natural sciences, the city might have numbered about four thousand inhabitants. It was still a military post—the residence of a Major-General of the United States Army. American officers, with rare exceptions, are gentlemen who respect culture,—and the old French families were not insensible to the progress of new ideas. The City of the Straits was holding out a welcome arm to the new comers from every State of the Union. Dr. Houghton was at once brought into close relation with the principal and leading men of Detroit;—the invitation had come from representative men. This close association, whether professional, or in connection with his scientific studies, was of signal service to him; he was not slow to see these advantages, and his rapid advance to the confidence of public men was not alone due to his own enthusiastic devotion to his profession and to science, but largely to the discernment of men of culture and attainments that distinguished the society of Detroit at that period. It has appeared to me that the following pages giving a few pen portraits of some of these early friends of Dr. Houghton would be welcome to those readers who can only know them by tradition :

General Lewis Cass.

When Dr. Houghton first arrived at Detroit, then a very young man, Gen. Cass was governor of the Territory, to which he had been appointed as early as 1814. He was a gentleman of unimpeachable patriotism; he was distinguished for gallantry in the war of 1812. The son of a New Hampshire farmer, he entertained a warm sympathy for the great working population of the territory. He had earned a reputation for literary culture. He felt a sincere respect for scientific studies. His early career as Governor of the vast region of the North-western Territory, and the conspicuous sagacity and wisdom shown throughout his long administration, made him a marked character of national significance. Gen. Cass had been one of those to invite young Houghton to come to Detroit to give a course of lectures on the sciences he was cultivating. The young men who came to Michigan from eastern States at that early day would bring letters to the Governor or would find ways to be known to him. It was the pleasure, as it was always in the power of Gen. Cass, to be of great assistance to these new comers, whether in business, in education, in the professions, or in the cultivation of science. Gen. Cass was a good judge of character, nor is it surprising that the young Professor of Troy should find a warm and efficient friend in the chief magistrate of the Territory.

Indeed, Houghton was so thoroughly imbued with this passion for science and so absorbed by the ambitious desire to develop the resources of the State, and to make new discoveries in geology, that it is not necessary to puzzle ourselves to define very exactly the complexion of his political creed. No doubt, in all respects he was a conservative in principle, as his father was before him. His sympathy for the people at large was very cordial and hearty. If we were called on to express by a phrase his political creed, we might say, he would be classed as a Democratic Republican, with strong proclivities to an administration that would secure the greatest liberty consistent with an efficient government, without respect to color, creed or race.

GOVERNOR STEVENS T. MASON.

Stevens T. Mason was hardly twenty-one years of age when he was elected Governor of Michigan. He was of the Virginia family of Masons. He came to Detroit with his father, who was private secretary to Governor Porter, to which post his son in a short time succeeded. The sudden death of the Governor, in 1834, left the Territory without a head and the young man was thus Acting Governor for a few months. He had an active shrewd friend in the Hon. John Norval, subsequently our United States Senator. Mr. Norval was a lawyer of ability and experience, and would be sought for in counsel. Mason was young, but had been trained in political ideas by a Virginia culture. His father was known as an astute business man; his ancestors for many generations had controlled political opinions, and were patriots of the best type. Handsome in person, Young Mason had all the elements of a popular favorite. Frank and outspoken like those of his race, genial in manner, abounding in gracious ways, beloved of his companions, but too popular to be a hard student; proud of a Southern pedigree, yet democratic in his intercourse with all classes. For a young man, his ideas were of commendable breadth, of high promise, of inflexible honesty; he was ardent and ambitious to distinguish himself. Appreciative of great qualities, and warm in his attachments, he cultivated the friendship of Dr. Houghton. He sympathized earnestly in the studies of the young scientist, and the moment the law was passed creating the department of the Geological Survey,

Dr. Houghton was placed by appointment at its head, as the only man in the State, in truth, competent to fill that position.

GEN. SYLVESTER LARNED.

The trying scenes of 1832, the first season of the cholera in Detroit, had taxed Dr. Houghton's skill in the treatment of this fatal malady. In the meantime his practice as physician was large and his reputation growing. This oriental scourge, which reached us in a mild form in '32, became fearful in '34. Among the early victims of the cholera which desolated Detroit in this season of dismay, was Gen. Sylvester Larned. The General was well known to the citizens of Detroit and of the State. A gentleman of noble and gracious bearing, a lawyer of distinction, in the prime of life and of health, universally respected and beloved, his sudden death gave a shock to the community. At the last stage of his sufferings Dr. Houghton had been called in at the special request of the patient; but he was fast sinking.

Dr. Houghton sat by his bedside all night and watched every pulsation with profound solicitude, to discover some favorable symptom, some gleam of hope. Gen. Larned retained his mental faculties up to the last moment. He met the inevitable fate with the calmness of a man at peace with all the world. He took Dr. Houghton by the hand and said he was satisfied that everything that science and skill could do had been done, and thanked him for his attentions, fidelity and sympathy. These were his last words. Not indeed that Dr. Houghton would be more faithful to duty than others of his profession in that trying season, but he was young and ardent, of more than usual gifts, and sympathized warmly with the sufferings of both rich and poor.

As in the investigations of science, so in the practice of his profession, he could vary old or prescribed methods. As a physician in large practice his success was great, uniting with his skill and knowledge the tender regard and care of a friend; the sound of his voice would cheer the desponding patient, and do as much for him as medicine.

DR. ZINA PITCHER.

There have been but few men in Michigan who have so identified themselves with the educational interests of the State as Dr. Zina Pitcher, a gentleman well advanced in years when young Houghton first cast his lines here. Dr. Pitcher was a brother of the former Lieutenant-Governor of New York. He was a man of enlarged culture, was well read in the science of medicine, was qualified to lecture on many questions of natural science. He attached himself very strongly to the young geologist, who was destined to leave the impress of his character so deeply engraved on the records of Michigan. Dr. Pitcher at one time was president of the Medical Society of the United States, and had received the appointment of Regent of the University. He was familiar with the ideas of advanced educators in all the States and in Europe. He was accustomed to mingle with men connected with government and with science.

His studies in natural science were not unworthy a man of liberal views. He took a high stand in the cause of schools, of academic and collegiate culture. No man in the State exercised a more wholesome influence on the opinions and the actions of public men, and in all systems of education or of charity.

He was a man of staid and distinguished manners, reserved and slow of speech. His thoughts came slow, and his manner was at first apparently cold. But this was the disguise, perhaps, of sensibility and warmth. Young Houghton, of a nervous and impetuous temperament, was the reverse of all this. His ardor was without disguise, and his ideas so rapid and so solicitous for expression, that they hardly found words fast enough. But on the principle, perhaps, that opposite natures are drawn toward each other, as certain chemical elements under definite conditions will coalesce, so Dr. Houghton was invited to become a partner in the firm of "Pitcher & Rice, surgeons and physicians." In all of Houghton's scientific studies he had a cordial and able friend and coadjutor in Dr. Pitcher.

Zina Pitcher had been at the Scientific School at Troy at the same time with Houghton, and the friendship and admiration he there felt for the young scientist, never for a moment abated.

Henry Nelson Walker.

It is not with a view of eulogy that we call to mind the early associates of Dr. Houghton, especially those who sympathized with him in his studies or aided him in his labors Among these intimate friends we must not omit the name of Henry N. Walker. They were boys together in Fredonia, New York, and young Walker soon followed his school companion to Detroit, where he pursued his study of law in the office of Chancellor Elon Farnsworth. A friendship beginning in the first bud and bloom of life had been kept warm and fresh up to the death of Houghton, in '45. A self-made man, like all men who are made of any value, Mr. Walker has occupied various positions of trust and responsibility in the State of Michigan.

A lawyer in successful practice, at one time Attorney-General of the State, as editor and proprietor of a daily journal of commanding influence, as vice-president of a bank, and president of the Detroit and Milwaukee railroad, he has not occupied a place that he was not in every sense competent to fill. His name will live in the history of the State as long as integrity and force of character shall be respected. Walker belonged to the Houghton School of Young Men, and throughout all the labors of the Geologist he found in him a tried friend in sympathy and counsel. It is to such men as

H. N. Walker, Douglass Houghton, Franklin Sawyer and John D. Pierce that the University is largely indebted for services and for many gifts.

This can be said of but few young men who, beginning life with no means save their own genius and purpose, have become benefactors to public institutions before even their own fortunes had been assured. The beautiful transit instrument attached to the observatory at Ann Arbor is a gift from the Hon. H. N. Walker, at a cost of not less than $4,000. At this time no other man of the State had bestowed a gift on this State University so munificent. Mr. Walker's death has occurred while we are writing the closing pages of this memoir of his early associate.

HENRY R. SCHOOLCRAFT.

The name of Schoolcraft has a conspicuous place in the early history of Michigan. His "Algic Researches," his "Discovery of the Sources of the Mississippi," and other well known works of a scientific nature, or relating to Indian dialects and customs, have made him known in every civilized land. He came to Michigan as early as 1828. He married a grand daughter of a Chippewa chief, and resided much of his time on the Island of Macinac or at the Sault Ste. Marie. He had received the appointment of Indian Agent, an agency that embraced a large extent of territory. He was familiar with many Indian tongues, and had investigated the principles of their various tribal dialects. The expedition to the sources of the Mississippi was organized by Schoolcraft, and was accomplished in 1832. Dr. Houghton, a young gifted scientist just settled in Detroit, but with the reputation already established of rare attainments, was appointed surgeon and botanist to this expedition, and the report he made of the flora of the region he traversed displayed the accuracy of a trained observer. It seems proper to mention Mr. Schoolcraft here, because Dr. Houghton was thus intimately associated with him, and because he was one of the ripe scholars in the territory who would appreciate the superior attainments of Houghton, as he was himself a distinguished scientist with a national reputation. In questions of Indian ethnology and the lingual peculiarities of the nomadic races of North America, there is no higher authority than Henry R. Schoolcraft. He was an ambitious author, with great confidence in his opinions; certainly a deep scholar in Indian antiquities, ingenious in his theories, with abundance of words and roots to sustain his views as to the similarity or diversity of races; a man of untiring devotion and industry, and voluminous in his publications.

To Mr. Schoolcraft, in concert with Dr. Houghton and Maj. Henry Whiting, the State owes the Indian names that have been adopted for most of the northern counties.

Major Henry Whiting, U. S. A.

It is with peculiar pleasure that we connect this name with Dr. Houghton. In the early days of Detroit few names were more conspicuous. In 1834 Col. Whiting had already been settled in the city for several years. He was quartermaster in the U. S. army; he was well and liberally educated. His culture was kept fresh by the habits of a student; his reading was extensive. He was a polished writer and a ready debater. He would often take part in the discussions before the Young Men's Society, and the Major did not disdain to pay homage to the muse of Poetry, and he wrote with grace and facility. He was the author of two published volumes of poems. Though more given to the amenities of literature, he was interested in questions of natural science. He had read several papers before the Historical Society, relating to the climate and waters of the upper lakes. These are published in a small volume, including discourses by Gen. Cass, Schoolcraft, and Maj. John Biddle. His studies, in fact, would lead him to sympathize with the pursuits of Dr. Houghton, and he did not fail to cultivate his acquaintance, and become an earnest and appreciative friend of the future Geologist. Mrs. Col. Whiting was a niece of Major-General McComb, a general of the national forces. She was a lady most interesting and lovely in person and manners, and she knew how to make her house the resort of the best people in the city, and the young persons who were desirous to improve their manners or cultivate conversational powers would be found at her house. Maj. Whiting had taken the precaution to study law during his spare moments, and was admitted to practice at the bar at Detroit. In this he was governed by a wise forethought, that he might wish at some future time to retire from the army, and would thus have a profession to fall back on.

Major Whiting was a rare example of an army officer rising out of and above the mere routine of a martinet, sympathizing earnestly but temperately with the new ideas involved in science and government. Handsome in person, tall and imposing in figure, of gracious and winning manners, his sympathies were quick and warm. At Lundy's Lane, more than twenty years before, under Gen. Scott, he had seen service, and was in the midst of a sharp conflict; brave and gentle as a true chevalier of the olden times. To know him and Mrs. Whiting was a passport to every house in Detroit. He was a true Christian gentleman, and his commendation would secure confidence and success.

His friendships were not lightly given nor hastily withdrawn. It was the countenance and friendship of such men that sustained Dr. Houghton throughout his brief and laborious career.

CHARLES C. TROWBRIDGE.

It is remarked by the late Hon. C. C. Trowbridge, that Dr Houghton on his first arrival at Detroit, youthful and even boyish as he was in appearance, was at once received into the best social and intellectual circles of the city without reserve. He took his place as one "to the manner born," as he was, indeed, in all respects; and it may be added in regard to the leading families who controlled the social standards in those early days, it was a way they had to accept the new comer for what he was capable of doing, for sterling qualities, without regard to family, station or money. The days of pretense, if they were ever to reach Detroit at some future period, at least would be postponed for many years to come. It has been seen, not only that the young scientist was cordially welcomed, but that very speedily he was recognized as a leader among the young men of the city with whom he associated.

Young Men's Literary Society.

Already it has been mentioned that the Young Men's Literary Society was largely indebted to Dr. Houghton for its early organization in 1832. In these generous labors he was united with Franklin Sawyer, a young man from Boston, of superior education and rare natural gifts; he was the first superintendent of public instruction in Michigan. Dr. Houghton would insist that Sawyer should be the first president of the new society thus formed, he taking the vice-presidency. The second year, however, the members elected Houghton as president. So of other associations and organizations looking to public improvements, young Houghton was among the first to give a helping hand. His young friend, William N. Carpenter, was associated with him in the Sunday school of the church in which he had been baptized as an infant.

At the time of his arrival at Detroit he would need assistance in preparing his apparatus for experiments, to illustrate his lectures on chemistry; and the Hon. John Owen, then a clerk in Dr. Chapin's drug store, would lend a helping hand.

Nor would young Owen resist altogether the enthusiasm of the youthful lecturer. Not only were the young men that surrounded Houghton inspired by his enthusiasm, but they seemed often to be inocculated with a passion for the sciences that he was cultivating; nor would they be insensible to the sterling qualities of honor, courtesy and probity that ever distinguished the young scientist, whose example indeed, was destined to inspire and raise the standard of culture of one entire generation.

It was at that period that George C. Bates, a student at law in the office of the Hon. Henry S. Cole, Attorney-General of the State, became a prominent character among his ambitious companions, conspicuous for grace of person and for style of public speaking quite irresistable to a popular audience. And Jacob M. Howard, of a logical cast of mind,—a deep student, made himself felt in our discussions, and gave promise for that distinction in a larger field, which in a few years after he won in the Senate of the United States.

We might go on and sketch thus briefly these word portraits of many other bright ambitious companions of young Houghton, but shall be obliged to restrain our pen, and confine it to a simple mention of some of these leading young men, many of whom have been heard of in the years that have followed.

John Talbot, of scholarly tastes, Morgan L. Martin, Henry Stringham, Lieut. Senter, H. N. Walker, Alexander Buell, Silas Douglass, Henry G. Hubbard, Franklin Sawyer, Henry Penney, Peter E. DeMill, George Reed, A. S. Williams, E. N. Wilcox, James V. Campbell, Samuel Douglass, George E. Hand, Stevens T. Mason, Marshall J. Bacon, Isaac Roland, George C. Bates, H. H. Emmons, Levi Bishop, Col. A. T. McReynolds, D. B. Duffield, Bela Hubbard, J. W. Waterman, Alvah Bradish, and others.

Most of these young men were brought into close relation with Dr. Houghton, either in business, in connection with the institutions of the State, or in the charities of the city. No doubt we have omitted many names that should belong to this group. But of the younger class, these will include the largest portion of the companions of Houghton from the period of his arrival in Detroit, in 1831, up to the time of the relinquishing his professional labors for the geological survey of the State.

It should be stated that most of these young men were early members of the Young Men's Literary Society, of Detroit.

It is not unsuitable to say, too, that there never has been a literary society established in any of the new States that has exercised a more wide-spread and solid influence on intellectual and aesthetical culture than this Young Men's Society, of Detroit.

Indeed, there are but few men of mark in Michigan, who, beginning their career in Detroit, have not felt and acknowledged its influence. Most of these have taken an active part, either by lectures or debates, or as efficient officials, sustaining its credit and activity with untiring zeal and patriotic devotion. If such a spirit as this that animated the founders of the Young Men's Society, of Detroit, could continue to preside over the conduct of a literary society, there is no good reason why its prosperity should not be perpetual.

PART II.

STATEMENTS REGARDING THE DEATH OF DR. HOUGHTON.

The following remarks are from the "Wolverine," a paper published at Flint, Mich., dated 1874:

No event in its day created more general and painful interest than the untimely fate of Douglass Houghton, cut off in the very prime of his manhood and the midst of his usefulness. No measure can be placed upon what Michigan owes him for the results of his early discovery and promulgation of the vastness and variety of her mineral wealth. His name was famous in both hemispheres, and his memory beloved by all who knew him. But a generation of men have passed off the stage since the crested waves of Lake Superior chanted their murmuring requiem over the remains of the distinguished scholar whom they held in their cold embrace, and a proposition being now before the Legislature to obtain for the new State Capitol Professor Bradish's full length portrait of Dr. Houghton, it has become a fitting time to revive some of the incidents connected with the loss of a man to whose scientific learning, indefatigable industry and fearless exploration in pursuit of knowledge, not alone Michigan, but the whole United States are so largely indebted.

Dr. Douglass Houghton was appointed State Geologist in 1838 by Stevens T. Mason, the first governor of the State of Michigan. He commenced his professional work at once.

In 1844, while making the geological survey of our upper peninsula, he discovered, first the large deposits of iron ore in Marquette county, and afterwards the copper in what was then known as Keeweenaw district, now embracing the counties of Keeweenaw, Houghton and Ontonagon. When his report was first published his statements were attacked by the celebrated Prof. Silliman in his journal, and also by the leading geological savants of Europe. It required but two years working of the mines to satisfy the world that the 'field geologist' of Michigan was right, and that some of the theories of parlor geology, however much they might be respected for their learning, must yield to the crucible test of actual demonstration.

The portrait, which it is proposed shall be purchased by the State, has been executed by Prof. A. Bradish, an artist of celebrity. It represents Dr. Houghton standing on the rocks close to the water's edge, with the pictured rocks forming the background. He is dressed in the free out-door costume of a working geologist, with his hammer in hand, his favorite black and white spaniel is standing by, partly in the water. The expanse of the entire of Lake Superior stretches off to the horizon, an archway of broken rock shelving down to the water, in the distance cascades, etc., fill up the picture. The likeness is said to be an excellent one. Petitions to the Legislature to purchase this portrait have been presented from some of the most prominent men and judges of art of our State, and referred to a select committee appointed to report upon the propriety of securing it for the State.

As a matter of interest to our readers, we republish from the Detroit "Free Press" of Oct. 28, 1845, the following recital of the melancholy circumstances attending the death of Dr. Houghton, made to the Hon. Lucius Lyon, by our fellow-townsman, Col. E. H. Thompson, who was near the spot when the accident occurred:

LETTER OF HON. E. H. THOMPSON.

FORT WILKINS, Lake Superior, October 21, 1845.
TO THE HON. LUCIUS LYON,
Surveyor-General, of Detroit:
MY DEAR SIR:—

Enclosed herewith I forward a statement of facts connected with the unfortunate end of Dr. Douglass Houghton, as given by the survivors of the melancholy catastrophy, Peter McFarline, his true and trusty voyager by flood and field for many years, and John Baptiste Bodrie.

I am aware that in a district of country duly organized with the usual county officers, the law, upon finding the body of Tousin Piquette, demanded an investigation from the hands of a coroner. This course was impracticable without removing all the witnesses to the Sault Ste. Marie, a distance of more than two hundred miles, and at this late season impracticable.

Thus situated, upon consulting with Col. Gratiot and others, it was considered as the best and only method of procuring the statement of the two survivors in the presence of witnesses to reduce it to writing, signed by them, with the certificate of those present of its correctness.

Upon this mode of proceeding I have acted in reducing the statements of McFarline and Bodrie, and trust that we shall meet with your approbation and that of the numerous friends of Dr. Houghton.

The original is sent to you, believing that through you in your official character, the intelligence should reach the executive department at Washington, in whose service he was engaged.

Amid the gloom surrounding the death of Dr. Houghton, it is a matter of congratulation to the world of science, but more particularly to our own State, that all his valuable papers connected with the geology and survey of the northern peninsula for the last six months are saved, with the exception of one small book containing the surveys of a fractional township between Eagle River and the Portage.

It is indeed strange that out of the many scientific men and hundreds of others who have coasted on the waters of our great inland sea during the past season, only the master spirit of them all should fall.

The ways of Providence are truly mysterious. The labor and toil of fifteen years, endeavoring to penetrate the veil which shrouds from our view many of the mighty events that preceded the history of our race, and which required only the magic of his pen and the power of the press to place him among the Humboldts of another sphere, is now lost.

Our country, nay, the world of science were looking with more than Argus eyes for his final report of the geology of the northern peninsula. Michigan beheld his scientific talent and moral worth with pride and admiration; but, alas! he has tracked the steps of glory to a watery grave.

I cheerfully avail myself of this opportunity to bear witness to the kindness of Colonel Gratiot and all connected with the mining works at Eagle River, in alleviating the sufferings of the survivors and in administering to their wants, as well as to his unwearied and indefatigable efforts in making with a sufficient force all possible exertions, but without success, to find the body of Dr. Houghton or that of his voyageur, Oliver Larimer.

I am,
    Very respectfully,
        Your obedient servant,
            E. H. THOMPSON.

STATEMENT OF TWO OF HIS VOYAGEURS.

EAGLE RIVER, Lake Superior, Oct. 14, 1845.

Statements of facts connected with the drowning of Dr. Douglass Houghton, Geologist of the State of Michigan, and two of his men, Tousin Piquette and Oliver Larimer, near Eagle River, on the night of the 13th of October, A. D. 1845, as related by Peter McFarline and John Baptiste Bodrie, survivors:

Dr. Houghton camped on the night of the 12th of October, at Eagle Harbor; on the morning of the 13th he started in his boat with the undersigned acting as voyageurs, with three barrels of flour, a bag of peas, a small quantity of pork, tent and bedding, and a traveling portfolio, for Eagle River, a distance of eight miles to the westward. On arriving at Eagle River they there took in some additional clothing for the surveying party and proceeded five miles still farther west to the store house of Hassey and Avery; they arrived there at noon and immediately commenced unloading the boat; after waiting some time, the miners at work on the location of Messrs. Hassey and Avery, came in to their dinner, and from some of them Dr. Houghton procured the key of the storehouse and deposited his provisions.

We all took dinner here, after which we started for Mr. Hill's surveying party, a distance of three miles on the lake coast. Dr. Houghton and McFarline then started into the woods on the line, and not finding Mr. Hill, he returned to the boat and found by the arrival of Tousin Piquette and Oliver Larimer that Mr. Hill and his men were two miles still further up the lake.

Dr. Houghton then started in his boat in pursuit of Mr. Hill with the undersigned, Tousin Piquette and Oliver Larimer; we met Mr. Hill and his party about sun down, and after remaining nearly an hour and transacting some business, we then put back with the same persons for the purpose of reaching Eagle River that night. We had nothing in the boat but some bedding and the portfolio; at the time of leaving there was a gentle land breeze and a heavy sea from the outside. Dr. Houghton took his usual seat in the stern as steersman, while four of us rowed the boat. On arriving opposite the Hassey location, McFarline asked Dr. Houghton if he was going to stop. Dr. Houghton replied, "No, for if I do not get to Eagle River to-night, Oliver will lose his passage down the lake." McFarline then stated to Dr. Houghton, that he was afraid that it was going to blow. Dr. Houghton said, "No, I guess not; a land breeze can't hurt us." By this time we were opposite the store house of Hassey and Avery. McFarline then told Dr. Houghton that he must go ashore at the warehouse as Oliver's baggage was at that place. At this we put into the landing, and after getting the baggage we then stood for Eagle River.

The wind was about the same as when we left Mr. Hill, except that it commenced snowing a little and growing dark; after rowing nearly three miles we found ourselves opposite a place called the Sand Beach. At this place the wind changed and commenced blowing from the northeast and snowing faster. In a short time we encountered a heavy sea caused by a reef projecting into the lake about a mile and a half. McFarline then asked Dr. Houghton to go ashore at the Sand Beach. Dr. Houghton replied, "We had better keep on—we are not far from Eagle River, pull away, boys, pull hard." At this, Bodrie spoke in the French language to McFarline, and said, "We had better go ashore." Dr. Houghton immediately inquired of McFarline, "What did Bodrie say?" McFarline told him, when Dr. Houghton replied, "We had better go to Eagle River to-night as we shall there have a new log house to dry us in." The wind and snow kept increasing, and after rowing some time, Dr. Houghton remarked once or twice, "Pull away, my boys, we shall soon be in, pull away," and encouraged us by similar expressions. We commenced shipping water and made but little progress. After knocking and rolling about among the breakers for over an hour and storming all the time, McFarline bailed the boat out and advised Dr. Houghton to put on his life preserver. The bag containing it was handed to him, he placed it at his side; instantly a heavy sea struck the boat and filled it.

Dr. Houghton then proposed going ashore. McFarline told him he could not land; that the coast opposite them was all rocks. Dr. Houghton immediately put the boat about, saying, "We must go ashore; we can do nothing here." Within two hundred yards of the shore, they shipped another sea which was followed by a larger billow, and the boat capsized with all hands under her.

McFarline was the first person from beneath, and upon rising to the top of the water, caught hold of the keel of the boat at the stern. Upon looking round, he saw a man's arm about half way out of the water. He instantly lowered himself and caught the man by the collar of his coat, and upon bringing him up, it was Dr. Houghton, who recognized him. McFarline told him to take off his gloves and to hold on to the keel of the boat. The advice was followed. McFarline still preserving his hold.

Dr. Houghton then remarked, "Peter, never mind me, try to go ashore if you can; I will go ashore well enough." Instantly a heavy sea struck the boat, throwing it perpendicularly into the air. It fell over backwards, and Dr. Houghton disappeared forever.

McFarline regained the boat, and upon getting in, discovered for the first time one of his companions, Bodrie, in the water and clinging to the bow. In this position they both remained some fifteen minutes, but saw nothing more of their companions. A sea washed them out again. McFarline drifted towards the rocks and got a loose hold. In a moment he was washed off and being carried to and fro against the rocks some three times. The fourth wave landed him on the top of a ledge of rocks, and by clinging to a crack or fissure in the rock, and getting hold of a small bush he succeeded in saving himself.

After landing he looked around him and could see nothing but the boat filled with water and the bedding floating. Soon he heard a voice among the rocks, asking in the French language, "Who is that?" McFarline replied, "It is me, Peter." The rescued man was Bodrie. We commenced looking about in every direction and hollowing, but heard no answer. We continued examining until we found ourselves growing chilly and stiff, when Bodrie remarked, "Well, we have lost our brothers; it may be that one of us will get to Eagle River to tell their fate."

We started, and on the way down McFarline fell several times from exhaustion and cold. Bodrie roused his companion up, and finally succeeded in reaching Eagle River between the hours of eleven and twelve at night. We told what had happened, and within an hour the entire coast was lined in search for the bodies, by miners and others who were near at hand.

(Signed) PETER McFARLINE,
BAPTISTE BODRIE.

EAGLE RIVER, Lake Superior, Oct. 14, 1845.

We do hereby certify that we were severally present when the above named Peter McFarline and John Baptiste Bodrie gave in their statements of the melancholy occurrence of the death of Dr. Houghton and two of his men on the night of the 13th inst., by drowning, and that the above is a correct statement as given by them.

E. H. THOMPSON, Michigan,
C. H. GRATIOT, Eagle River,
J. HOUGHTON, JR., Detroit, Mich..
J. T. WHITING, Eagle River,
JOHN HAWKS, M. D., Rochester, N. Y.,
ALGERNON MERRYWEATHER, Mich.
BELA HUBBARD, Detroit.

In the spring of 1846 the remains of Dr. Houghton were found not far from the scene of the disaster in the previous October. They were half covered with sand, but easily identified. They were interred in Elmwood cemetery, Detroit, now covered by the monument raised to his memory by Mrs. Houghton.

The night of Houghton's death and the day following, the snow that had commenced at dusk fell to the depth of three feet.

RESOLUTIONS OF THE COMMON COUNCIL OF DETROIT.

CITY CLERK'S OFFICE, DETROIT, Nov. 27, 1845.

At a special session of the common council of the City of Detroit, held Wednesday, Oct., 29, 1845, the following preamble and resolutions were adopted:

WHEREAS, The lamentable intelligence has reached us that our late esteemed fellow townsman, Dr. Douglass Houghton, has met with a sudden death on the waters of Lake Superior;

AND WHEREAS, The relation which the deceased so lately sustained with us as mayor of the city and ex-officio president of this board, renders an expression of respect and regret proper on behalf of this council; therefore,

Resolved, That the members of the common council of the city of Detroit, cherish the most profound respect for the memory of the deceased, and deeply deplore the mournful event which has deprived this State of a man whose talents, acquirements and services have adorned her history and promised still more to enrich her annals, which has deprived this city of a valued, esteemed and most useful citizen, society of an amiable, interesting and beloved member, and his family of an affectionate and devoted head;

Resolved, That we tender our sincere condolence to his afflicted family upon the occasion of their sad bereavement;

Resolved, That as a further mark of respect, his honor, the mayor, be requested to call a public meeting of our fellow-citizens to be held to-morrow evening at 7 o'clock at the city hall;

Resolved, That this expression of our feeling be entered on our records, that a copy be furnished the family of the deceased and published in our proceedings in the papers of the city.

ROBERT E. ROBERTS,

Clerk.

THE CENOTAPH AT ANN ARBOR.

In the beautiful University grounds at Ann Arbor, Mich., has been erected a square monument of lime stone, designed for four tablets, and surmounted by a broken column. Two of the sides are already occupied by white marble tablets to the memory of Professors Whiting and Houghton. The one to Dr. Houghton bears the following inscription:

TO THE MEMORY OF

DOUGLASS HOUGHTON, M. D.,

PROFESSOR OF CHEMISTRY, MINERALOGY AND GEOLOGY IN THIS UNIVERSITY, AND GEOLOGICAL SURVEYOR GENERAL

IN THIS STATE.

IN SCIENCE LEARNED, IN ACTION PROMPT, WHILE BOLDLY ENGAGED IN PUBLIC DUTY, BY THE OVERTURNING OF A BOAT IN LAKE SUPERIOR, HE PERISHED. SINKING, NEVER, ALAS! TO BE SEEN AGAIN UNTIL "THE SEA GIVE UP THE DEAD."

OCTOBER 13, 1845,

Aged 36.
.

THE TRUSTEES OF THE UNIVERSITY OF MICHIGAN THIS STONE HAVE TAKEN CARE TO PLACE.

PART III.

THE HOUGHTON PORTRAIT.

As early as 1834 Mr. Alvah Bradish was a resident citizen of Detroit, a young man and an artist, closely associated with Dr. Houghton, and on intimate terms with his family.

He had unusual facilities for the study of his countenance and his person. The portrait he painted from life has always been considered an excellent likeness of Dr. Houghton. It is, indeed, the only portrait in oil that he ever sat for. This was before the days of the daguerrtype or the photograph.

With this original portrait before him, and with a perfect knowledge of Dr. Houghton's person, the artist has designed a full length portrait, standing at the water's edge, with the pictured rocks of Lake Superior forming a back ground. It has been widely seen and approved by all who knew Dr. Houghton.

It was offered to the legislature of Michigan for purchase; a bill for its purchase was brought before the legislature in 1879. Prof. Bradish was in the capitol by invitation of Gov. Croswell, and all the members of the two houses had visited his room. Besides the full length of Dr. Houghton, a full length of Dr. Henry P. Tappan, first president of the University, was on exhibition; also a full length portrait of that eminent statesman, the Hon. Lewis Cass, so long governor of Michigan while a territory; besides other distinguished citizens of the State. These large paintings were original works by Prof. Bradish.

During the winter more than three thousand citizens had visited the studio to see these historical portraits, but mainly, it may be said, to pay their respects to the pioneer geologist of the State. Nearly one thousand petitions had been sent to the legislature, coming from all parts of the State, urging its purchase.

So many years had elapsed since the time of Houghton's death that some hesitation might be looked for among members who had yet to become acquainted with the career of the first geologist of Michigan. But so well persuaded were the leading members of the legislature of 1879 that this recognition of his services was just and patriotic, that in the senate there were only one or two votes adverse, while in the House the bill for purchase was passed by a very large vote, the members satisfying themselves that the memorial portrait offered by Prof. Bradish had every claim to authenticity, and that it was a faithful representation of the subject of this memoir.

The bill was promptly signed by the governor, Charles Croswell. It passed into the hands of the board of auditors of this State, who had been authorized by it to purchase the portrait for the State. It still lies there.

The Proposed Monument.

If the writer has shown excessive zeal to perpetuate the memory of Houghton, it should be remembered that he is among the few now living who knew him well, that he is the only artist that ever painted him from life—it being ten years before the advent of the photograph—that most of his associates have passed away, and that life is too precarious to leave these varied materials and records to the arrangement and handling of a stranger.

For several years past the author has been solicitous in obtaining materials bearing on Houghton's life and services. His zeal is warmed by the remembrance of his character, his steady friendship and his enthusiasm in the cause of science, in which he lost his life.

The Michigan legislature was in session at Detroit, then the capital of the State, when the news of the death of Dr. Houghton reached the city. The loss was deemed a public calamity by the representatives. A bill was introduced expressing the general feeling, making an appropriation for a monument to be erected on the shore of Lake Superior, near Eagle River.

But at that time the financial condition of the State was so depressed that it was thought advisable to postpone action until a later season, and a sum more suitable and more in accordance with public sentiment could be secured.

If it is surprising, it is hardly creditable, that the monument contemplated by the legislature of '46 has not been followed up by some popular action. One would expect among the enterprising and intelligent citizens of the upper peninsula especially, that almost a spontaneous expression in this direction would have been seen before this date. At Elmwood cemetery, where Dr. Houghton's remains were deposited, there is a plain granite shaft, erected by his widow, that will inform the passer by of the last resting place of Houghton. One of the free schools of Detroit has received his name, in honor of one so zealous to promote popular education. A cenotaph, plain and inexpensive, stands within the grounds of the University Campus. A name that is so cherished in this State will not perish. A few years hence passengers traversing the waters of Lake Superior, from the deck of steamers will scan the southern shore along the coast near Eagle River. They will remember what name has been associated with all this region, and especially with the perils of storm and disaster; they will look for some sign that the memory of such a man has not been forgotten. These travelers may not always be disappointed. The time is soon to come when they will discover some monument booming through the mist, perhaps a simple granite shaft broken midway, as the life of Houghton was shattered and broken, and the story of his marvelous energy and courage will be read again and again with ever renewed interest.

The good missionary Marquette died in the performance of duty somewhere near the shore of Lake Michigan, but the precise spot or the time is not known. La Salle, the most courageous and intrepid explorer of the great inland lakes and the waters of the Mississippi, perished amid the wild savannahs of lower Louisiana, not a scientist but eager to make discoveries and to add new lands to the rule of a sovereign who could not heed their importance. He fell by assassination, but no one can name the spot where he perished.

The adventurous explorer of Florida, De Soto, stimulated by motives less pure perhaps, perished on the banks of the Mississippi, and was buried in its waters. It may be remembered that these courageous pioneers were in the midst of a race or races of nomadic habits, who had no written language, kept no records and had no history. There are good reasons and some apology for our ignorance of the last moments and final resting places of these adventurous heroes. But there can be no apology for our indifference or neglect of the memory of those whose services are conspicuous, whose persons are remembered, whose labors have enriched the State, and whose fame is a part of the inheritance of the present generation of men in Michigan. In the county of Roscommon there is a beautiful lake some fifteen or twenty miles in length which bears the name of Houghton. It was the way our people had to honor the names of men who were devoting their energies to the service of the State. But so easily and rapidly will errors become installed in the popular thought, that an eastern gentleman sojourning a while on the banks of this secluded lake, was taken by a resident to a point of land overlooking the waters, and was shown the very spot where Dr. Houghton was drowned!

The reader will not censure the author for offering the following quotation from a gentleman well known to the citizens of Michigan. In a report to the legislature, the Hon. Lyman D. Norris speaks of Houghton's death as "truly a sad loss to the State of Michigan. An enthusiastic lover of science for itself, and for no selfish end, with a constitution that seemed never to know fatigue or fear, labor or danger, he had with all a kindly, loving heart, that drew to itself all who were brought within its circle. Simple as a child, and unassuming as he was scholarly, he wrote his name on the history of this State, there to remain forever. The influence that such men have live after them, and if there is anything of unsensational enthusiasm in the advocacy of the writer of this report, of such geologic work as would most gratify the spirit of that great and good man of science (if permitted to participate in the cares of this mortal life), it springs from the recollection of many months of intimate intercourse had with him in the earliest days of our University.

"His small, compact form, sinewy figure, crowned with a dome-like brain, usually bent downward like a full head of wheat, as he sauntered across the college campus, surrounded by his then 'baker's dozen' of the students of those days—always welcome companions to him—is one of the memorial pictures never to be effaced. Then with his forward and downward look he seemed ever to be interrogating Mother Earth and asking for her secrets, while no rare bug or beetle, or blade of grass, or stone, escaped his notice, but was seen and examined and taken as the text for many pleasant and instructive lectures to the loving group that stood around him."

Testimonials.

After the death of Dr. Houghton the Hon. Bela Hubbard and Mr. William A. Burt were appointed and requested to prepare reports based on the field notes and other materials of Houghton's uncompleted labors. As Assistant State Geologist, Mr. Hubbard submitted a brief but comprehensive report of these labors. In conclusion he says: "In attempting this duty the undersigned cannot be unmindful of the very meagre and imperfect sketch here presented, when compared with whatever proceeded from that master mind, whose genius first developed and whose indomitable energy tracked through all its difficulties a system not only intricate in itself but novel to science, and in a region at that time destitute of all ordinary facilities for scientific investigation.

To the same active and philosophical mind we owe the system of the union of the geological with the lineal surveys of the land of the United States, the first experimental results of which are now returned to this department."

This memoir of Dr. Houghton had been nearly completed before the author had seen the report of Mr. T. B. Brooks to the Board of Geological Surveys of the State of Michigan. This able report had escaped his notice, being absent from the State when it was first made, but he cannot deny himself the satisfaction of giving to the reader these generous words of an able scientist, competent to appreciate the genius and the labor of his predecessor.

From the report of T. B. Brooks to the Board of Geological Survey of the State of Michigan, Vol. I, page 12:

"The honesty, skill and enthusiasm with which this field work was executed, resulted in the collection of a large amount of geological data, which at the completion of the survey would have left little to be done save the final report, with which the master mind should classify, group and harmonize these facts, and thereby develop nature's laws from the mass of materials collected.

" Dr. Houghton's untimely death by drowning on Lake Superior while in the midst of his labors prevented him from performing this crowning work. Anyone familiar with the geology of the upper peninsula and who will peruse the manuscript notes left by Dr. Houghton, will be convinced that his views regarding the geology of the older rocks were far in advance of his time, and such only as geologists years after arrived at, and those which are but now, thirty years after he recorded them, universally accepted. In 1843 the financial troubles of the State of Michigan, arising out of the five million loan, as it was called, were of such a character as to cause the legislature to withhold the annual appropriation for the geological survey, which then had been for several years in successful operation under the directions of Dr. Houghton. Thoroughly interested in his scientific work, and believing that the best interests of the State and the cause of science demanded the continuance of the survey, Dr. Houghton solicited from the general government the aid which his own State felt unable to grant, and succeeded in obtaining in the appropriation for the public survey of the upper peninsula of Michigan an additional allowance per mile, to cover the cost of the geological work.

"In order to expedite the work and insure the best scientific results from the adoption of his plans, Dr. Houghton himself took the contract from the government for completing the survey of the upper peninsula which had previously been begun in 1840, under the direction of the Hon. William A. Burt, U. S. Deputy Surveyor. In 1844 Dr. Houghton commenced operations under his contract, the field work being in charge of Mr. Burt, who received in compensation therefor the extra allowance granted by the government.

"It is proper to add that Mr. Burt entered with deep interest into Dr. Houghton's plan, and had during his surveys in the lower peninsula collected for him many specimens and important geological information not required by his instructions"

WM. A. BURT AND HIS SOLAR COMPASS.

In 1844 a party consisting of Mr. Burt, Jacob Houghton, younger brother of Dr. Houghton, and others (young Houghton being the barometer man), was engaged in establishing township lines and making geological observations as previously described. On the 19th of September, while running the eastern line of town 47 north, range 27 west, the great iron township as it proved, they observed by means of the solar compass a remarkable variation in the direction of the needle.

Mr. Houghton, who kept a diary, says: "On the evening of the 18th of September we reached the lake and established the northeast corner of town 47 north, between the Chocolate and Carp rivers. We then run west the township line, and camped at the town corner, on the east side of Teal Lake, on the 18th September. On the morning of the 19th we started running the line south, between the ranges 26 and 27. So soon as we reached the hills to the south of the lake the compass man began to notice the fluctuation in the variation of the magnetic needle. We were, of course, using the solar compass, of which Mr. Burt was the inventor, and I shall never forget the excitement of the old gentleman during the changes of the variation, the needle not actually traversing alike in any two places. He kept changing his position to take observations, all the time saying: 'How would they survey this country without my compass? What could be done here without my compass?'

"It was the full and complete realization of what he had foreseen when struggling through the first stages of his invention. At length the compass man called for all to come and see 'a variation that would beat them all.' As we looked at the instrument, to our astonishment the north end of the needle was traversing a few degrees to the south of west. Mr. Burt called out, 'Boys, look around and see what you can find.' We all left the line, some going to the east and some to the west, and all of us returning with specimens of iron ore, mostly gathered from out crop This was along the first mile from Teal Lake. We carried out all specimens we could conveniently." (See Appendix 'E,' vol. 2, Geology of Michigan, unpublished manuscript at the University. These extracts and comments and notes are by Mr. T. B. Brooks, who had the compilations of these volumes in charge, a work of great interest, and performed with ability and fidelity.)

Discovery of Gold in the Mineral Region.

Immediately after the death of Dr. Houghton, in 1845, the report became current that he had added to his discoveries of copper, silver, iron and lead, that of gold, but as his notes of that year were lost with him, it became generally supposed that there was no foundation for the rumor. As passing years brought no confirmation through further discovery—a generation, in fact, having passed away before the existence of the precious metal became a practical fact—the alleged discovery by Dr. Houghton was long treated as a myth.

It will be remembered by those who have read the foregoing pages that Dr. Houghton was at that time carrying forward the connected linear and geological survey of the mineral region under a contract with the government, consequently he had several parties of surveyors in the field. Among them was Mr. Samuel W. Hill, who is well known throughout the Lake Superior region. We here copy from the "Marquette Mining Journal" his statement, which would seem to set the question at rest:

Samuel W. Hill's Recollections of Dr. Houghton's Gold Discovery on Lake Superior.

S. W. Hill, who was with Dr. Houghton on his geological survey of the Marquette iron region about forty years ago, said that he was sent up with a party of men to where Negaunee now stands, and they pitched their tents a hundred rods northeast of the city, where the Doctor was operating at the mouth of the Chocolate River. One day the Doctor visited their camp to see how they were progressing at that end of the survey. He arrived at the camp in the afternoon, and, after resting and refreshing himself, he took a pick and went out among the hills. Returning just before darkness set in, he said: "Mr. Hill are you aware we are in a gold region?" Mr. Hill replied that he was not. "But," said the Doctor, "we are;" and he took some specimens of rock from his haversack which were quite richly charged with gold. Mr. Hill asked the Doctor if there was much of it. Dr. Houghton answered that he had not examined the ground very closely, and also said he did not wish anything said about it just then, as they had already had some trouble with the men, and if these should become aware that they were in a gold region they might desert them to hunt for it themselves.

Unfortunately, that fall Dr. Houghton was capsized in a squall at Eagle River and drowned, and all his notes were lost with him. Mr. Hill says the Doctor came from a northeast course—not from the northwest, as I had been previously informed—and that he could not have been over a mile or so away, which would be about on a range with the Ropes vein. Mr. Hill also said the specimens then found were sent to Detroit, and Jacob Houghton, a brother of the Doctor, had some of the gold extracted and made into a breastpin, which he wore for years.—[T. Meads, in Marquette Mining Journal.]

A Memorial Window.

It has been reserved for a stranger to do what State and citizens have failed to accomplish, viz., to erect at and near the scene of his scientific labors and triumphs, some suitable memorial of Dr. Houghton.

As we go to press the following notice comes to hand of a beautiful memorial window put up in St. Paul's church, Marquette. The article is copied from the "Marquette Mining Journal," January, 1889, and is from the pen of Hon. Peter White:—

A Houghton Window—The Beautiful Memorial Window just Placed in St. Paul's Church.

Mr. A. Langfear Norrie, a New Yorker by birth, after passing seven years in London and other parts of England acquiring his education, returned to his native country seven or eight years ago. Hearing almost fabulous stories of the mineral wealth of Northern Michigan, and of the new iron fields steadily being opened up here, he was seized, notwithstanding his great inherited wealth, by the laudable ambition of achieving success through his own personal efforts, unaided by wealth or friends, and he came to Michigan almost immediately after his return. He made Marquette his headquarters and, donning the garb of an explorer, joined the hardy class always to be found in the forests of the upper peninsula looking for timber or mineral wealth.

He traversed the Marquette and Menominee regions, subjecting himself to all the hardships of life in the wilderness, and then struck into what is now known as the Gogebic range, and within a couple of years had located the great Norrie mine, which in the season just ended shipped over 400,000 tons of Bessemer ore. A simple reference is made to these facts to explain Mr. Norrie's friendly feeling for Marquette, where he was always welcome, and where by the qualities within him he made many warm friends. In the last two years he has resumed his residence in New York, but is still an occasional visitor to his Michigan home.

While here he had heard and read of the exalted character and service to the State of Dr. Douglass Houghton, as the first Michigan State Geologist, and of his sad fate. This suggested to his mind some suitable memorial. With this in view he wrote to a prominent citizen of Marquette an offer to put a Houghton memorial window in St. Paul's church in this city, and pursuant to his instructions the offer was made to the rector and vestry of the church as a Christmas gift, December 25, 1887. It was promptly accepted on that day, and Mr. Norrie at once ordered the window from the celebrated firm of Clayton & Bell, London, Eng. At the suggestion of Mr. D. F. Charlton, the architect, Mr. Norrie ordered a brownstone tracery, instead of the wood sash, in which to set the window. This was cut here by James R. Lawrence, and is in itself a work of art.

The window is now in place in its brownstone fittings. The reporter has examined it, and only regrets his inability to adequately describe the beauty of finish, harmonious blending of color, exquisite design and perfect loveliness of its *toute ensemble*, the same attributes of perfection being found in each separate figure. It is a poem in glass. The emblems can be only imperfectly described, and the reader should visit the church for himself and see the window with the sunlight streaming through it. In the lower right hand corner appears the "Salutation"—Mary saluting Elizabeth before the birth of John the Baptist, while in the lower left hand panel is the "Annunciation"—the angel Gabriel announcing to Mary the coming birth of Christ. The two panels forming the centre section of the window are really one in design, and represent the "Nativity" and the "Adoration"—Mary and Joseph with the child in the manger, and the visit of the three wise men, kings of the east, one with gold, another with frankincense, and the third with myrrh. The beauty of the three faces, and figures is wonderful. It is noticeable that the artists follow the ancient tradition, and picture one of the kings as a Nubian. The upper panel, circular in form, also relates to the design of the centre section. It represents the "Glorification"—the song of the angels, and the star throwing its light down upon the stable in Bethlehem for the guidance of the kings.

The window is mediæval in design and finish, and is striking in the attention paid to details. It is perfect in its smallest part, and the richness of coloring cannot be surpassed. Between the lower panel and the center section is the inscription from Isaiah, "The Gentiles shall come to Thy light and kings to the brightness of Thy rising," while across the bottom, just above the sash, are the words, "Douglass Houghton, M. D., State Geologist, born Troy, N. Y., Sept. 21, 1809; drowned Eagle River, Mich., Oct. 13, 1845. Presented Xmas 1887, by A. L. N."

Dr. Douglass Houghton was the first State Geologist of Michigan. He was appointed immediately on the admission of this State into the Union, at about the same time that, as a result of "The Toledo War," Michigan acquired the upper peninsula. In May, 1840, Dr. Houghton came to Lake Superior and the upper peninsula in canoes and small boats, accompanied by Bela Hubbard and Columbus C. Douglass as his assistant scientific expert geologists. Of the same expedition was Frederick Hubbard, in charge of instrumental observations, H. Thielson, civil engineer, Charles W. Penny and six Canadian oarsmen.

The State has gained much knowledge and information through the work of this commission, but the boat occupied by Dr. Houghton was capsized and he was drowned October 13, 1845, off Eagle River. He had completed his summer's work on this peninsula, and was returning home with all the notes of the season's discoveries and observations, all of which were lost with him.

In this connection it may not be inappropriate to copy a tribute to Dr. Douglass Houghton by an upper peninsula State senator in 1875, in an address before both houses of the legislature that year. It is here given:

"At length, in 1841, the first report of the geological survey of the upper peninsula was made by the Michigan State Geologist, Dr. Douglass Houghton.

"Here I must pause, for Douglass Houghton is a name which no true Lake Superior man, or Michigan man, ever passes without a tribute, perhaps unspoken but none the less striking, deep and pure, in the bottom of his heart.

"The world has now but just turned from the pageant which followed to an illustrious tomb the scarred and weather-beaten frame of that great man, Dr. Livingstone, who gave up his life to his God humbly kneeling by his rough couch in the wilds of Africa, where no white man's foot had ever trod, in magnificent solitude.

"We have here no enormous London, no rich and cultured people, bowing in enthusiasm before the throne of intellect, science, genius and heroism; no titled, hereditary lords and sovereigns in funeral train; no vast and sombre monumental pile where rest in peace the ashes of the mighty dead.

"We are a rough, practical, money-making race. Seldom in our busy day can we pause to ponder on the goodness of a by-gone friend, and we shudder to think how soon the stream of life will close over our heads after we, too, have followed.

"But we have great, warm, working, western hearts, which the icy waters that were his winding-sheet cannot chill, and they shall be our Westminster Abbey, Douglass Houghton's mausoleum. We will fix our eyes on his noble life and death, and by striving with generous ardor to emulate them, erect to him the imperishable memorial which history ever grants the teacher, and, perhaps by God's grace, may follow him to heaven."

PART IV.

LETTERS OF DR. HOUGHTON.

TO HON. AUGUSTUS PORTER.

This letter to the Hon. Augustus Porter, member of Congress from Detroit, is in reply to one of inquiry copied from the "National Intelligencer," Washington, D. C.:

DETROIT, December 26th, 1840.

MY DEAR SIR,—

Yours of the 17th inst. has just come to hand, and it is highly gratifying to me that steps have been taken in relation to the Sault Ste. Marie canal at an early day in the session. The importance of this work to Michigan is appreciated by but few of our citizens, and its importance in a national point of view is hardly appreciated at all.

The fact is, the great mass of our people are disposed to look upon the upper peninsula as having a climate so rigorous and a soil so poor as wholly to unfit it for agriculture. Now, both these suppostitions are without ground, and I will venture to say that the soil and climate as a whole are better adapted to the purposes of agriculture than that of the New England States. I do not speak on this subject without knowledge, for I have traversed the length of Lake Superior by canoes, oar and sail boats, five times; have ascended frequently, though not always, to the sources of every stream entering the lake from the south side; have crossed from the lake to the Mississippi River by three different lines, and have made many hundred miles of traverses of land where I did not follow the course of the stream. The Indians, after leaving the immediate shores of the lake, raised corn, and it was a sure crop. The average latitude of the south coast is nearly 46 deg. 30 min. In only one respect do I imagine there has been an over-estimate of the resources of this district, and this is with timber. The amount of pine compared with what has been usually supposed, is, I imagine, small. The quantity of sugar maple is vastly greater than has been supposed, and frequently this is of the most magnificent growth I have ever seen. The exports of this district for the present must consist chiefly of peltries, fish and minerals. Upon the two first of these the last census will give you full statistical returns, and I would add that the fishing is conducted under very great disadvantage and increased expense in consequence of keeping vessels constantly upon the lake with a crew under pay, while they necessarily lie idle during a large portion of the year.

Of the mineral resources of the country I am unable to speak as definitely as could be wished, for the reason that my field notes are not yet reduced to form. Much time is required to place the observations for geological locations of fixed points in such a shape as to make a whole, and until this is done I am unable to fix the precise limits of the mineral region.

Ores of zinc, lead, iron and manganese occur in the vicinity of the south shore of Lake Superior, but I doubt whether these, unless it be zinc and iron, are in sufficient abundance to prove of much importance. Ores of copper are much more abundant than either of those before mentioned, and a sufficient examination of them has been made to satisfy me that they may be made to yield an abundant supply of the metals. I do not mean by this that copper is to be found in that region, as is the popular opinion, pure and without labor, but that capital may be safely invested in raising and smelting of these ores with profit to the capitalist.

The district which is believed to contain the chief of the copper ores lies upon the south side of the lake and towards the westerly end. It stretches partly parallel to the lake for a distance a little less than one hundred and thirty miles, and has an average breadth of three to four miles. These dimensions are given a little at random, but they cannot vary far from the truth. This district only reaches the shore of the lake at a single point; from this it stretches off on a crescent form about twenty-eight miles inland, and again approaches within half a mile of the coast. The mineral district of Lake Superior bears a very striking resemblance, in a geological point of view, as in all other respects, to that of the celebrated copper and tin district of Cornwall and Devon, England, and its area is vastly greater. The veins of ore traversing the mineral district of Lake Superior, in those portions I have examined closely, are of very frequent occurrence, and range from a few inches to fourteen feet in width. I do not now recollect (I write without a reference to field notes) that I traced any of those veins over a mile in length, and most of them less, but the difficulty of tracing them depended on the covering of earth and the obstacles from the thickness of the timber and the undershrub. The average width of the worked veins in Cornwall is about four feet, which is considerably less than the average of those of the district examined near Lake Superior. I brought from Lake Superior on my return to Detroit this fall from four to five tons of copper ores, and am now busily engaged in making an analysis of them. Thus far they have proved equal to any ores I have ever seen, and their value for purpose of reduction cannot be doubted. The average per cent. of metal is considerably above that of the ores of Cornwall. While speaking of the ores I am reminded of the beautiful specimens of native copper which came out with the ores in opening some of these veins. They are not very abundant, but some of them are very fine. In opening a vein with a single blast, I threw out nearly two tons of ore, and with this were many masses of native copper, from the most minute specks to about forty pounds in weight, which was the largest mass I obtained from that vein. Ores of silver occasionally occur with the copper, and in opening one vein small specks of native silver were observed. There are as yet, however, no evidences of the existence of this metal in sufficient abundance to be of practical value.

It has been my desire in all examinations connected with these important subjects to be sure and not deceive myself, and to draw no conclusions but such as are strictly based on observation.

The collection of minerals I have brought from the regions of Lake Superior have turned the heads of most of those persons who have examined them, but it is not so with myself, for I know full well the many difficulties and embarrassments which will surround the development of the resources of this district of country. That it will eventually prove of great value to our citizens and to the nation there can scarcely be a shadow of doubt, but the time when this can be done must in a great measure depend on the general policy of our government. This should be a liberal one, and such as will give stimulus to individual enterprise, while it will prevent a monopoly. The construction of the Sault Ste. Marie canal will add very much to the facilities, and in fact at this time without it nothing could be done except at enormous and ruinous expense.

I hope to see the day when instead of importing the whole of the immense amount of copper and brass used in our country we may become exporters of both.

DOUGLASS HOUGHTON,
State Geologist.

TO RICHARD HOUGHTON.

It would seem that the plan of Mr. Lucius Lyon, mentioned in the following letter, in reference to the appointment of Dr.

Houghton as Naturalist, was not carried out, for in June following we find him on Lake Superior, connected as surgeon and botanist with the Schoolcraft expedition, as will appear in a subsequent letter.

Richard, to whom this letter was addressed, was then at Lockport, N. Y.:

FREDONIA, N. Y., Feb'y 21, 1832.

To Richard Houghton:

DEAR BROTHER:—As I suppose that Lydia and Sarah, who have scribbled on the other side, have given you the most important news respecting our mighty city and its citizens, I will briefly attend to my own matter. Since you left here I have heard from Secretary Cass through Mr. Bates Cook, and he talks favorably. There is now no vacancy in the medical staff of the army, but there is a bill before the House for increasing the number, and I presume it will pass.

I have received from Mr. Lucius Lyon, agent or commissioner to settle some of the Indian boundaries at Galena, Ill., an invitation to accompany him the ensuing season, in settling the Indian bounds under the Treaty of Prairie du Chien, of 1830, in the Northwest territory, as naturalist. He will apply to the war department for a direct appropriation for that purpose, and he offers to furnish me forty dollars per month from his own pocket, in addition to which he will defray my expenses from the time I leave home until I return next fall. The route is as follows: Beginning at the Mississippi one hundred and fifty miles above Galena, and running up the Iowa River to its source, thence to the upper forks of the Des Moines River, thence to Calumet River and down that river to the Missouri, somewhere near Council Bluffs, then down the Missouri River to the Western boundaries of the State of Missouri, thence north on said boundary to the northwest corner of the State, thence by a circuitous route to the upper forks of the Des Moines River as aforesaid. The lines of the Iowa River and across the Des Moines will be treble, one line on each side of the centre line, and at a distance of twenty miles from it. The greater part of the route will be through a country almost wholly unexplored. It will undoubtedly afford a rich field for investigation, particularly in the department of botany, and should an appropriation be made for that purpose will afford a handsome salary. If I do not receive other orders from the war department I shall probably leave here for Galena as early as the first of April. My route will be down the Ohio, and up the Mississippi by the way of St. Louis, and my return in the fall by the way of the Illinois River to Chicago, and across the peninsula of Michigan to Detroit.

I shall look for further instruction from Mr. Lyon in about twenty days, when I will write more upon the subject; other things which I mentioned to you will be deferred until next fall. My business is so urgent that I shall not be able to visit Lockport as I anticipated. Remembrances to Mr. Brown and family. Please write me immediately.

Your brother,
DOUGLASS HOUGHTON.

TO RICHARD HOUGHTON.

Dr. Houghton had been appointed as surgeon and botanist to the Schoolcraft expedition for the discovery of the sources of the Mississippi. This letter is to his younger brother Richard, who fell a victim to the cholera two years after at Detroit:

AMERICAN FUR CO. POST.
FOND DU LAC, June 24, 1832.

MY DEAR BROTHER:—

We arrived at this place, which is twenty-four miles beyond the head of Lake Superior, on the St. Louis River, last evening. I was much surprised upon our arrival, at the village-like appearance which it presents. There are several capacious log buildings and these are surrounded by a stockade, and this gives it almost the air of a fort. Directly in the rear of the post, the hills rise almost to mountain heights and upon the opposite side of the river they are seen stretching as far as the eye can reach in either direction. The trading clerks and voyageurs of the American Fur Co. who trade west and north of the head of Lake Superior, about two hundred in number, are now collected here, and in addition to these there are between two and three hundred Indians of the band now situated at this place, now present, and adding our own party we can muster between five and six hundred persons, so that you can well imagine we have lively times. Some of these half French and half Indian traders have traversed during the winter most of the country bordering on the upper Mississippi River, while others have been as far west as the Rocky Mountains.

Mr. Aiken, the director of the company in this section of the country is now here—his headquarters at Sandy Lake. He is European French, I suppose, is affable and intelligent, and has been in the Indian country more than twenty years. I also met here a German physician with whom I was before acquainted, who has engaged in the Indian trade, and passed the last winter at Rainy Lake. All the traders will leave here to-morrow for Mackinac, for the purpose of receiving their annual supplies. This day is Sunday, and we are stationary. To-morrow our baggage will be arranged in packages smaller than is usual, weighing ninety pounds, and will commence passing around the falls of this river upon the Portage, which is nine miles in length. The Portage is, in consequence of excessive rains, nearly impassable, and for this reason it is calculated that our voyageurs can only carry two packages each, weighing one hundred and eighty pounds, at a load. Between this and Sandy Lake it will be necessary to make about seventeen miles of portage, which will alone occupy about six days. Our precise route is but just determined We will proceed from this place by the Grand Portage, St. Louis River Portage Aux Coteau, Savannah River, Savannah Portage, Sandy Lake and Sandy River, to the Mississippi River. From thence ascend the Mississippi River, pass by Little Lake Winnipeg to Upper Red Cedar Lake, and from thence to Lac La Bishop; from thence return by another route to Upper Red Cedar Lake, then proceed by Leach River to Leach Lake, thence by a series of portages and small lakes to the source of the River de Carbeau, the great southwest fork of the Mississippi, thence descend the River de Carbeau to the Mississippi, and the latter stream as far as fifty miles below the Falls of St. Anthony, thence we will proceed by the St. Croix River and River Brule, with only a short portage to Lake Superior, which we will enter from the southern shore about four hundred and sixty miles above the Sault Ste Marie. We hope to complete this immense journey so as to arrive at the Sault Ste. Marie between the middle and the last of August. You can scarcely imagine the difficulties which we will be obliged to encounter, and they certainly beggar description. Although I am now twelve hundred miles from you, I consider this the place where I in reality commence my journey.

I find the vaccination of the Indians an irksome task, chiefly in consequence of the great numbers. Last evening after our arrival I operated upon two hundred and forty at one sitting, and I shall complete the band to morrow. As yet I have only found a few who had never heard of vaccination. It is astonishing to learn the fearful dread they have of the small-pox. When I commence operating they crowd around me with their arms ready, and anxiously wait their turn. I keep an accurate list of the number, age and sex of those vaccinated, together with the tribe and band to which they belong.

The season is hardly sufficiently advanced to admit of an extensive collection of plants, but I am doing more than could have been expected. I received another letter from Prof. Torry, respecting my plants of last year, after my arrival at the Sault Ste. Marie, and I was much gratified to learn that the opinion I had given respecting those which I supposed to be undescribed species was supported by the New York botanist. This will give me fresh courage to push the subject this season. My mineral collection, as yet, has been but small. I wish you to write me at the Sault Ste. Marie, so that it can reach there by the 20th of August. We have good health so far, and while our men have hard times upon the portage I have more leisure to make my scientific examinations than I could under other circumstances. To-morrow morning I expect to take up the brachial artery in a case of advanced aneurism.

Love to all members of the family,
Your affectionate brother,
DOUGLASS HOUGHTON.

TO HON. JACOB HOUGHTON.

DETROIT, Dec. 20, 1834.

DEAR FATHER:—

I have neglected writing you much longer than I intended, but this has arisen wholly from fatigue of business, leaving me with hardly sufficient energy to sit down to write what was not an absolute necessity. Since our return to the city our health has been constantly good, I think mine has hardly ever been better. Lydia seems contented, and I think she is pleased with our place. In business I am still prospering; it is constantly and rapidly increasing, and that among the most respectable citizens. My charges, which are perfectly good, from the time of my return from Fredonia to the first of January, although the town has been healthy, will amount to between one thousand and thirteen hundred dollars, the time being less than thirteen months.

I had proposals some time ago from a physician whom I supposed to be doing the most business in the city, for a co-partnership, and though I was convinced that if my health remained good it would be of no advantage to me, I was upon the whole disposed to look upon it rather favorably. We compared estimates of our charges, and I was astonished to find that mine exceeded his by several hundred dollars for the last year.

I confess that I was not without some little feeling of gratification that I was able to make such a comparison with one who has been in business here sixteen years. The result was that we concluded to join our business as soon after the first of January as the new office can be fitted up, but a perquisite will be allowed me worth some four or five hundred dollars a year.

I have just closed the purchase of two city lots near my president residence, and situated near the centre of the city on a pleasant street only one hundred and twenty feet from Main street. They cost me sixteen hundred dollars; of this I pay six hundred dollars down, and the balance is to be paid in equal payments of one and two years with interest. I propose to build on these lots next summer. They are fifty-three feet front and sixty feet deep. I think I will be able to build two substantial brick houses for four or five thousand dollars, without involving myself, against which I intend to guard rigidly. One I propose to occupy myself, and the other will rent readily for three or four hundred dollars per annum. I consider the purchase of the lots so much of a bargain that I would not release them for five hundred dollars, and I do not doubt from their situation that they will be worth double their present cost in two years time. I have finally determined to invest all my earnings in lots and buildings, and in order that the income may be permanent I will build nothing but of the most durable kind. Temporary structures will give greater profit at present, but in the end the erection of such would be bad policy. Should my present practice continue for four or five years, and my life and health be spared, I may be able to return to Fredonia with a handsome support for my brothers and sisters who may require it. But after all, it is not for myself that I toil, nor is it for myself that I rejoice in my pecuniary success. I rejoice in the prospect that I will be able to free a kind and indulgent parent from the toil of business for which his age unfits him. I feel that I have much to repay, and I only hope that my life may be spared to repay it. I only wish to be able to labor successfully that it shall be done. I desire to invest what I have already made so that the interest may go towards the education and support of the family, and when I have once done this the income will be regular. I have been anxious to hear from Alexander, but he does not write me. His proper education I look upon as a matter of great importance; his success in life depends upon it. I daily become more and more convinced of the utter inability of an uneducated man to occupy any prominent situation without much humiliation. I have not written this about Alexander because I feel any less interest in the other members of the family. I know no division of interest, but I feel that I already want the assistance of Alexander, and as if he would be fitted to occupy a situation which I have now in view. I constantly think of you all. Though I have said nothing of mother, aunt, Sarah and Jacob, it is not from a want of thought. I look anxiously for the time when I may set myself down by you. I may not be able to do this very soon, but I shall labor with no less pleasure to be able to add to the comforts of all the members of the family at home.

Your affectionate son,
DOUGLASS HOUGHTON.

At this date, 1834, he was in full practice of his profession, but great opportunities were then opened to young professional and business men to lay the foundation of fortunes. Dr. Houghton's knowledge of business and high credit would lead him to enter with energy the field of real estate investments. Mr. Henry G. Hubbard was associated with him in the purchase of real estate. His father, the Hon. Thomas H. Hubbard, of Utica, N. Y., had met Dr. Houghton in Detroit, and was inspired with great confidence in his business qualifications and his transparent integrity of character. Mr. Hubbard was a gentleman of ample fortune, but of a careful and cautious nature, and the fact that he did not hesitate to entrust the large sum of $20,000 to Dr. Houghton as a loan shows a rare confidence in his character, and is a pleasing evidence of these qualities of order, sagacity and probity that even then were marked traits of Dr. Houghton.

One of those investments it may be worth while to notice particularly as showing not merely good judgment of the young real estate operator, but his influence over men.

The Brush farm, now in the heart of the City of Detroit, was then managed by Edmund A. Brush, whose policy was opposed to the sale of any portion, but to lease instead. No one had been able to prevail upon the owners to part with the title to a single lot. Dr. Houghton determined to try his skill upon the hard head of Mr. Brush. Meeting him one day, the conversation led to some chaffing upon the subject of real estate management, in which the Doctor bore pretty hard upon the obstinate refusal of Mr. Brush, so different from the custom of other men, to sell. "I will sell," said Mr. Brush, "if I get my price." "Well, now, what would you take for those ten acres north of Gratiot street?" "I would take $10,000," said Brush, naming what he considered a good round price and beyond the means of his interrogater. "Done," said the Doctor, and the bargain was consummated before it was allowed to get cold. Dr. Houghton associated Henry G. Hubbard with him in the venture, which proved profitable. The tract is known as the "Houghton Section."

The Doctor felt it as a duty to himself and to his family not to neglect these opportunities for investments. But these new business complications, with his professional engagements, were now telling on his health, and he was forced to relinquish to some extent his practice.

It should be remembered, however, that Dr. Houghton did not give up at any time his interest in science, and the trip mentioned in the following letter was in part to make certain examinations in reference to the salt springs.

TO HON. JACOB HOUGHTON.

DETROIT, April 2, 1836.
DEAR FATHER:—

Your two letters were received last evening, and I have but a moment to answer them in, as I am about making a short trip into the country this morning. I shall be gone some eight or ten days.

You will have seen by the *Detroit Journal* before you receive this, that Dr. Rice and myself have dissolved our partnership by my withdrawing from the profession. The fact is that the measure was necessary for common prudence, as I have stretched my arms so wide that my profession was a loss rather than a profit. Mr. Hubbard has returned, having perfected through his father, an arrangement by which we are enabled to draw for $20,000 with additional sums when required. This was perfected by the elder son, Henry G. Hubbard, who has been indefatigable in assisting us. The truth is I appear to have gained the perfect confidence of the banking interest here, and it is giving me a powerful engine for perfecting my plans. I design to pursue such a course as to retain that confidence.

I purchased yesterday 2,600 acres of pine lands which cost $1.25 per acre, worth now from $5.00 to $10.00 per acre. The tract embraces three valuable mill seats. I have sold a small tract which I purchased about two weeks ago for $5.00 per acre.

On my return from the country, if possible, I shall visit Fredonia, and I shall wish Lydia and Sarah to return with me, and if you think it best, it will be well for Alexander to be prepared to go to Gambia at the same time.

I shall be able to remain with you only a day or so, as I will be obliged to return here promptly. Later in the season I hope to spend a longer time with you.

Your affectionate son,
DOUGLASS HOUGHTON.

These investments, it will be observed, were all made previous to the connection of Dr. Houghton with the Geological Survey. While State Geologist, Dr. Houghton was scrupulously careful to avoid speculations of all kinds, even those that could not be supposed to derive any aid from his position and opportunities. All proffers of the kind he declined, from fear of private motives being attributed to his actions. Would that all men in public station were equally uncompromising.

TO HON. JACOB HOUGHTON.

DETROIT, January 17, 1841.

DEAR FATHER:—

Your letter of the 11th inst. has just come to hand, and it reminds me how very remiss I have been in writing you, but between sickness and overwhelming pressure of business, my mind has been incessantly occupied.

My rheumatism has so far left me that I am able to attend to my official duties, and were it not for the great number of hours I am compelled to work, there can be no doubt that my health would be completely restored. The disease was the result of excessive fatigue and exposure, and I do not imagine it will be of any permanent injury to my constitution. I have now been busily engaged for several days in analyzing minerals from Lake Superior localities, preparatory to my report, which will be sent in on the 1st of February. As yet I have scarcely touched it, and the remaining time is short. Our Legislature is in session, and I believe the department over which I preside is in greater favor than it ever has been before, for which reason I anticipate but little embarrassment.

The publication of the maps of the department is steadily progressing; and the engraving which is done at Washington, D. C., will require my personal attention, and if health will permit I shall leave home for that city as early as the 15th to the 20th of March, which will enable me to attend the Geological Convention at Philadelphia, the first week in April. My down trip will probably be either by the way of Columbus or Cincinnati, but I hope to be able to return by the way of New York, in which case I shall spend a day or two with you, somewhere between the 15th of April and the 1st of May.

I shall probably be required to spend the coming season in the Lake Superior country, but this is not certainly determined. Some difficulty is about occurring with respect to our boundary on the west, with Wisconsin. I refer to State line between Green Bay and Lake Superior. If any action is had upon the subject, I suppose my services will be required there, which will divert my labor for a time from the Geology Survey. At any rate I have the prospect of another season of severe labor before me.

We are all well, and Hattie is as fat and mischievous as ever. She says, "ask grandpapa if he is not coming to see her some day." The Fredonia boys are all well. Stephen Snow has been sick, but has now recovered. Dr. Silas Douglass is in the United States service stationed at the Arsenal at Dearborn. He is doing well; is associated with a fine, gentlemanly corps of officers who are highly educated. He is improving in every way, and is receiving good pay. We are suffering terrible pecuniary embarrassment in our State; not so much in consequence of our home debts as from deranged condition of the currency. It is almost impossible to procure a draft or such money as may be transmitted east at any rate of exchange.

I am gradually bringing my own affairs into such condition as to be unembarrassed. The amount of taxes I am called on to pay, together with some minor debts, have rubbed hard, and I have found it exceedingly difficult to make the end of the year meet. My tax for the last year was about $2,000, and this added to other expenses you know is no small item to raise in these times of embarrassment.

It is now somewhat doubtful whether I will remove to Ann Arbor in the spring. My house there is finished, and is quite a splendid mansion; but I am not desired to be upon the ground until the institution is fairly organized, and at least a sufficient number of the faculty to make a society of our own. Harriet joins with me in sending love to all members of the family. I am anxious that Jacob should pursue his studies industriously and prepare himself for a situation at West Point. Say to Lydia that I had a letter from Mr. Bradish a few days ago, and shall answer it soon.

Your affectionate son,
DOUGLASS HOUGHTON.

JACOB HOUGHTON, ESQ.

TO HON. JACOB HOUGHTON.

DETROIT, March 13, 1841.

DEAR FATHER,—

I have just returned from an exceedingly fatiguing journey which has called me from home for a time of nearly three weeks, for which reason your letter of February 19, is just received. The unlooked for intelligence of the death of my young protegé, Charles Morrison,* could scarcely be more keenly felt were he my own son. I had watched his progress in all that could serve to elevate him to

---

*A young Indian half-bred.

the rank of a highly intellectual man, with pride, and I had looked forward with pleasure to the day when he should return to his parents and to the country from which he came, to aid in bringing about a moral and intellectual change in that whole country. I had looked upon him as the pattern which his associates from the same region of country, would follow. But how vain are all our hopes! The very prop upon which I was resting has been taken away. It is however, to be hoped, that this calamity may not act unfavorably upon others now at the school in Fredonia, or discourage others from entering the institution. It would be well for you, jointly with Mr. Palmer, to write to Mr. Morrison. It would check any unfavorable impressions and be a consolation to his father. If some lady would write to Mrs. Morrison, no doubt it would console her much, and might lessen objections that might be likely to grow up against sending children out of the country to school. I wish all the effects of Charles to be preserved with the utmost care, together with all his letters and papers. Mr. Snow is just on the point of starting for Fredonia, and I have but a moment left to write you. During my absence from the city, and without any knowledge whatever, on my part, I have been elected mayor. Upon first hearing the result, I had determined to refuse to serve. But my friends advised differently, and I have consented to qualify, which must be done to-morrow. The duties are exceedingly arduous, and it will be impossible for me to perform them with satisfaction to myself, for which reason, I will probably resign after two or three weeks. My duties during the current year will be more arduous than ever, though it is likely I shall be absent from home comparatively little. My health is much improved though not fully restored. I had intended to write to Mr. Palmer, and you will please say that I have only been prevented by the constant interruption of a crowd of office seekers and friends, so that I have been unable to do so.

In great haste, I am,
Your affectionate son,
DOUGLASS HOUGHTON.

JACOB HOUGHTON, ESQ.

TO HON. JACOB HOUGHTON.

DETROIT, Nov. 14, 1841.

DEAR FATHER:—

In consequence of the great pressure of business by which I have been surrounded since my return from Lake Superior, I have delayed writing you much longer than had been intended. Although my health during the summer was poor, I have nevertheless been able to accomplish a large amount of work, and have done much towards the completion of the field work of the geology and topographical part of the survey. My health is now steadily improving and will, I think, eventually be fully restored, though it probably never will be such as to permit the performance of as active duties as those that have already been done.

I am now busily engaged, in addition to other duties, in arranging the immense mass of materials that have been steadily accumulating during the five years that we have been engaged in the work, for my final report. But this report will not probably appear until two or three years from this time.

Our University at Ann Arbor has commenced operations, and there is a tolerably strong class, but at the present juncture I do not think it prudent for me to remove to that place, though it is possible I may think it advisable to do so in the coming spring. My pecuniary affairs seem to demand that I should remain here for a time, for my private business during the progress of the geological survey has suffered very much. In the unsettled condition of monetary affairs by which we are surrounded it is exceedingly difficult for me to make the ends meet, and this year it has not been done, the result of which is that I have to renew my attention to business to avoid falling into deeper difficulties hereafter. We have the dawn of brighter days in our State, but for the present it is exceedingly difficult to proceed in any direction without suffering loss. The large amount of unproductive real estate which is on my hands embarrasses me much in the way of payment of taxes, and unless the wheel should turn up

I shall be compelled to suffer sacrifices to meet these. Jacob is now attending the University in this city, and is making good progress in his studies. Columbus returned in safety, and I sent him immediately to Midland county, where I have men at work at the salt springs. This saved me an arduous journey, which it was desirous for me to avoid at this season of the year.

Our salt springs are succeeding well, and I have gained quite a victory upon a subject which by many of our citizens was regarded as visionary—but no matter to what improvements out attention may be turned, or however important, there are those who at first would doubt and throw cold water.

Although I do not propose to remove to Ann Arbor for the present, I shall spend some little time there before the winter sets in, in arranging a portion of the collections. This collection of specimens, which is exceedingly choice, has now been a long time in boxes, and our people are desirous to have a portion at least so arranged as to permit examination.

I learned by Columbus that the Misses Oaks will remain at your house for a time, to which I make no particular objection if they prefer to do so. They are the daughters of an old and particular friend, and I feel a deep interest in their welfare. They will, without any doubt, make good progress in their studies and endear themselves to our people. The young boys will require careful watching, and above all they must be kept apart as much as possible, for one object is to break up all association as much as can be done.

I hope to visit you in the spring, when on my way to the annual convention of Geologists, and trust to make a longer visit than the last time. Martha, who has been in charge of our domestic affairs since the confinement of Mrs. H., has been ill from fatigue, but is now quite recovered. Samuel Walker and Mr. Snow are all in good health and in active business.

Please remember me to mother and all of the family, as also to Misses Oaks and the young boys, not forgetting Charles

Morrison, to whom I wish you to say, that I look to him to set an example to the other boys of manly conduct, associated with studious habits.

Your affectionate son,
DOUGLASS HOUGHTON.

JACOB HOUGHTON,
      New York.

PART V.

GENERAL SUMMARY AND SYNOPSIS OF THE WORK DONE UNDER THE FIRST GEOLOGICAL SURVEY OF MICHIGAN.

The following summary will serve to show the great extent of the field covered by the investigations under the first organized geological survey, the amount of labor involved, and the general results so far as they are given to the public in the annual reports. These have been for a long time entirely out of print.

As since the close of that survey, by the untimely death of the State Geologist, the State has again entered upon the detailed work of geological survey, the results of which are before the public in several printed volumes, covering much of the same ground, it is deemed unnecessary to republish more fully than the statements here contained.

In regard to a portion, however, particularly the report of 1841, the matters treated of being not only original but so important that they have constituted the basis of all subsequent investigations, it has been deemed advisable to republish a large part in full.

SUMMARY AND SYNOPSIS OF THE WORK PERFORMED BY THE GEOLOGICAL SURVEY OF MICHIGAN UNDER ITS FIRST ORGANIZATION.

The original Act for the organization of a State Geological Survey was approved by Governor Mason, February 23rd, 1837. (Laws of Michigan, 1837, page 14.)

It provided for the appointment of a State geologist, and it appropriated annual sums, increasing from $3,000 the first year to $12,000 the fourth year.

Dr. Douglass Houghton, of Detroit, received from Governor Mason the appointment, and his first report was made to the governor, January 25th, 1838 (37 pages). It sets forth that at as early a day as a sufficient corps could be organized the geologist proceeded to a rapid and general reconnoisance of such parts of the State as the limited time would permit.

These examinations had chiefly for their object the determination of the rock formations, their extent and order of super position.

Of the annual reports which he is called upon to make he proceeds to say, that they "should only embrace a brief abstract of such facts as may be deemed of immediate practical importance or tend to a general development of the resources of the State, or as may serve to show the progress of the survey, for which reasons these portions which may be considered of a strictly scientific character will be omitted until the final report will be made."

The report then proceeds to describe the general character of the peninsula, particularly of its northern portion, about which much misconception prevails. It then briefly describes the rocks of the lower peninsula, the superficial extent of country occupied by them, so far as determined, and their places of outcrop. These pages are followed by a particular account of the brine springs of the State, with sundry analysis and comparisons with the springs of other States, and some practical conclusions. It then alludes to the beginning made in the departments of zoology and botany, under the direction of Doctor Abram Sager, and of the topographical map of the counties which were in progress, being reduced from the original returns of the United States Survey.

This preliminary report was followed February 1st, 1838, by an appendix containing, "with a view to facilitate the progress of the survey, certain queries proposed to the people of the State, with suggestions to the proprietors of lands that they forward to Detroit specimens of minerals, rocks, marls, peat, petrifactions and soils," all which was intended to interest the people, and draw out facts for future investigation.

REORGANIZATION AND REPORT.

During the winter of 1837-8 the survey was reorganized on a larger basis (Laws of 1837-8, p. 119), and with particular reference to the provision made, in addition to the geological department proper, for zoological, botanical and topographical departments, it appropriated the annual sum of $12,000 for the years 1838 to 1841. The following corps of officers was appointed by the governor on the nomination of the State geologist:—

Douglass Houghton, Geologist.
Abram Sager, in charge of zoological department.
John Wright, in charge of botanical department.
Sylvester W. Higgins, topographer and draughtsman.
Columbus C. Douglass, assistant to the geologist.
Bela Hubbard, assistant to geologist.
William P. Smith, in charge of mechanical zoology.

On the 22nd of March, 1838 (Laws of 1837 8, p. 119), a new act received the approval of the governor, reorganizing the survey on a more comprehensive plan, and with more detailed provisions. Under this act, January 1st, 1839, the

State Geologist sends to the legislature a report (eight pages) in relation to the improvement of State salt springs, under the provisions of an act approved March 24th, 1838. In this the geologist refers to his visit to the principal salt wells of Ohio, Pennsylvania and Virginia, for the purpose of comparison and analogy, "those of New York being so very differently situated, geologically, that a satisfactory comparison with them can scarcely be instituted at this time."

He describes the mode of occurrence of our salt springs, the probable depth of the boring required, and the best method of improvement. Details are given of the preparatory work done on Tittawawassee River in Midland county, and the embarrassments which beset operations, owing to the unsettled state of the country, the distance from supplies, and the sickness of those employed, and the small amount of the appropriation for this purpose, also to the necessity for the presence of the State Geologist in person at other and remote points, all which caused temporary abandonment of the work.

THE SECOND ANNUAL REPORT

was made to the legislature, February 4th, 1839 (thirty-eight pages). It mentions the organization of the geological board, in accordance with the act of March 22nd, 1838, "in such a manner as to constitute a geological and mineralogical, a zoological, a botanical and a topographical department."

That "the heads of the departments took the field at an early day and continued their arduous duties until the inclemency of the season compelled a suspension of labor, since which time they have been busily engaged in arranging a great amount of information which has been obtained in such a manner as may eventually be made available."

The individual labors of the State Geologist had been chiefly devoted to an examination of the coast of those portions of our State bordering on Lakes Huron and Michigan; also to "a general examination of some of the central and southern counties, preparatory to the more minute examination, which has been commenced and which it is proposed to renew with the first opening of spring."

This report of the geologist details the topographical and general character of the northern portion of the peninsula west and north of Saginaw Bay, a portion then but imperfectly known, and also the general character of the rocks of that portion, showing their line of bearing, and the connection of our geology with that of the neighboring States.

Special remarks follow upon the clays, marls and gypsum of the peninsula.

An interesting portion of the report is devoted to a consideration of the change of elevation in the waters of the great lakes, "which were then at a higher point than had been known for many years, a subject of great interest practically in connection with lake harbors and with the agricultural interest of the State." Dr. Houghton distinguishes the then high stage of the waters, from the fluctuations due to annual and temporary causes. Many facts are stated, going back to the beginning of the century. In leading to his conclusions, viz., that the increase is due to increased rain fall, he points out the fact that the waters of the interior lakes and streams have also risen, and that these changes have not been peculiar to Michigan, but manifested over the whole western country. He refers also to the succession of cold and wet seasons which prevailed in 1838.

This whole subject had been heretofore clouded in much mystery and theory, and the data and reasoning of Dr. Houghton were the first to throw light on the real causes.*

Reference is made to the progress of the geological and the botanical departments, and to the collections made for the University.

In the topographical department maps of the several counties had been projected on a scale of two miles to the inch, a size which enables him to place upon them most of that information which will be required for the use of town and county officers, as also the complete geology and topography of the country. "Upon these skeleton plats the assistants were required to fill up the deficiencies, and return the same with the streams carried out across the interior of the sections; the soils, marshes, timbered lands, openings, prairies, woods, etc., etc, as well as the geology and topography accurately delineated."

The documents occupying this second annual report contain:

No. 1 — Report of Dr. Abram Sager, zoologist of the survey. Appended to his report Dr. Sager gives, in a catalogue of ten pages, the results of his labors in his department for the past year, being of such mammals, birds, reptiles, amphibia and molusca as had come under notice in the State, and adds that of many of the species contained the requisite

---

*It may please the interested reader to find the whole theory of lake fluctuations practically discussed by Bela Hubbard, in his "Memorials of a Half Century," 1888. He has had the advantage of half a century of observations to add to those of Dr. Houghton, and he shows, further, the nature and extent of the connection between the lake fluctuations and the general phenomena of climate of the lake region.

number (the law required seventeen specimens of each species to be preserved) have been procured, and of some a much larger number than was required, with a view to exchanges. "Altogether a considerable amount of material has been collected towards forming a history of the subjects of our investigations."

No. 2—Report of Dr. John Wright, botanist of the survey, sets forth that his examinations have been made in the two most southern ranges of counties; that he has been enabled to examine between eight hundred and nine hundred native and naturalized species of phenogamous or flowering plants, and to collect specimens of each, amounting in all to about nine thousand, all in an excellent state of preservation. When not too large the entire plant is preserved, roots, stems, leaves, flowers and seeds. He confines for the present the notice of the plants to a catalogue of their names, reserving a detailed account for the final report. This catalogue occupies twenty-eight pages.

No. 3—Next follows report of S. W. Higgins, topographer of the survey. The topographer details the methods pursued to obtain complete maps of the several counties, and regrets the absence of a thorough hydrographical survey of the lakes by the general government. This had been commenced when Gen. Cass occupied the war department, but had extended only from the foot of Lake Huron to Middle Island. (Since the date of this report the whole chain of lakes and their connecting rivers has been systematically and accurately surveyed, and charts published showing meanderings, windings, etc.)

This report describes with much detail never before collected, the situation of Michigan relatively to other portions of the continent, and to the mountain chains, table lands, streams, etc., giving tables of elevations, and depths and areas of all the lakes.

It touches upon the subject notably treated by Dr. Houghton, of the great rise in the waters of the lake during the last five years, with some data extending back to 1814, and comes to the same conclusion, that the causes must be looked for in the increased quantity of rain fall. Accompanying this report was a map of the State, exhibiting projections of all the levels which had been taken across the State, in the course of engineering operations on the various works of public improvements; also the general profile of heights collected from all sources and tabulated for reference. He states that "maps of twenty counties are in a state of forwardness, five being finished, to which during the next year a large number would be added." Drawings will also be given of such remains of ancient works and tumuli as are scattered through St. Joseph, Kalamazoo and other counties.

No. 4—Report of C. C. Douglass, assistant geologist. Gives details of the geology, etc., of the central counties, including examinations of the coal district; the coal beds of Ingham and Eaton counties, with their associated rock formations are particularly described. Much information of a practical nature is embodied, relative to the soils, rocks, marls, springs, timber, etc.

No. 5—Report of Bela Hubbard, assistant geologist. Includes the supervision of Wayne and Monroe counties, their general topographical and geological features, their rocks, clays, soils, and agricultural characters. The report refers to the subject then of so great an interest, the encroachment of the lake waters during the past two years. He says, "Many acres of formerly arable lands in both counties are now embraced by the waters. Numbers of orchards, the growth of a century, have become a prey to the flood, and families of the old French inhabitants are driven from the homes till now occupied from childhood."* It alludes to remedies which may be resorted to, to afford protection against these encroachments. Some important remarks are made regarding road constructions, and in derogation of the inadequate methods usually obtaining.

A glossary of geological terms closes the document.

THE THIRD ANNUAL REPORT OF THE STATE GEOLOGIST

(thirty pages) was made to the legislature February 3d, 1840. It gives a general description of the topography and geology of the southern slope of the upper peninsula, to which the formal attention of the State Geologist was principally directed during the season of 1839. This embraces the numerous and intricate islands and channels skirting the north shore of Lake Huron and in the Ste. Marie's River, and the range of hills extending westwardly from this river as far as Bay du Noquet. In this district of Michigan is embraced that interesting group of limestones and sandstones now included within the Paleoozoic times, as upper and lower silurian rocks. The limestones are characterized by abundant fossil remains, of which a large collection was made. The lowest rocks of this series is the Lake Superior sandstone.

*See note page 138.

The true position of this rock has been subject of dispute among geologists, but it was shown by Dr. Houghton to rest upon the primary or azoic rocks, and to be referable to the Potsdam sandstone of New York.

A few pages of the report are given to the clay ironstone of Branch county, and the bog ore of Kalamazoo and other counties, which the State Geologist was particularly instructed to examine. The gypsum and marl beds of the State are again referred to, and a general reference to the geological and topographical departments, which in the plan of organization are mutually dependent.

The Geologist refers to the departments of zoology and botany, which unfortunately, owing to the failure of adequate appropriation, consequent upon the embarrassed condition of the State finances, had become suspended by the resignation of the assistants in those departments.

The documents accompanying the third annual report, contained:

No. 1—Report of S. W. Higgins, topographer, January 12, 1840, accompanied by an engraved map of Wayne county, illustrative of the scale and method adopted for the county maps in progress. The topographer states that since the date of his last annual communication his time has been occupied in the drafting office, mostly in compiling and adapting to the scales of the proposed maps the details of information furnished in the progress of the geological survey and of the United States linear surveys. Among the most arduous of the labors of the department was the procuring of copies of almost all the original patents. The importance of these is shown by many instances of conflict between these original patents and the section lines of the subsequent United States surveys, by the fact that of 130,000 acres of these lands, "no maps existed which can be in any manner depended upon, while these lands include a large portion of the coast line from Monroe to Lake Huron.

He enumerates the following counties as among those of which the material of the maps in progress are completed or nearly so, viz., Wayne, Jackson, Lenawee, Calhoun, Branch, St. Joseph, Cass, Berrien, Livingston, Washtenaw, Ingham, Eaton, Hillsdale, Monroe, Oakland, Genessee, Ionia, Kalamazoo and Van Buren.

The concluding seven pages of this report contain items of information whose interest is not diminished but rather increased by the lapse of time. They are, therefore, here copied in full:—

Roads and Highways.

The roads and highways of our State claim a remark, as excelling in many particulars those of the east, both in respect to their uniform grades and their passable condition at all seasons of the year. The cause of the first mentioned superiority is common to most of the western country, viz., the even and level nature of the surface, which is at most gently undulating or rolling, with the total absence of mountains or high hills. The second arises from the nature of the soil, it usually containing much sand and gravel in its composition.

The roads in the openings and plains offer to the traveler a variety of routes, with the choice of diverging at pleasure, the scattered oaks leaving sufficient space between for the passage of horses or carriages, while the prairie is one wide, unbounded highway, where no obstacle is present for pursuing whichever course curiosity may direct. These roads require the expenditure of little or no labor to keep them in repair.

The only exception to the above remark is found in those roads which, commencing at the different frontier towns on the eastern coasts, lead across a low, timbered belt of country for the distance of six, ten and fifteen miles, and where the soil, as in some other districts, is clay. In these districts they require to be worked at no inconsiderable expense, to keep them passable during the wet periods of the fall and spring.

The Chicago Turnpike or Trail.

Among the most noted of the highways of the State, the "Chicago road" claims a particular notice. It was formerly to the western tribes of Indians, the Sauks, Foxes, Winnebagoes, Menomonees, Potawatamies, etc., what the national road from Cumberland to St. Louis now is to the whites. They were constantly traversing it in periods of war and peace, or when treaties were negotiating and different and distinct tribes were to be represented.

The Sauks from the Mississippi, in great numbers, in late years were accustomed, by this route, to reach Fort Malden to receive their annuities from the British government.

There were no parallel trails across the peninsula, and the trails from the Potawatamies in Indiana and Illinois, and from the Foxes, and Menomonees, etc., of the northwest, all joined near the south bend of Lake Michigan, and uniting into one led directly to Detroit.

Persons even well acquainted with the appearance of an ordinary Indian path are astonished at the width and depth of the track which is visible in places to this day.

Such was the directness and facility of this route that the United States made an appropriation some time after the erection of a territorial government for the northwest, causing a survey to be made of it from Detroit to Chicago, and letting it in sections for the construction of a turnpike.

This trail is supposed to be as long as any other within the territory of the United States, being two hundred and forty miles from Detroit to the point where it received those diverging trails from the south and north-west, and the length of some of its branches cannot be less than three hundred miles further, while numerous smaller ones enter from different directions, by which means the early pioneers of the west easily threaded their way through these regions, and into the valley of the Mississippi beyond.

Natural Woods of Michigan.

The arrangement which this subject calls for properly belongs to the department of botany. Nevertheless, without attending to the details which should accompany a catalogue of an entire flora, it will be sufficient to exhibit generally the geographical boundaries of such of the larger productions as are required for constant use, either in farming, building, or for the market.

Oak is the predominant growth of the peninsula. Among the varieties, the white is in the greatest abundance.

The shingle or laurel oak, and the red oak, are next abundant. And the burr oak, though not usually found intermixed in common with the other varieties, abounds, notwithstanding, over extensive areas, not unfrequently to the exclusion of other kinds.

The surest indication of a good soil accompanies the last mentioned, and the finest and largest crops of wheat are there produced, for the reason that the soil contains a larger amount of calcareous matter.

Dividing the peninsula by an east and west line, nearly corresponding to that of the northern railroad, a botanical map would represent the northern portion as having by far the greatest burthen of timber, possessing a proportionable quantity of the different varieties found elsewhere in the State.

Marked limits may be given to those districts in the southern portion, where a few groves of pines are found.

Their localities are in the vicinity of the water courses of Kent and Ottawa counties, and among the timbered lands of Allegan, extending in comparatively small tracts along the borders of Lake Michigan, nearly to New Buffalo, in Berrien. In crossing the State through the interior counties none are met, until reaching the central part of Genesee, Lapeer and St. Clair. Here they are again found in the same range of northern townships, where they first occur, in the counties before mentioned.

North of this belt or zone, which is the natural boundary between the oak openings and plains of the south, the forest abounds promiscuously with the white, yellow and Norway pine, white cedar, tamarack, ash, oak, birch, sugar maple, sycamore, beech, lynn, elm, white wood, black walnut, etc.

There are, however, extensive districts nearly continuous from Ottawa, Kent, and Ionia counties, northward, of openings and small prairies, particularly a few miles inland from White River, and from Great and Little Sable points. But on ascending the Maskego River until reaching its source, thence north, on both sides of the Principal Meridian, extensive tracts occur, in many instances free from a mixture of other timber, while in other places the sugar maple and beech are not unfrequently found commingled with pines of immense girth.

The fact of the white wood and black walnut accompanying the sugar and beech, as seen occupying the districts inland, from the Sable points, in towns 13, 14, 15, 16 and 17 north of ranges 14, 15, 16, 17 and 18 west, would, to the most ordinary agriculturist, demonstrate the superiority of the soil, and, when taken in connection with the limited tracts of oak openings and the great amount of the most valuable timber, it seems difficult to determine any preference of the southern over the northern portions of the State.

The soil is not considered of so good a quality on the eastern side of the peninsula, immediately along the shore of Lake Huron, owing to its low, level and sandy qualities, consisting chiefly of the debris of sand rock. Consequently the timber is generally stunted, and consists, in greater proportion, of birch, tamarack and cedar.

Where pine occurs it is mostly too small to be profitably made use of. But at every advance inland both improve.

The face of the country throughout the northern interior is high and rolling, or undulating, and appears to one acquainted with the southern part of the peninsula to bear a close resemblance in its general contour.

It may be considered, then, as a question fully decided, that more than one-half of the State is heavily timbered, in that part lying above the northern railroad; that the sugar and pine are here the most common, as well as the most valuable timber; that the other kinds are found in situations equivalent to their occurrence further south, upon streams and bottom lands, or upon plains and openings.

No tree is held in higher estimation by the Indians than the sugar maple, and no source of complaint is more grievous than a separation from it by removal to places where it is not found.

The pine, if not wasted or wantonly destroyed by fire or otherwise, will furnish an abundant supply for a long time to come.

Variation of the Magnetic Needle.

The surveys of Michigan were intended to correspond with the true meridian, excepting those of Mr. Greely, before mentioned, which were made without an observation to determine the true north. There appears, however, a variation between his first and last surveys of about one degree.

This difference is palpable on tracing the lines along the first donation lands, to the rear of the "back concessions," so called, but the time which elapsed between running the front and rear lines may account for this in some measure, being about three years, during which, it is well known, there must have been a greater or less alteration in the magnetic meridian. The needle, in this instance, was attracted westward.

Mysterious as the movement of this instrument is accounted to be, were greater attention devoted to an examination of the causes that effect it, instead of a diminished confidence in many of its results, its habits, though governed no doubt by a subtle influence, would be intimately known, and its uses appreciated accordingly. The rights of our citizens to their property is closely connected with this inquiry.

Columbus, in his first voyage to America, first noticed the deflection of the needle, and since that time the subject has engaged the unceasing attention of the scientific, particularly for the last few years, insomuch that measures are now taken, both in Europe and America, to investigate fully the causes which are known constantly to affect it.

In 1835 the line of no variation was known to run longitudinally through about the middle of Lake Huron, the variation on the shore twelve miles above the foot of the lake was 6 min. east; on Pointe aux Barques, in lat. 43 deg. 51 min. 36 sec.; seventy miles from the foot of the lake it was 1 deg. 38 min.; twenty miles west of Pte aux Barques on the same parallel it was 2 deg. 6 min.; farther west, at the mouth of the Saginaw River, in lat. 43 deg. 36 min. 30 sec., 2 deg. 19 min. east; at the same time it was 2 deg. 10 min. at Detroit, lat. 42 deg. 18 min.

This line of no variation, has had, for the last eighteen years, a slow and perceptible movement westward, whereby continual changes are observable in the magnetic meridian.

The rate of movement, from 1810 to 1322, was from 2 deg. 48 min. to 3 deg. 13 min. 22 sec., equal to 25 min. 22 sec. increase of east variation. From 1812 to 1828 a decrease from 3 deg. 13 min. 22 sec. to 2 deg. 50 min.; (yearly difference, 4 4-10) and for the last twelve years, up to 1840, a decrease 2 deg., 50 min. to 2 deg. ; (yearly difference, 4 min. 10 sec.) 2 deg. being the variation at this time at Detroit, where the above observations were taken.

The progress made in the surveys of the public lands during the last three years has further developed this subject.

FIRST GEOLOGICAL SURVEY OF MICHIGAN. 149

In 1837, on Lake Michigan, near the mouth of Grand River, the variation was 4 deg. 30 min. east; thirty miles north, on the south side of Little Point aux Sable, it was 6 deg. 15 min. east; and twelve miles further, on the north side of the same point, 6 deg. 00 min.; at the mouth of Pierre Marquette River, seventy-eight miles above Grand River, 4 deg. 34 min. east.

In 1838 the north boundary of town twenty-four north, range 16 west, on the shore of Lake Michigan, ninety-nine miles above Grand River, in lat. 44 deg. 31 min., it was 4 deg. 30 min. east; thirty miles east on the same parallel, 2 deg. 50 min. east; sixty miles east on the same parallel, 2 deg. 45 min. east; ninety miles east, same parallel, at the principal meridian, 2 deg. east.

The magnetic meridian of Detroit, then, would pass at this time diagonally across the State, having a bearing from Detroit to the mouth of Saginaw River, thence to where the township line number twenty-four intersects the principal meridian, passing off the northern boundary of the State into Lake Michigan near the Little Traverse Bay, and intersecting the western extreme of Point Wabashance.

Further data could be furnished were it thought necessary, but the foregoing is presumed to be sufficient to call the attention of practical surveyors to the importance of accurately making and recording their observations.

Diurnal Variation.

Besides the absolute variation, a daily motion has been observed constantly to accompany the needle.

The amount of this variation corresponds to the temperature, and therefore at the period of the united heat of the earth and atmosphere the diurnal variation will be greatest. This variation tends to increase the *absolute* western, and decrease the eastern variation, because the north end of the needle in this case invariably points to the west.

Messrs. John Mullett and W. A. Burt are the only gentlemen who have communicated to me their observations. These were made without a thermometer to determine the degree of temperature, yet during several summers, the correspondence of their observations, with those made elsewhere, agree as to the amount of variation, the mean of August and September, being 14 min. Mr. Burt found the maximum for one day 40 min., but it is probable that other causes were in combination.

Errors Arising from Incorrect Observations.

The known inaccuracy of the first public surveys, undoubtedly arose from errors in making observations to ascertain the variation, and shows a recklessness to obligation, which was probably induced by the newness of the country, and apparent distance of detection.

The fairest portion of the State was subdivided with this evident want of skill, and with a carelessness in the first surveyor* which has already resulted in a vast amount of trouble and absolute loss, to a portion of our citizens.

The area embraced by these surveys may be traced on the map, commencing at the south boundary of the State; thence northward forty-eight miles to the base line; thence fifty-four miles up to town No. 9, N ; thus passing along the meridian of seventeen towns, of six miles square. Range lines, intersecting these meridians at right angles, were also begun at the southern boundary of the State, at the principal meridian, and closing on the eastern border of the State.

The lines throughout this whole tract were run at a variation differing but little from 4 deg. 39 min.

The error lies in a too great variation of about 1 deg. 30 min., as is proved:

1st. By platting these surveys in connection with those since made, where a convergency, too great, of two miles is observable on a meridian of fifty miles.

---
*Mr. Wampler.

2d. By the incorrect manner in which the surveys themselves close; in many instances, a difference of 2 deg. and 3 deg. being necessary to meet the exigence.

3d. From the records of actual observations, made both before and since.

4th. From the improbability of the variation ever having been so great at or near Detroit.

In 1810, Col. Jared Mansfield records the variation at Detroit, at 2 deg. 48 min. 00 sec. east.

In 1822 Messrs. Mullett and Lyon, do., 3 deg. 13 min. 22 sec. east.

Between the time of the above two observations, during the years 1816, '17 and '18, the error was committed, and if Mr. Wampler, who performed the surveying, was right, then from 1810 to 1816 the variation had increased from 2 deg. 48 min. to 4 deg. 39 min., making a difference of 1 deg. 51 min. in six years, or equal to 18 min. 30 sec. each year, an unheard of phenomenon on this meridian, when it is further considered that in 1828 it was reduced to 2 deg. 50 min., decreasing in a ratio of 4 4-10 min. per year only, and 4 min. 10 sec. being the average annual decrease since that time.

I am inclined to attribute the error to a neglect of observing the motion of the north star at the time of observation. This star revolves around the pole once in 23 hours and 56 minutes, and when at its greatest eastern or western elongation is 1 deg. 34 min., nearly, from the pole. The western elongation was, no doubt, substituted for the meridian, which it was intended to observe, whereby the error occurred.

Little, if any, attention was afterwards manifested to correcting this error, and it is doubtful whether a suspicion existed in regard to it, for being satisfied with having obtained an observation at one point at the beginning of the survey, three years were afterward consumed in establishing town lines, without an alteration of 5 min. of a degree, advancing with each line westerly over a space of 100 miles, as in the instance of towns Nos. 17 N.

Now, so far as the best information collected up to this time in regard to the increase of magnetic variation (which is stated by Prof. Loomis in the American Journal of Science, Vol. 34, to be about 1 deg. in 60 English miles), these lines on the western boundary of the survey should have been run at a variation of 1 deg. 40 min. greater than on the eastern. Hence arises the cause of that series of fractional townships adjoining the principal meridian, throughout the extent of this survey.

Decrease of Elevation in the Waters of the Lakes.

All that is necessary to observe on this subject is a notice of the decrease in the level of the waters of the great lakes during the past year.

It is a question, I believe, satisfactorily determined at the present time that there exists no perceptible tide in them which can be referable to planitary influence, yet for a long time to come, it is presumed, the ordinary fluctuations produced by atmospheric agency will be considered a *tidal wave*, nor will the persuasion be easily dismissed that so great an expanse of water can remain unaffected at least to some degree.

The question is also as fully determined as to their general rise for a succession of years, and then their general subsidence to a certain minimum, the actual degree of which as well as the maximum, were not recorded previous to the year eighteen hundred.

Their elevation in 1838 was given in my report of last year. The waters had then attained to five feet three inches. This proved to be a greater flood than had occurred within the last century.

Table of elevation and depression in the waters of the Lakes, compared with that of June 1, 1819.

	Feet.	Inches	Feet.	Inches
August 21, 1838, highest stage,			5	03
September, " decrease,	0	03	5	00
October, " "	0	09	4	03
November, " "	1	00	3	03
December, " " same,			3	03
January, 1839, "	1	08	1	07
June 10, " increase,	2	01	3	08
July 31, " "	0	03	3	11
Sept. 20, " decrease.	0	09	3	02
Oct. 28, " "	0	09	2	05
Nov. 27, " " same,			2	05
Jan. 30, 1830, "	1	08	0	09

No. 2—Report of C. C. Douglass, assistant geologist, Jan. 12, 1840. This report states that the time of the assistant has been chiefly occupied with a detailed examination of the northern and western counties so far as the United States surveys had extended.

After describing many extensive deposits of marl and clays, Mr. Douglass describes the coal bearing rocks included in one division of these counties, with observations upon the range and extent of this series of rocks in this State. Local details are given of the lower and upper coal groups and their associated sand and lime rocks and shales, with sections of the rocks at various localities.

No. 3—Report of B. Hubbard, assistant geologist, Jan. 12, 1840, details his examinations in the southern range of counties, mostly west of the principal meridian. These examinations have embraced the collection of all facts of a geological and agricultural character which could serve to illustrate the capabilities of the soil, and the general wealth and resources of the country. In connection with these objects he adds, "I have been able to fill up the skeleton maps furnished by the State Topographer of each town in the several counties, in such a manner as to afford at once a complete view of the soils, timber and topographical details, courses of streams, village and mill seats, and all recorded roads of the townships, to correct errors in streams and lakes arising from inaccurate surveys, and to plat a great number of lakes, streams, etc., which were altogether omitted in the notes of the original survey. The topographical features of the district are described in general, the extent of timber, soils and scenery, followed by the general geological structure of that part of the State, with such economical considerations as are deducible. A table is given of the superposition of rock strata in Hillsdale county, some account of the extensive tertiary and diluvial deposits, with the accompanying clays, marls, peats, tufas, bog ores, boulders and conglomerates. Mr. Hubbard describes an ancient lake ridge, whose course was traced for more than sixty miles, parallel to Lake Erie and Detroit River. This ridge had a width of several hundred feet, a somewhat conical form, and a height of about twelve or fifteen feet above the flat land on the lake side. It is composed of layers of coarse and fine gravel and beach sand reposing upon the clays which constitute the subsoil of the contiguous country. No doubt remains that this ridge once constituted the boundary of an immense expanse of water, which became afterwards circumscribed to the dimensions of the present lake. It is ascertained that this ridge has a uniform elevation above Lake Erie of 107 or 108 feet.

"It is plain that this ridge could not have been formed during that turbulent state of the waters which brought upon the rock covered surface of the country its immense deposit of diluvium, but must have resulted from a quiescent state of the waters." He then proceeds to speculate upon the results of the supposed elevation of the waters of the lake to the height of this ridge, in the distribution of land and water surfaces, and the immensely broad and continuous sea which must have filled the valleys of the St. Lawrence and the Mississippi, "in which whatever of dry land remained were as islands in the deep. But one theory is possible, namely, that the elevation of the lakes relatively to the land was the result, not of their increased actual elevation but of the diminished elevation of the land itself.

"The facts and suppositions above stated lead to several important conclusions in determining the alluvial deposits of the peninsula as distinguished from those which are classed as diluvials, and they indicate three great eras since the formation of the newest rocks.

"1st. After the elevatory process had commenced and land appeared above the surface, at this period was formed the immense mass of diluviums.

"2d. When the upheaving force became stationary at successive intervals, during which periods lake alluvions would be forming over the area then occupied by the waters.

"3d. The era of present levels, when the lakes assumed their present forms in successive order, beginning with the most elevated."

―――

Jan. 9, 1840, the State Geologist presented a report relative to the improvement of salt springs (seven pages).

The subject details the steps which had been taken for the erection of the machinery required for the borings at the State salt wells; the contract made with a practical mechanic from Kenawha, Virginia; the failure of the contractor to fulfil his undertaking, in consequence of assigned fears as to the health of the country, and he details embarrassments which beset the prosecution of the work, and the onerous duties devolving on him as State Geologist, which prevented absolutely a personal direction of the improvements in progress.

After giving an account of the condition of the buildings, shops and engines at the Tittabawassee and Grand River borings and the extent of the borings accomplished, and that a point had been reached where the expense in future would be comparatively small, he states that in consequence of the embarrassments existing in the Internal Improvement Fund, and in the failure to receive the installments of the appropriation, and which compelled the Geologist to provide means from his private resources, it became necessary to suspend operations in the month of September. He prays a release from the duties and responsibilities connected with the superintendence of the improvement of the Salt Springs, as incompatible with the proper discharge of the duties imposed upon him as State Geologist.

THE FOURTH ANNUAL REPORT

Of the State Geologist bears date Feb. 1, 1841 (88 pages). The Geologist states that his "individual labors during the past season, 1840, had been chiefly devoted to surveys connected with the northern slope of the upper peninsula, and regrets that the hardships to which he has been exposed in conducting the field work over the wilderness portions of our State have so far impaired his health as to render it impossible to enter into so minute details as had been anticipated.'' He then enters upon a

General Description and Topographical Features of the Upper or Northern Peninsula.

The topography and general features of the upper and lower peninsulas differ so widely from each other, that, with the simple exception of a part of the easterly extremity of the upper peninsula, they scarcely admit of a comparison. The wide contrast exhibited by the two districts is wholly dependent upon geological differences, and these are so strongly marked that they could not fail to attract the notice of the most superficial observer.

In the last report I had the honor to lay before you, some general references were made to the topography of the southern slope of the upper peninsula, which embraced simply those portions bordering on Lakes Huron and Michigan, and extending from Point de Tour to Monominee River.

Although the rocks of the district extending from Point de Tour to Chocolate River, upon the northerly or Lake Superior slope, belong to an older series than those lying south, and are different in composition, the general features of the two districts, nevertheless, bear a close resemblance. Easterly from Point Iroquois, the country is for the most part flat, or but slightly elevated, and the near approach of the rock to the surface so far prevents the descent of the waters as to give rise to extensive districts of wet and swaly land. Westerly from point Iroquois to Chocolate River the country is more elevated and has a much smaller proportion of wet land. A range of hills, having an elevation varying from 300 to 600 feet above Lake Superior, commences a little easterly from

Point Iroquois, and stretches very nearly west, or but a few degrees north of west, until the western escarpment again appears upon the coast, giving rise to the elevated hills of which the Pictured Rocks and Grand Island form a part. The outline of this range of hills has the most perfect regularity, being unbroken and uniformly covered with a dense growth of timber.

West from Chocolate River, to our boundary line at Montreal River, the physical character of the country is widely different from that of the district before referred to. This country is made up of a series of irregular, knobby ranges of hills that have a general easterly and westerly direction, with intervening valleys of flat or gently rolling land. These hills not unfrequently rise to a height of from 600 to 900 feet, very near to the immediate coast of Lake Superior, and at a distance of 15 to 20 miles south from the coast, portions of some of the ranges rise to a height of 1,200 to 1,300 feet above the level of that lake. The ragged and broken outline which this district presents, when viewed in detail, from the lake, contrasts in a striking manner with that of the country lying east from Chocolate River, for instead of the regular and unbroken range of hills uniformly covered with a dense forest that occur in the latter districts, we have a series of ranges of broken hills, with knobs not unfrequently nearly or quite destitute of timber. The escarpments of these hills are sometimes so abrupt as to render them difficult of ascent.

The only exception to the general easterly and westerly direction of these ranges of hills, occurs in that range constituting the Porcupine Mountains. These mountains rise somewhat abruptly almost upon the immediate coast of Lake Superior, at a point 37 miles north-easterly from the mouth of Montreal River, and from this point they stretch inland, in a direction which, for the first thirty miles, is very nearly south-south-west, after which their course is more westerly, and in the direction of the sources of the Wisconsin River. The most elevated points of the Porcupine Mountains, near to Lake Superior, attain an altitude of very nearly 950 feet, but several of the knobs, at a distance inland, rise from 1,100 to 1,300 feet above the level of the waters of that lake.

The valleys, before referred to as separating these ranges of hills, are uniformly heavily timbered, and by far the largest proportion of this timber is beech and maple.

The length of the hilly or mountainous district, estimating in a direct line west from Chocolate River to the boundary line on Montreal River, is very nearly one hundred and sixty miles, and it does not probably extend, at any point, more than 20 to 25 miles south of this line. Estimating this hilly district to extend regularly 20 miles south of a line drawn from the points before mentioned, the greatest width of the district would be opposite Keweenaw point, which extends 67 miles north from this line, making the total width at this point 87 geographical miles. The very great irregularities of the coast, with the numerous deep bays and projecting points upon the north, together with the irregularities of the ranges of hills upon the south, cause so great variations in the width of the district, that it is impossible, with the present information upon this subject, to estimate the width of the district with any great degree of accuracy. Keweenaw Bay, of Lake Superior, stretches 60 miles, estimating from the extremity of Keweenaw Point, into this hilly or mountainous country.

South from the range of hilly country alluded to, and extending to green Bay, the country at first becomes more level and finally flat, though with several regular and unbroken ranges of hills. In topography and general character it more nearly resembles that district of country which lies east from Chocolate River.

Of the district of country lying between the hilly country and Green Bay, less is known than of any other portion of the upper peninsula. The extent of my duties did not permit me to extend my examinations very far into it, nor was I enabled to obtain any information as to its general character.

The streams which discharge their waters into Lake Superior upon its south shore, are invariably short, and with very few exceptions, the quantity of water they discharge is small. This remark, in fact, may apply to the whole of the region of country surrounding that lake, for this immense body of water is completely surrounded by hills that, at no great distance from the lake, fall away more or less rapidly. Thus, while many of the streams discharging their waters into Lake Michigan, Green Bay and the Mississippi River, have their sources near to the south shore of Lake Superior, so also, many of those streams which discharge their waters northerly into Hudson's Bay, have their sources near to the north coast of the lake. The near approach of the summit of the ranges of hills surrounding the lake, to the immediate coast, leaves the area of country draining into Lake Superior, comparatively small.

The most important of the streams entering Lake Superior upon its south shore and within the limits of our State (commencing near the foot of the lake and enumerating westwardly), are the Tequoimenon, Train, Chocolate, Death, Yellow Dog, Huron, Portage, Fire Steel, Ontonagon, Iron, Presque Isle, Black and Montreal rivers. Besides these, there are innumerable creeks, which are usually known to voyageurs as rivers, for this term is applied indiscriminately to all. The waters of most of these streams are remarkably transparent and pure, with brisk currents and numerous cascades, and they almost invariably contain an abundance of the brook trout, a circumstance which I mention from the fact that this fish is scarcely known in the streams of the southern peninsula.

The Tequoimenon River, which is the only stream east from Chocolate River that in reality breaks through the range of sandstone hills, before mentioned as extending westerly from Point Iroquois, has its embouchure about 18 miles south from White Fish Point, and near the foot of the lake. The discharge is through loose sands, and there is an average of 4 to 4½ feet water over the bar. Having passed the bar, the water for a distance of 7 to 8 miles varies from 10 to 15 feet in depth.

Some of the sources of this stream approach very nearly to Lake Michigan, being directly at the base of the range of lime rock hills, referred to in my third annual report.

The Toquimenon River, with the exception of a distance of some four to five miles, while passing through the range of sandstone hills before alluded to, is, through its whole course, a sluggish stream, though at many points having a strong, deep current. The character of the river in its passage through the range of hills referred to, is totally changed, for it has there numerous chutes and falls, with almost continuous rapids. At one point the whole body of water contained in the stream is precipitated by a single leap from a height of 46 feet, and the effect of this fall is much heightened by the elevated and overhanging rocks that bound the river on either side.

Most of the small streams discharging into Lake Superior between the foot of the lake and Chocolate River, have their sources to the north of the elevated range of hills mentioned, or minor branches only decend from those hills.

Chocolate River, which discharges its waters into Lake Superior at a point 146 miles very nearly due west from the Saut de Ste. Marie, is a stream of considerable magnitude, though in consequence of the loose sands at its mouth it is difficult of entrance at ordinary stages of water even with barges of moderate draught, but when once the bar is passed the stream is found to be deep, and for several miles has a width varying from 80 to 150 feet.

This stream will be made a point of reference in the strictly geological portions of this report, for it winds along near the line of junction of two widely distinct geological districts, the general features of one being characterized by its ragged and broken hills, while the other is not less marked by its generally level or regularly undulating surface.

(11)

Chocolate River takes its name from the dark color of its waters.

Those streams which occur between Chocolate River and Keweenaw Bay, are, with the exception of Huron River, small; though were we to refer to the published maps of this district, we would suppose that some of these streams were of very considerable length. But with the exception of Huron River and River Des Morts, I believe they all have their sources in small lakes lying along the bases of the elevated hills already described. These hills rarely recede farther than three to five miles from the coast, and the length of the streams forming the outlets of the lakes referred to, is governed wholly by these features.

Ontonagon River, which is one of the most important of the rivers discharging its waters into Lake Superior, upon its south shore, has its embouchure very nearly fifty-five miles east, or rather north-easterly, from the western boundary of the State, at the mouth of Montreal River. Ontonagon River has its sources in a very great number of mountain lakes, situated in part upon the south-easterly spurs of the Porcupine Mountains, and in part in the hilly district formed by the easterly and westerly ranges of hills before described, which ranges, upon this portion of the coast, curve very considerably to the south. Some of the sources of the Ontonagon River approach very near to the sources of the Chippewa River of the Mississippi. The great number of small tributaries of the Ontonagon, which are simply the outlets of the small lakes referred to, are concentrated into two, principally branches, that finally unite and form the principal river, at a distance of about eighteen miles from the coast of Lake Superior. The smaller tributaries are mostly mere torrents, with frequent perpendicular falls, and high banks, sometimes of precipitous rock. The main stream, from the junction of the two principal branches to within five or six miles of the lake, is rapid and shoal, but below this the stream is comparatively still, and with a good depth of water. The mouth of the Ontonagon River is obstructed by a bar of sand, over which there is usually, at low stages, about six feet of water.

The principal rivers west from Ontonagon River, and within the limits of our State, have already been stated to be Iron, Presque Isle, Black and Montreal Rivers. These streams are all short, and the amount of water discharged by each separately is comparatively small. Their waters descend from the elevated mountain region immediately south from the coast, and since the whole streams are concentrated before passing from these elevations, their waters are discharged in body and they descend with very great rapidity. A greater variety of grand and beautiful scenery than that presented by some of these streams in their descent to the lake, taken in connection with the rugged and wild character of the country, can scarcely be conceived. I was particularly struck with the great variety of picturesque views furnished by Black River, in its descent from the elevated country on the west side of the Porcupine Mountains to Lake Superior. The stream was estimated to fall about five hundred feet in a fraction over four miles, and this descent is made up by a constant succession of falls, chutes and rapids, which continue with so little interruption that the waters for the whole distance may be said to be constantly white foam. The stream is bounded upon either side by banks elevated from one hundred to three hundred feet, sometimes sloping away from the stream, somewhat gently, and again rising in mural precipices of rock, separated from each other by so short distances as to appear scarcely sufficient to permit the passage of the waters of the river. The most considerable fall does not exceed fifty feet, and they are usually from ten to thirty feet in height, but their constant succession and variety add much to its interest.

Montreal River is a comparatively small stream, made up of numerous small tributaries that rise among the ranges of hills to the south-west and south-east of its mouth. The passage of the river through the range of hills near the lake, gives rise to several very considerable water-falls, as also to much rugged and wild scenery. Almost directly at the place of embouchure into Lake Superior, there is a perpendicular fall of about 40 feet. This stream, it will be recollected, forms a portion of the boundary between Michigan and Wisconsin.

By the act admitting Michigan as a State into the confederacy, and in which her boundaries are defined, it does not appear to have been the intention to include within her limits any portion of territory lying upon the north shore of Lake Superior, but in consequence of the peculiar shape of the coast at that point where the *national* boundary line "last touches Lake Superior," at the mouth of Pigeon River, a direct line to the mouth of the Montreal River, if followed literally, would throw within the State of Michigan several small rocky islands, together with a few miles of the south cape of Pigeon Bay, situate on the north coast. This boundary leaves in Wisconsin the whole of the Apostles' group of islands, near to the south coast, while it includes within Michigan, Isle Royale, situate near to the north coast of the lake.

Isle Royale is little less than an island of rock rising abruptly from the lowest depth of the lake, in irregular hills, to a height varying from 100 to 450 feet above the level of the lake. The island has a length of a fraction over 45 miles from north-east to south-west, and a breadth varying from 3½ to 8 miles. The most northerly point of the island is very nearly in latitude 48 deg. 12 min. 30 sec. north, and the parallel of longitude 89 deg. west from Greenwich, crosses the island a little east from its centre. Its nearest approach to the main land is near its north-westerly end, where it is separated from a point of the north coast, a few miles east from Pigeon River by a distance of a fraction less than 13 miles. Isle Royal is separated from Keweenaw Point of the south coast, by a distance of 44 miles, and the elevated hills of this point may be distinctly seen from Isle Royale when the atmosphere is clear.

Nearly the whole of the north-westerly side of Isle Royale is a continuous, elevated, rocky cliff, which will scarcely admit of a landing, but the south-easterly side, together with the easterly and westerly ends, are deeply indented with bays, which form secure harbors. The north-easterly end is made up of a series of elevated, rocky spits, with intervening bays. These spits of rock continue for a length varying from 10 to 12 miles, with a width scarcely exceeding half a mile, and altogether they may not inaptly be compared to the hand with the fingers half spread. The bays have a sufficient depth of water to admit vessels of the largest class to enter nearly one-third the whole length of the island.

Much of Isle Royal is absolutely destitute of soil, and the island has a most desolate appearance, but notwithstanding this it is of immense value for its fisheries, which are as yet scarcely appreciated.

General Geology of the Upper Peninsula.

The geology of the upper or northern peninsula of Michigan, when compared with that of the southern or lower peninsula, bears a striking contrast, for while that of the district last referred to is uniformly regular, with rocks, which, though rarely exposed to view, are few and for the most part but little disturbed, over large areas of country, the upper peninsula embraces a much greater number of rocks, distributed over a somewhat smaller district of country, and a portion of which are so much disturbed as to render their delineation exceedingly complex and difficult.

The widely different topographical features of the easterly and westerly portions of the northerly part of the upper peninsula would lead the most casual observer to infer that the geological features of the different districts would be equally distinct, and in this he would not be disappointed.

I have already referred to the rugged and broken character of the country extending westerly from Chocolate River to our boundary at Montreal River, and have also attempted to define its general length and breadth. This district, which is essentially made up of primary, trap and metamorphic rocks, with intervening sedimentary rocks, usually occupying the valleys and out boundaries, may be estimated to cover an area equal to a little more than one-fourth of the whole of the upper peninsula. To the east and south of this district the rocks are wholly sedimentary, consisting of a series of sandstones, limestones and shales.

With a view of rendering the local details of the separate formations more intelligible, I will first describe in general terms the rocks occurring in so much of the peninsula as has been examined, together with their general extent. This will necessarily involve a repetition of a very small portion of the report last made, upon the subject of the limestones of the south and east portions of the peninsula, but since the examinations of the past year have enabled me to add another member to the limestone group, and to define with more certainty its outline, this may not be devoid of interest.

1. *Primary Rocks.*—The rocks constituting what may be considered as the true primary group of this region are chiefly granite, syenite and syenitic granites. The members of the group are first seen upon the south coast of Lake Superior, constituting a rocky point known as Little Presque Isle, a little south-east from River Des Morts. These rocks frequently appear upon the coast north westerly, nearly as far as Huron River, and the Huron Islands, off the mouth of Huron River, belong to the same group. West from Huron Islands no rock appears upon the coast which, in a strict sense, I should regard as primary. The rocks of this group rise upon or near to the coast, in irregular and broken ranges of hills, to a height varying from 300 to 700 feet above the waters of the lake, and these hills, or ranges of hills, are continued in a south-westerly direction. The precise limit of the primary rocks to the westward, has not yet been determined, but they are known to extend nearly or quite to the sources of the Wisconsin River.

A portion of the south-westerly prolongation of the Porcupine Mountain range is made up of rocks belonging to the primary group, but its precise limit here has not yet been determined.

2. *Trap Rocks.*—Flanking the primary rocks already described on the north and north-west, are a series of ranges of hills stretching in a direction generally south-westerly and northeasterly, which attain an altitude of from three to nine hundred feet above the lake. They are more regular, or rather less broken in outline than the primary hills; a change, however, which in the transition is noticed to take place gradually from one group to the other, or in other words the knobbed character of the ranges becomes less and less apparent as we cross them in a north-westerly direction, or from the primary range. These hills are composed of rocks, differing at first but slightly from those of the primary group, but gradually the difference becomes more and more apparent as we proceed northerly. The rocks of those hills nearest the primary range may possibly be regarded simply as rocks of that group, more or less altered, though the rocks of the outer ranges are plainly trap. The range of these rocks, which may be said to commence at the very extremity of Keweenaw Point, extends, after a slight curve to the north, in a general south-westerly direction, gradually receding from the coast, until at the crossing of the Ontonagon River, it is nearly 25 miles inland. Westerly from Ontonagon River the range becomes confounded with the northerly portions of the Porcupine Mountains, while west from these mountains a portion of what may be considered the same range of rock has taken a more westerly course and approaches the coast, until at the crossing of the Montreal River it is but a few miles distant from Lake Superior. West from the Porcupine Mountains a second range of trap is continued at a distance of from fifteen to twenty miles inland. The trap range of Keweenaw Point may be estimated to compose one-third the entire width of the point, and the south-easterly portions of the range are

made up of compact greenstone, while those portions to the north-west are amygdaloid.

The ranges of hills constituting the north-westerly part of Isle Royale, and extending its whole length, are of similar rocks, and single knobs of well defined trap rock occasionally occur in the very midst of the primary region before referred to, upon the south coast; the proofs of the character of which will be shown as we advance.

3. *Metamorphic Rocks.*—Flanking the primary rocks on the south, is a series of stratified rocks consisting of talcose, mica and clay slates, slaty hornblende rock, and quartz rock; the latter rock constituting by far the largest proportion of the whole group. In traversing the country south-easterly from little Presque Isle, the point referred to as the most south-easterly prolongation of the granite, this last rock passes almost insensibly into a serpentine rock, which has a regular jointed structure, sometimes approaching to stratification; continuing in the same direction we find a series of hornblend slates, talcose, mica and clay slates, resting against the serpentine rocks, and still farther to the south-east the rock becomes almost uniformly quartz. The rocks of this group dip irregularly to the south and south east, while the cleavage of the slates is very uniformly to the north.

The rocks of the metamorphic group stretch into the interior in a westerly or rather south-westerly direction, forming the south-easterly part of the hilly region.

Rocks referable to this group also occur upon the north coast of Lake Superior.

4. *Conglomerate.*—The rock to which I shall restrict this term does not occur well characterized at any point east from the district referred to as the commencement of the trap group, nor has it been noticed resting upon any of either the primary or metamorphic rocks, but is invariably seen resting upon the trap rocks. Commencing upon the north side of the trap, at the extremity of Keweenaw Point, the conglomerate

flanks the trap upon its northerly side, as far west as the boundary of our State; nor does it stop here, for the same rock is seen at intervals as far west as the head of Lake Superior. A similar rock also rests upon the trap of Isle Royale, facing the south-east.

In the course of the range of conglomerate upon the south shore, it forms a nearly continuous range of hills, with somewhat steep escapements, but with a generally rounded outline. These hills sometimes rise to a height of from three to five hundred feet above the level of the lake.

The conglomerate attains a very great thickness, being greatest at its westerly prolongation, and it gradually thins out as we proceed north-easterly; but the irregularity in thickness is so very considerable that variations of several hundred feet are not uncommon within the space of a few miles.

The conglomerate rock of the south coast dips in mass irregularly to the north and north-west, while that of Isle Royale dips to the south-east.

5. *Mixed Conglomerate and Sandstone.*—The rock or rocks to which I have affixed the above name consists of an alternating series of coarse conglomerates and red sandstones, resting conformably upon the conglomerate rock before described. In strictness, these rocks should probably be considered as a member of the conglomerate itself, but for the sake of convenience in description I have deemed it desirable to separate them.

This mixed rock was only noticed, as before stated, resting upon the conglomerate, and this only between Point Keweenaw and Montreal River. Its thickness immediately west from and upon the flanks of the Porcupine Mountains, is very considerable, but it wedges out rapidly both easterly and westerly, and on the east, near the extremity of Keweenaw Point, it wholly disappears.

The mixed rock dips regularly to the north and north-west.

6. *Lower or Red Sandstone and Shales.*—The red sandstone, with its accompanying red and gray shales, occupies a much larger extent of the country bordering upon Lake Superior than any other single rock or group of rocks. It rests upon the primary and metamorphic rocks, immediately west from Chocolate River; upon the conglomerate and mixed rocks from near Eagle River, of Keweenaw Point, west to the head of Lake Superior; upon the primary trap, metamorphic and conglomerate rocks of the north shore of the lake, and upon the conglomerate rock of Isle Royale. It is this rock which forms the basis of the level plateaus or valleys occupying the spaces between the several ranges of hills south from Lake Superior, and west from Chocolate River. In these last situations this rock is frequently seen undisturbed to surround the bases of isolated knobs of granite, though when near to or in contact with knobs or trap there are invariable evidences of very great disturbance.

The rocks of this group attain their greatest thickness at their westerly prolongation, gradually thinning out as we proceed easterly.

With the exception of that portion of the coast extending from Point Iroquois, at the foot of the lake, to Grand Island, the predominating rock upon the immediate coast, both on the south and north shore, is this red sandstone; for even the primary trap and conglomerate rocks are almost invariably skirted with a band of it. It is also over this rock that the waters of Lake Superior are discharged at the Sault de Ste. Marie.

The sandrock forms the chief portion of the group, the shales occurring rather, as beds than otherwise, as will be hereafter described.

The red sandstone both upon the north and south shores of Lake Superior invariably dips into the basin of that lake, which may therefore be regarded as a synclinal axis.

7. *Upper or Gray Sandstone.*—Upon the south shore of Lake Superior, and extending from Point Iroquois to Grand

Island, a sandstone occurs, differing widely in its appearance from that before described. This sandstone rests *unconformably* upon the red sandstone, the former dipping gently to the south or south-east, while the latter dips very considerably to the north or north-west.

The elevated range of hills before described as commencing a little easterly from Point Iroquois and extending to the Pictured Rocks, are composed of this rock. From the Pictured Rocks, the range of hills curves more to the south, stretching very far to the south-west, but its precise limit is not yet determined.

In its easterly prolongation the gray sandstone thins out rapidly. It is last seen at the Neebesh Rapids of the Riviere Ste. Marie, on the east, at which point, in consequence of not having been sufficiently examined farther westerly, it was confounded with the red sandrock in the last report which I had the honor to lay before you.

8. *Sandy Lime Rock.**—Resting immediately upon this upper or gray sandstone is a sandy limerock, which, although nearly wanting at the very easterly extremity of the peninsula, as we proceed westerly occupies a more important place. This rock, which, as its name implies, is intermediate between a sandstone and limerock, may be seen on Sailor's Encampment Island of the Riviere Ste. Marie, as also at several points in the vicinity of Monusco Bay, from whence it stretches westerly, occupying nearly the central portion of the peninsula for a distance of at least sixty miles; from which its precise range and limit has not yet been determined. The outcropping edge of this rock appears at a level very considerably below that both of the sandstone to the north, and of the limestones to the south. Its width for the distance mentioned varies from ten to fifteen miles, and it dips uniformly to the south-south-east.

The sandy limerock has not yet been examined with sufficient care to admit of accurate description. It contains but

---

*The names which have been affixed to the several sand and lime rocks are regarded as merely temporary, and are introduced, for the present, barely to facilitate description.

few fossils, but those few are sufficiently characteristic, were there no other considerations, to separate it from the lower limerocks and shales.

Upon the sandy limerock to which reference is above made rests the lower limerock and shales, and upon this last the upper limerock, both uniformly dipping to the south or southeast. These limerocks were described in general terms, in my third annual report, and although many additional facts have been gathered respecting their character, range and extent, it is, perhaps, unnecessary to lay them before you at this time. I will barely add, with respect to them, that the suggestion there mentioned, that a more careful examination of these limestones would render a farther division of the groups necessary, has been fully confirmed.

I had hoped to lay before you a profile section of the rocks of the upper peninsula, but the impossibility of having it engraved in time to accompany this report has led me to defer it. I regret this the more since many of the facts connected with a full understanding of the economical portion of this report are so intimately dependent upon the general geology of the country that in the absence of correct maps, and without a profile section of the rocks, I fear it will be impossible for me to render the most important portion, so far as regards the prosperity of the State, intelligible.

As it is, I can only, in the place of this, lay before you a general section of the rocks of the upper peninsula, together with their thickness, so far as the same has been satisfactorily determined. This section is intended simply to represent the order in which the several rocks rest upon each other.

Having already described in general terms the range and extent of the rocks of the upper peninsula, so far as the same have been examined, the limits of the present report will admit of nothing more than a general description of the characters of these rocks, and I shall not attempt a minute description of any members of the series, except such as are more or less connected with subjects which are supposed to be of immediate practical importance.

Section Illustrative of the order of super-position of the Rocks of the Upper Peninsula.

		Thickness in Feet.
9.	Tertiary Clays and Sands.	
8.	Upper Limerock Group (embracing as members the Drummond Island and Mackinaw limestones).	
7.	Lower Limerock and Shales.	
6.	Sandy or Intermediate Limestone.	
5.	Upper or Grey Sandstone,	mean 700
4.	Lower or Red Sandrock and Shales,	extreme 6,500
3.	Mixed Conglomerate and Sandrock,	extreme 4,200
2.	Conglomerate Rock,	extreme 5,260
1.	Metamorphic, Trap and Primary rocks.	

PRIMARY ROCKS.

Although the usual ternary compound of quartz, feldspar and mica, occurs but rarely in the primary, in the vicinity of the coast of Lake Superior, and in fact but rarely in any portion of the range which I have visited, nevertheless, the great mass of rocks included within this range, may, in a broad sense, be called granite. The compound above referred to is more common in the westerly than in the easterly portion of the range. The more common rock is made up of quartz, feldspar and hornblende, giving rise to a very dark colored syenite; occasionally mica enters sufficiently into the compound to form syenitic granite, and sometimes the place of the hornblende in the syenite is supplied by schorl or tourmaline, thus giving rise to a schorl rock.

The rocks of the southeasterly portion of the primary range of hills are more clearly defined as granitic rocks, than those situated more northerly, for they are more distinctly and largely crystaline in structure, and quartz enters much more largely as a constituent into their composition. As we proceed north-westerly, from the south-east boundary of the primary, over the several broken ranges of hills, we find the character of the rocks in mass almost imperceptibly changing. The quartz as a mineral gradually forms a less important part, and it finally almost wholly disappears, leaving a binary compound of feldspar and hornblende, which then assumes a granular structure, constituting greenstone. The intermediate rock, between the syenite and greenstone ranges, may not inappropriately be called a syenitic greenstone.

The primary rocks which appear in the vicinity of Lake Superior, in the several ranges of hills extending from a point opposite little Presque isle,* to Huron river, are essentially either syenite or syenitic granite. The rock, as a whole, is extremely compact, and the constituent minerals are mostly in small crystals, though occasionally the feldspar assumes a more largely crystaline form.

The granitic rocks, so far as the range has been examined, in a southwesterly direction, are largely traversed by dykes, that are almost without exception made up of materials in all respects indentical with the greenstone, before alluded to, as forming the more northwesterly ranges of hills. The courses

---

*A little south-east from River Des Morts.

of these dykes or veins are invariably marked by striking changes in the character of the rock traversed, and in the larger dykes, the evidences of the changes produced by the heat of the injected matter, extend to several hundred feet upon either side of the dyke itself. The connection between the rocky matter composing these dykes and the ranges of greenstone, lying northwest, is clearly identified, not only by the perfect similarity in mineral character, but also from the fact, that as we proceed in the direction of the ranges of greenstone, the dykes become much more frequent, until at length it becomes difficult to determine which of the rocks predominate in quantity.

These facts serve to throw much light upon the relative ages of the several ranges of hills, or in other words, serve to show the order in which they were severally uplifted; facts which will be more fully shown when we come to consider the present position of the overlying sedimentary rocks. These facts are not only important, to enable us to understand the many changes which have taken place, with regard to the relative position of the land and water, but they are rendered of practical importance for the reason, which I think may be satisfactorily shown, that the mineral region of the upper peninsula, to be hereafter described, is strictly confined to only the outer portion of the rocks of a single epoch.

The veins and dykes of greenstone, referred to as traversing the granite rocks, do not, in this portion of the group, appear to have any regular magnetic bearing, for they traverse the rock in all directions. Veins of any other matter are very rarely seen traversing the granite. In a single instance, what was regarded as a true vein of porphyry, having a width of nearly three feet, was noticed, which vein is crossed, at angles of 53° and 107°, by a vein of greenstone, having a width somewhat less than that of the porphyry. In this instance, the greenstone is clearly the most recent vein.

The veins of greenstone traversing the granite, vary from a mere line, to 50 or 60 feet in width. The intimate blending of the material composing these veins, together with the chemical differences, causes them to disintegrate or waste away more rapidly than the rock they traverse; the result of which is, that deep grooves are frequently left in the granite, the simple result of the wasting away of these dykes or veins. This is peculiarly the case upon the coast of the lake, where the rocks are subject to the action of the waves, which have, in some instances, so removed the debris as to leave long and narrow bays, with high perpendicular walls, occupying simply the space once occupied by the dyke. The Huron islands, which are simple elevated granite knobs, appear, upon first examination, as a mass of rocks, completely rent in many places, with portions separated from each other by narrow clefts, having perpendicular walls of great height. While these rents are of sufficient width to admit of being traversed by small boats, the perpendicular walls are so little varied in their elevation as scarcely to leave a point, in these narrow passages, where a landing can be effected. A careful examination of these passages shows them to be simply the spaces once occupied by dykes or veins of greenstone, which having disintegrated, and the detrital matter having been removed by the action of the waves, has left the walls of the more enduring granite rock, unbroken and almost untouched.

Upon the north coast of Lake Superior, well defined granite and syenite, or syenitic granite, occasionally appear upon the immediate coast of the lake, but more frequently these rocks are flanked on the south by greenstone, with occasional narrow bands of sandstone ; thus precisely reversing the magnetic order of those rocks upon the south coast.

TRAP ROCKS.

Were we to consider the rocks of the district under consideration, strictly in their chronological order, those rocks which I propose to treat as trap rocks, would undoubtedly *follow* those slates and quartz rocks which are considered as metamorphic, and which may be regarded as identical in time of uplift with those rocks before alluded to, as being intermediate between the granitic and trap rocks. The almost insensible gradations by which the granitic rocks pass into the greenstone of the trap formation, and the near analogy of the whole of the rocks of both formations, to each other, renders it more convenient, at the same time that it is more simple to follow the arrangement or order that I have adopted.

I have already stated that in passing from the granitic region on the south side of Lake Superior, in a direction northwesterly, we cross a series of ranges of hills, varying in height from three to nine hundred feet above the lake, and that in pursuing this course, we observe that the character of the rocks gradually and almost insensibly change, until at length they become well defined greenstone.*

The rocks of the outer or northwestern range of hills, which were clearly the last of the series of uplifts, bears more unequivocally the evidences of igneous origin, than either of the outer ranges alluded to. The rock upon the south flank of these hills, is invariably very compact greenstone, while upon the north-westerly line it is almost equally invariably an amygdaloid, or at least, has an amygdaloidal structure. The causes of this difference of structure of the rock, upon the opposite sides of this range of hills, when carefully examined upon the ground, are very apparent, for it is evident, as will hereafter be shown, that the uplift of the rocks of this range of hills was wholly upon the south-easterly side, and while the rocks of this portion were in a solidified state, or in other words, that a point in Lake Superior may be regarded as a fixed axis of the uplifted mass. That this was the case, is shown by the fact that the sedimentary rocks to the south or south-east are scarcely disturbed, so far as regards this range of hills, while the sedimentary rocks on the north or north-westerly side are

---

*In the present report, I use the term *greenstone* in its generic sense, applying it to all the compact rocks, of a granulated structure, belonging to the trap range. By far the larger proportion of these rocks are greenstone, in its most restricted sense, or in other words, are composed of feldspar and hornblende; but the term is also used to include rocks which in a strict sense would be considered as altered syenite, syenitic, granite, hornblende rock and angitic rock.

The term *amygdaloid*, I apply, as it is usually applied to that portion of the rock having a difference of form simply, without any reference to the constituents of the rock. This generic use of terms is employed for the reason that the limits of the present report will not allow any thing more than a very general consideration of the subject. The term *trap* is used in such a sense as to include both the greenstone and amygdaloid, though it may sometimes prove that the amygdaloid has had its origin from the fusion of the lower portions of the sedimentary rocks.

invariably tilted to a high angle near the range of hills, which angle gradually decreases as we pass farther and farther from the hills themselves. These sedimentary rocks, which upon the north side always dip *from* the range of trap hills, are in their close proximity to the trap inclined at angles varying from 45 deg. to 85 deg. Dykes of from fifty to four or five hundred feet are of frequent occurrence, traversing these sedimentary rocks, but the widest of these have invariably been protruded between the strata of the sedimentary rocks, and consequently have the same general inclination. The result of these frequent dykes, which occur at comparatively short distances from the main body of trap, is that the sedimentary rocks frequently so far lose their original character as scarcely to be recognized.

The rocks of the complete north-western escarpment of this range of hills were evidently in an intense state of ignition while in contact with the sedimentary rocks, as is clearly shown by the very great changes which have taken place in the rocks last alluded to. In fact, I am disposed to refer the origin of much of the amygdaloid rock to the fusion of the lower portions of the sedimentary rocks referred to, for the reason that as we pass south from this junction the amygdaloid rocks wholly disappear, their place being supplied by greenstone; and again, so intimately are they blended that it is frequently impossible to determine where the amygdaloid ceases and the upper sedimentary rocks commence. Fragments of the sedimentary rocks, the characters of which can be clearly recognized, are not of rare occurrence, imbedded in the amygdaloid rock, a circumstance which although by no means conclusive, should not be overlooked in considering this subject.

I would not wish to convey the idea that the amygdaloid rocks have their origin exclusively from the altered sedimentary rocks, but simply that the change in the structure of the trap from greenstone to amygdaloid may and no doubt does depend upon the proximity of the sedimentary rocks to the trap while the latter was in a state of ignition.

I have been compelled to tread upon grounds which may, perhaps, be considered theoretical, but it would appear to be necessary in order to convey a proper idea of the condition of the rocks composing the range of hills under consideration. These views, however, would not have been alluded to at this time had it not been for the fact that an understanding of all that relates to the mineral resources of this portion of our State is more or less intimately connected with this portion of the subject.

Although the general range of the trap hills has been already given, I will define as nearly as is in my power the line of junction between the trap and sedimentary rocks upon the north escarpment, premising that the elevation at which this junction takes place is usually at a height of from 100 to 500 feet above the lake, and only in a single instance does this line reach the coast of the lake. Commencing almost directly at the extremity of Keweenaw Point, this line passes in a south-westerly direction, gradually receding from the coast; it crosses Sturgeon or Portage Lake near its centre, after which it recedes still more rapidly from the coast, until finally it is seen to cross the upper forks of the Ontonagon River, and soon after the whole is apparently lost in the range of the Porcupine Mountains, which last range has a course so much to the south-west as probably to completely intersect the first range mentioned. On the west side of the Porcupine Mountains the range of hills and the line of junction appear again, but many miles farther north than they would have been looked for; from thence the true line gradually approaches the coast, until, at its point of crossing the Montreal river, it is but about two miles above the mouth of that stream.

To the north and north-west, through the whole of the distance described, this trap is bounded by hills of conglomerate and sandstone, more or less elevated, but usually not exceeding 400 feet. To the north-west of these hills of sedimentary rocks, a dyke of trap is seen to extend for many miles along the line of coast of Keweenaw point, and so great is the width of the dyke, that unless carefully examined, its character might easily be misunderstood. It lies in a plane parallel to the stratification of the sedimentary rock by which it is embraced, and with that rock dips to the north-west The dyke is chiefly made up of greenstone, but not unfrequently large portions of the mass consist of amygdaloid, in which the amygdules are filled or composed of quartz, chalcedony, agate, calc. spar, zeolite, etc.

The dykes just referred to, so far as their relation to the amygdaloidal portion of the trap is concerned, as also the many others similarly situated with respect to the superincumbent sedimentary rocks, will be regarded in the same light as contemporaneous veins, though they are only contemporaneous with the uplift of the strata, and not with their deposit. But there is still another class of veins which not only traverse a portion of the trap rocks, but also the upper sedimentary rocks, and which may be regarded as true veins. These last mentioned veins traverse the rocks at a high angle with the line of bearing of the sedimentary rocks, as also with the line of junction of those last mentioned with the trap rocks. The composition of these veins is widely different from that of the contemporaneous veins or dykes before referred to. As this subject will be treated more at length in a succeeding portion of this report, I deem it unnecessary at this time to refer more particularly to the subject.

A single knob of trap appears under circumstances which add very much to its interest, at what is usually known as Presque Isle, an elevated rocky point immediately north-west from Riviere Des Morts, and almost directly within the granitic region. This point of land has its origin from the simple elevation of a mass of trap rock which rises on the north in abrupt cliffs varying from 20 to 60 feet in height. The trap is mostly greenstone, though portions of it are so largely impregnated with a dark colored, almost black serpentine, as to deserve the name of serpentine rock.

The knob of trap under consideration is possessed of additional interest, from the unequivocal evidence of uplift, as also from the manner in which these evidences are exhibited. The cliffs of trap occupy the very extremity of the point, while the neck and central portions are made up of conglomerate or trap-tuff and sandrock resting upon the trap. These upper rocks also appear upon the immediate coast, in cliffs of from 20 to 60 feet in height, and in many places they are seen resting directly upon the trap. The stratification of these sedimentary rocks has been very much disturbed, and they invariably dip at a high angle in all directions from the trap itself. The character of both rocks, at the immediate line of junction is almost completely lost, and the evidences of change most unequivocally marked. But the most curious feature of the whole is that the sedimentary rocks for a distance of several hundred feet have been completely shattered or broken into minute fragments, which, having retained their original position were again cemented by the injection of calcareous matter. This injection has filled the most minute fissures, and so perfect is it that in looking upon the face of a mural cliff of these rocks, the veins may be easily seen at a distance of many rods, forming as it were, a complete net work over the cliff, and so minute is it that a single hand specimen frequently contains many hundreds of these veins.

This knob of trap, like the rock before described, is also traversed by veins of a date subsequent to the uplift of the rock.

The whole of the north-western portion of Isle Royale is made up of trap, and in truth that rock constitutes by far the largest proportion of the rocky mass of the island. The two northerly ranges of hills already alluded to as traversing the island in its greatest length are wholly trap. The most northerly range of hills is composed almost exclusively of greenstone, while the rock of the south or south-easterly range becomes more decidedly amygdaloidal in its structure; thus reversing the order which these portions of the rock bear to each other upon the south shore of the lake.

The ranges of hills immediately bounding Lake Superior upon its north coast are almost invariably either well defined trap or altered syenite, while the decidedly primary rocks usually appear in ranges of hills to the north of these; thus following the reversed order of the rocks upon the south coast.

The character of the trap rocks of Lake Superior has perhaps been sufficiently described to answer the purpose for which this hasty sketch is intended; and I will only add that they are usually distinctly jointed, and where they approximate to the sedimentary rocks, there is not unfrequently so distinct a cleavage opposed to the joints in direction as to give the appearance of stratification. The jointed structure of the trap rocks sometimes, though rarely, passes to what may be termed a rudely columnar structure. Upon one of the long rocky points forming the north-easterly extremity of Isle Royale this rock assumes the columnar form, and the columns are tolerably well defined, having a height of from 80 to 90 feet. The columns are also seen, but less perfectly developed, forming the coast of a small rocky island two or three miles south from the point last alluded to. These are the only points in the trap of Lake Superior where I have noticed the rock to assume this form.

METAMORPHIC ROCKS.

The general direction of the rocks composing this group, has already been described, and they are confined exclusively to the range of hills lying upon the south-east side of the granitic rocks. The general direction of these hills is south-west and north-east.

The outline of the hills of the metamorphic group is less broken than either the granitic or trap ranges, but these rocks sometimes rise in abrupt conical peaks, closely resembling those of the granitic rocks.

The area of country occupied by rocks of this group is less than that of either the primary or trap, the general average width not exceeding six to eight miles. The precise limit of the group in a south-westerly direction is not known.

It has already been stated that Chocolate River is the boundary on the south-east, between these and the sedimentary rocks, and that they extend in a north-westerly direction from this stream to the granite, against which they rest. The group is made up of an alternating series of talcose and mica slates, sometimes graduating into clay slates, with quartz and serpentine rocks, the quartz rocks constituting by far the larger proportion of the whole mass. Since it would be nearly impossible to describe the alternations of these several rocks, in such a manner as to be understood without the aid of a diagram or section, no attempt will be made to do so.

The cleavage of all these rocks is usually north or north 10 deg. west, at an angle which in the main varies but little from 80 deg., but the mass of the group appears to dip regularly to the south or south-west. The talcose slates and quartz rocks alternate frequently with each other, and with the rock which has been called serpentine rock less frequently.

The quartz rock is usually distinctly granular, though it is sometimes compact, with a conchoidal fracture. It usually separates by cleavage into masses or strata, having a considerable degree of regularity, and varying from a few inches to several feet in thickness. The rock is usually more or less regularly jointed.

The rock which for the sake of convenience I have denominate serpentine rock bears a close resemblance to greenstone, being essentially composed of granular feldspar and hornblend, with which serpentine is intimately blended. This rock only occurs in the talcose slate as we approach the granitic region, and possibly a more close examination may show it to be a simple series of dykes lying parallel to the line of cleavage of the slate rocks.

The metamorphic rocks are occasionally traversed by trap dykes. The group of rocks under consideration has been comparatively little examined, and the more minute details connected with it will be taken up at some future time.

Conglomerate Rock.

The lower of the sedimentary rocks to which I have attached this name appears to be invariably connected with, or to rest upon, the trap rock, nor has it been noticed to any extent in connection with either of the other lower rocks, for it wholly disappears as we approach the granitic and metamorphic groups. Of all the sedimentary rocks this is the most variable in thickness, and not unfrequently does a few miles make a difference of several hundred feet. The conglomerate rock may without doubt be considered as a trap-tuff which was gradually deposited or accumulated around the several conical knobs of trap during their gradual elevation, and which would necessarily occupy the complete spaces or valleys between the several irregular ranges of knobs or hills.

If we regard this conglomerate rock in this light, we will at once perceive why the rock should be variable and irregular in its thickness.

The pebbles of which the mass of the rock is composed consist of rounded masses of greenstone and amygdaloidal trap, of which the former make up by far the larger proportion, and scarcely a pebble of any other rock than trap enters into its composition. These pebbles vary in size from that of a pea to several pounds weight, but the average size may be stated at 1½ to 2 inches in diameter. The pebbles are usually united by a mixed calcareous and argillaceous cement, more or less colored by iron, and so firm is this union that the most compact and tough of the greenstone pebbles will frequently break through as freely as the cement, and crevices and narrow veins are frequently seen passing indiscriminately across the pebbles and cement. This fact is the more worthy of notice since the pebbles are almost without exception made up of the hardest and most indestructible portions of the trap rock.

The conglomerate rock can scarcely be said to occur in such form as to be well defined, in any portion of the country, excepting upon the northern flank of the outer trap range, before referred to. On the outer or northern side of Keweenaw Point, the conglomerate commences near the extremity of the point, and extends several miles westwardly, forming a series of abrupt and precipitous cliffs upon the immediate shore, as also a range of well defined hills a little in the interior, which hills have an elevation varying from 200 to 300 feet. After appearing for a few miles upon the coast, this rock gradually stretches into the interior, following the line before described as the most northerly boundary of the outer trap range of hills, and invariably occupying a place to the north of this range, and it may be observed, nearly or quite continuously, as far as Montreal river, which stream it crosses at a short distance above its mouth, thus making its complete length within the limits of Michigan, computing its southerly curve, something over 140 miles, but the rock does not cease at Montreal River, for it may be seen at short intervals in the interior as far westwardly as the head of Lake Superior.

At the trap knob of Presque Isle conglomerate is imperfectly developed, but on the south-westerly side of Isle Royale it is more perfectly developed, flanking the hills of trap upon the southerly side.

The conglomerate rock is imperfectly stratified in masses of immense thickness, and it dips upon the south shore of Lake Superior regularly to the north and north-west,* usually at high angles varying from 30 to 85 deg., while upon Isle Royale and the north shore the dip is reversed, being south and south-easterly, or in other words the rock upon all sides dips in the direction of the lake basin.

Upon the south shore of the lake the thickness of this rock was not estimated at any point west from Montreal River, a little east from which it attains its greatest thickness, being, as estimated, 5,260 feet. In addition to the great variations in thickness over comparatively small districts, the formation

---

*This variation in the dip is in conformity with the variation in the direction of the trap hills.

wedges out as we pass easterly along the range, and so rapid is this change that near its easterly prolongation the thickness was estimated at something less than 1,000 feet.

The greatest estimated thickness of the rock upon the north coast is a fraction less than 2,300 feet.

I have already stated that this rock is frequently traversed by dykes of trap, which are usually parallel to the line of stratification and dip of the rock. These dykes, which have sometimes a thickness of 50 to 60 feet, and even several hundred feet, are sometimes continuous for many miles, and are many times repeated. In addition to the dykes just alluded to the rock is frequently traversed by veins of a more recent date, which traverse alike the trap and conglomerate rocks, always at very high angles with the line of bearing of the conglomerate. These veins, which are usually more perfectly developed near the line of junction of the two rocks, or for a distance of a few thousand feet upon each side of the junction, are clearly true veins, and since, with a few unimportant exceptions,, they are the only veins belonging to this range which are metalliferous they will be considered more fully under a separate head.

MIXED CONGLOMERATE AND SANDROCK.

This rock formation is made up of an alternating series of conglomerate and red sandstones, which rest comformably upon the conglomerate rock last described, dipping with that rock into the bed of Lake Superior. The mixed rock was not noticed upon the north side of the lake, or upon Isle Royale, but upon the south shore the rock was traced continuously for a distance of about 130 miles, extending from a few miles westerly from the extremity of Keweenaw Point to Montreal River. It follows the line of the conglomerate before described, stretching from Keweenaw Point in a south-westerly direction,, and again curving to the north-west, forming, as it were, a crescent between the points before mentioned, the result of which is that the rock only appears for a very limited distance upon the coast of the lake, at Keweenaw Point.

From a point about eighteen miles easterly from Montreal River the rock wedges out rapidly as we proceed westerly from that point, and as we continue towards the head of Lake Superior the rock wholly disappears or becomes merged in the conglomerate rock below and the sandrock above. The greatest observed thickness of this rock is 4,200 feet.

The conglomerate portion of the mixed rock consists of strata of conglomerate, varying from a few feet to several hundred feet in thickness, and it is composed of materials in all respects resembling those constituting the conglomerate rock before described, and these materials are united by a similar cement.

The sandstone portion of the formation occurs in strata of very nearly corresponding thickness, and the two rocks may be said to form nearly equal portions of the complete mass. But the material of which this sandstone is composed differs widely from that of the true sandrock lying above, for while the latter is chiefly made up of quartzose materials the former is composed of materials bearing a close analogy in composition to those of the conglomerate rock itself; or in other words the sand consists chiefly of greenstone, so much comminuted as when cemented to compose a coarse sandstone. It will thus be seen that the members of this formation differ only in the degrees and fineness of the material, and the character of this material will explain sufficiently why the true conglomerate, and the mixed rocks are referable to the same origin, for the materials of the several members of the group have their origin and trap rock, and as a whole may perhaps be regarded as a trap-tuff.

The coarser conglomerate of the formation is scarcely separated by lines of stratification, and the strata appears usually in mass embraced between the strata of sandstone, but the stratification of the latter rock is perfect, and it bears evidence of having been deposited in shoal water, in the very abundant, perfectly defined ripple marks which it exhibits through its complete range.

No fossils were noticed in connection with either the mixed rock or the conglomerate lying below it.

Dykes of greenstone occasionally appear in the mixed rock, but less frequently than in the rock below. These dykes almost invariably occupy places between the strata of the rock, and correspond in position to the direction and dip of the rocks by which they are embraced, or in other words, the rocky matter composing the dykes appears to have been injected in a plane corresponding with that of the stratification of the embracing rock. As in the conglomerate below, these dykes have produced very great changes in the color and structure of the mixed rock bounding them upon either side.

In addition to these, the mixed rock is occasionally (though less frequently than the rock below) traversed by veins or cross courses of a more recent origin than the dykes (which latter they usually cross at a high angle), their course usually being at an angle of at least sixty degrees, opposed to the line of bearing of the mixed rock. These cross veins are usually made up of calcareous spar or a sub-granular limestone, and more rarely of some variety of quartz and imperfect trap rock, the latter of which is usually of the amygdaloid variety.

RED SANDSTONE AND SHALES.

That rock to which I have applied the name of red sandstone is emphatically the chief rock that appears upon the immediate coast of the south shore of Lake Superior, and the same remark will apply, in a more limited degree, to the complete coast of the lake. A traveler proceeding westerly along the coast, from Grand Island to the head of the lake, would imagine he had seen little else than red sandstone, and in fact, were he to confine his examinations to the immediate coast, he would see no other rock for nineteen-twentieths of the distance. From Grand Island westerly to the mouth of

Chocolate River, no other rock is seen in place, and from Chocolate River to Keweenaw Point, embracing the complete width of the primary, metamorphic and trap ranges, the hills forming these groups are almost invariably surrounded or flanked at their bases by this sandrock, so that even along this portion, the hills are, for a large proportion of the distance, cut off from the lake by a narrow belt of the rock under consideration, and westerly from Keweenaw Point to the head of Lake Superior no other rock appear upon the coast, if we except several trap dykes in the vicinity of the Porcupine Mountains, and a series of more recent deposits of clay and sand that appear west from Keweenaw Point. This sand rock also occurs upon the southerly side of Isle Royale.

The material of which the red sandrock is composed differs widely from that of the sedimentary rocks before described, for while the rocks last referred to are made up of materials clearly of trappean origin, and in which the material is very rarely quartz, the rock under consideration is composed of materials, the predominating portions of which are clearly derived from the granitic and metamorphic rocks, and in which quartz occurs abundantly, though with this, there is usually associated more or less sand, that has all the characters of the comminuted trap, constituting that portion of the mixed rock before referred to. Magnetic iron sand sometimes becomes a constituent of the red sandrock, and occasionally continuous strata of several inches thickness, are almost wholly composed of this material. The material composing this rock is usually cemented by calcareous matter highly colored by the per oxid of iron, though not unfrequently these are associated with argillaceous matter.

While the chief mass of the rock is a coarse grained, somewhat compact sandrock, there are portions of the formation where there are well formed red and grey flags, and red and green shales, forming, as it were, beds of a very considerable thickness and occupying large districts of country. These red and green shales are more largely developed in that district extending from Granite Point westerly to Keweenaw Bay, and upon the south side of Keweenaw Point, extending from the head of the bay to near the extremity of the point they are particularly largely developed. These shales more usually occur in alternating bands of deep red and green colors, the red usually largely predominating, and they are made up of argillaceous matter, with sand, the whole of the materials being of extreme fineness.

On the south-east side of Keweenaw Bay, near its head, an argillaceous rock appears, and extends for a short distance along the coast which is an anomaly. The rock is evidently embraced in, or rather may be said to constitute a member of the sandstone series, but it differs widely from any other rock seen in connection with it. This argillaceous rock sometimes appears in the form of a slate, though its most usual form is that of compact strata, frequently of several inches thickness, and which closely resembles indurated clay. A peculiar appearance is given to this rock by the innumerable layers or very thin strata which compose the mass, being of different colors, sometimes red, grey and dark brown, alternating in the same hard specimen.

The material of which this argillaceous rock is composed possesses an extreme degree of fineness, and is so soft as readily to be cut with the knife, which qualities render it a fit material for the manufacture of pipes, to which purpose the Indians of the country have long applied it. It has also been applied to use in sharpening tools, but its softness is a serious objection to its use for that purpose.

A similar argillaceous rock also appears at several other points in the interior or southerly from that already described, but as yet I have been unable to determine its thickness at any point. The finely represented bands or zones, which may fairly be supposed to represent the original lines of deposition, are very much contorted, and in such a manner as to lead to the conclusion that this change must have taken place very soon after the deposition of the rocks and while they were still in an unindurated state.

The rocks belonging to the red sandstone formation bear the evidence of having been almost universally deposited in shoal water, for ripple marks occur abundantly at all points where the rock takes on the decided character of sandrock, and these ripple marks may frequently be seen, for many rods together, as distinctly and clearly defined as they are at the present day in the loose sands forming the bottom of some of the shoal bays of Lake Superior. Fossils are rare in the red sandstone, and in fact, I have never seen any other than fucoides, of which there are three species, that are tolerably well defined.

The red sandrock is less frequently traversed by dykes of trap than either of the rocks before described, though dykes were sometimes noticed traversing the whole of the several rock formations up to and including the red sandstone. Upon portions of the north coast, where the conglomerate and mixed rocks are more frequently wanting, and where the red sandrock is brought more nearly in contact with the trap, these dykes are of more frequent occurrence. It is deserving of remark, that where the lower rocks are either wholly or in part wanting, the red sandstone usually becomes of a deep brown color, and the material of which the sand is composed, gradually changes from that before described to greenstone.

I have already stated that the sandrock, at its westerly prolongation, attains its greatest thickness, which was estimated at 6,500 feet, but as the rock continues easterly it gradually and quite regularly diminishes in thickness, and beyond Saut de Ste. Marie the thickness is very inconsiderable. The average rate of diminution which takes place in the thickness of the rock as we proceed easterly, was shown by a great number of observations upon the south-westerly portions of the coast of Lake Superior to be a fraction over fifteen feet to the mile, but this rate of decrease could not be satisfactorily estimated upon the lower or easterly half of the coast. The red sandrock thins out as we proceed southerly or inland from the coast at a still more rapid rate, as was most satisfactorily shown where it is connected with the several primary, metamorphic and trap ranges of hills, for all or nearly all the valleys, after passing the outer or northerly range of trap hills are based upon this sandrock, and since we have every reason to believe that this sandrock was deposited in part during the gradual elevation of the several chains of hills it would follow that over those districts which were last elevated the rock would attain its greatest thickness. I have already alluded to the order in which the several ranges of hills appear to have been uplifted, and since more particular reference will be made to this hereafter I leave the subject for the present.

The red sandrock south from Lake Superior, as well as upon the immediate coast, dips regularly northerly, while that upon the north coast dips invariably southerly, or, as has already been said of the lower rocks, this rock dips upon all sides regularly into the basin of the lake. The quantity of dip is exceedingly variable, being always very much increased as it approaches the trap, and diminishing as it approaches the primary and metamorphic ranges.

The line of cleavage of some of the members of the lower sandrock and shales is frequently irregular and opposed to the true stratification of the rock.

Upper or Gray Sandrock.

The only remaining rock which separates the red sandrock from the limestones lying to the south is a gray or brownish sandrock, that is almost wholly composed of grains of quartz, usually feebly cemented with calcareous matter. The composition of this rock differs from that of the lower sandrock, in being more exclusively quartz, while in epoch of deposition the rock under consideration should not be confounded with that of the red sandstone. It has already been stated that the red sandrock of the south coast dips regularly northerly, while the upper or gray sandstone dips equally regularly south or south-easterly, in which respect the last mentioned rock conforms to the limestones resting upon it, while it rests itself upon the uptilted edge of the red sandrock below.

I have already stated that this rock was first noticed rising in hills at a point not far distant from Riviere Ste. Marie, and south-east from Point Iroquois; from this point it stretches westerly in an elevated and very regular chain of hills that are upon the coast, as far as Tequoimenon Bay, westerly from which the shape of the coast is such that these hills do not again appear upon it, until we reach that precipitous portion of the lake coast known as the Pictured Rocks, where the fury of the waves, aided by frost, has acted upon the feebly cemented material of which the rock is composed to such an extent as to leave large portions of what was originally the northern escarpment of these hills along this coast in high mural and overhanging precipices. Westerly from the Pictured Rocks the ranges of hills which are composed or made up of this rock stretch in a south-westerly direction, passing completely to the south of the primary, trap and metamorphic regions. The westerly prolongation of this rock has not yet been determined.

The upper sandrock, like the lower, abounds in clearly defined ripple marks, and its line of cleavage is very irregular, frequently being opposed to the line of stratification over very considerable districts of country. Two indistinct species of fucoides were all the fossils noticed in connection with it.

I was unable to obtain any observations upon the thickness of the upper sandrock, which were satisfactory, but from the imperfect observations which were obtained I was led to conclude that the average thickness as far westerly as the Pictured Rocks does not vary very far from 700 feet. The upper sandrock, like the rocks before mentioned, wedges out as we proceed, in an easterly direction.

TERTIARY CLAYS AND SANDS.

As in the lower, so in the upper peninsula, the older rocks are more or less covered by deposits that may be severally arranged under the above head. To these deposits it is my intention at the present time barely to allude.

Stratified clays and sands similar to those skirting the borders of the lower peninsula are seen at many points, and continue for long distances upon the coast of Lake Superior; and they are also largely developed at many points in the interior of the country. These deposits sometimes attain a thickness of from 200 to 300 feet, and they are spread over the less elevated portions of the district The character of these clays and sands bear a close resemblance to those described in a previous report, as occurring upon the lower peninsula.

ECONOMICAL GEOLOGY.

Rocks.

The series of limerocks resting upon the sandrock last described were noticed in the report which was laid before you at a previous session, and the limits of the present report will not permit me to refer to them more fully at this time. My observations will, therefore, only include those rocks which lie below the limestones. It will be borne in mind that the whole of the group of limestones are embraced in the southerly portion of the upper peninsula, and that their outcropping edges do not reach within many miles of the coast of Lake Superior. This is an important fact, for it shows the whole of the northern part of the upper peninsula to be deficient in materials for the manufacture of lime, which are, in truth, wholly wanting.

Materials adapted to the purposes of building abound throughout the district of country under consideration, and though they vary exceedingly in value for that purpose, yet no portion of the country can be said to be without a supply.

Among the most valuable of the materials for this purpose the syenites and syentic granites deservedly rank first, and they occur of a quality which may be advantageously worked at various points in the primary range. Some of the syenites near the coast of the lake are so situated as to be readily quarried, and they may be made to furnish a beautiful and durable material for building. The color of these syenites is usually a very dark gray, from the predominance of hornblend in the composition, but this is by no means invariably the case.

The metamorphic group scarcely furnishes a fit material for use as a building stone, for the structure of its schists would be an effectual bar against their use, and the difficulties of working the quartz rock will probably prevent that rock being applied to that purpose.

Some of the compact greenstones and altered syenites of the trap range may be made to furnish an excellent building stone, which, although in powers of resisting the action of disintegrating agents may be less than that of the unchanged syenite, nevertheless possess a very great degree of durability. The greenstone ranges of hills frequently for very considerable distances are made up of rock in which the jointed structure is so perfectly developed that regular blocks of a convenient size for building may be obtained with comparatively little labor.

The conglomerate rock is scarcely applicable to use for purposes of building.

A very good building stone may be obtained from many portions of the lower or red sandstone formation, and though the cement of this rock is usually not very perfect, yet frequently such changes have taken place in the rock that it has almost taken on the character of granular quartz rock, in which cases its durability is very much increased. The strata of this rock are usually of a convenient thickness to admit of being easily quarried, and they are so regular that the stone will require but little dressing.

The upper, or gray sandrock, being almost uniformly but feebly cemented and sometimes decidedly friable, is of less value as a building stone than either of the rocks before mentioned. Those portions of the upper sandrock where the calcareous cement is perfect, but not sufficiently hardened, might be rendered much more capable of resisting the action of the elements if allowed to remain under shelter a sufficient length of time to allow this change to take place.

The value of the limestones of the southern part of the peninsular, for the purposes of building, as also for the manufacture of lime, was mentioned in a previous report upon the geology of that district of country. As has already been stated, these limerocks do not reach within many miles of the coast of Lake Superior, and it is certainly to be regretted, that the shore of the northern portion of the peninsular is destitute of this important material. Nor have I seen any marls of sufficent extent in the district to admit of application to any of the purposes to which it is applicable, or to supply, even in part, the deficiency in limestone. All the lime which would appear to be capable of being applied to practical purposes is that of the calcareous spar, composing the veins traversing the sandrock, and these are not only rare, but they are also of very limited extent.

MINERALS AND MINERAL VEINS.

In considering this portion of the subject, I propose to treat the minerals of the different formations separately, so far as the same can be done, and, although this method will necessarily cause some repetition, it will enable me to show more perfectly than could otherwise be done, the connection between those minerals that may be regarded as of practical value and the rocks to which they belong.

As a whole, the rocks of the upper peninsula are deficient in *number* of minerals, though some few individual *species* occur abundantly.

Minerals of the Primary Rocks.

The following list can by no means be regarded as perfect, but it will serve, at least, to convey an idea of the small number of minerals which are found in connection with the rocks of this group:

    Schorl,   Mica,
    Tourmaline,   Feldsdar,
    Hornblende,   "   red,
    Actynolite,   Quartz.

FIRST GEOLOGICAL SURVEY OF MICHIGAN.   197

Minerals of the Metamorphic Group of Rocks.

Quartz, common,   Iron, scaly red oxid of,
"   milky,   "   hæmatite,
"   greasy,   "   pyritous,
"   tabular,   Steatite,
Serpentine, common,   Novaculite.

Of the minerals enumerated as occurring in the metamorphic rocks, the milky variety of quartz is abundant, sometimes composing almost entire ranges of hills. The novaculite is also abundant, but of coarse variety. This last is associated with the talcose slates. The remaining minerals appear either disseminated or forming druses in the quartz rock, though sometimes they occur in thin beds or veins, in the talcose slate, which beds conform to the line of cleavage of that rock. Although the hæmatite is abundantly disseminated through all the rocks of the metamorphic group, it does not appear in sufficient quantity at any one point that has been examined to be of practical importance.

Minerals of the Trap Rocks.

Quartz, common,   Steatite, common,
"   smoky,   Asbestus,
"   milky,   Amianthus,
"   greasy,   Calcareous spar,
"   radiated,   Copper, native,
"   mamillary,   "   pyritous,
"   drusy,   "   black,
"   amethystine,   "   red oxid of,
Chalcedony,   "   azure carbonate of,
Carnelian,   "   green carbonate of,
Jasper,   "   "   " ferruginous,
Agate, common,   Lead, sulphuret of,
"   fortification,   "   carbonate of,
Augite,   Iron, pyritous,
Actynolite   "   red oxid of,
Serpetine,   "   hydrate of,
"   pseudomorphous,   "   silicate of,
Chlorite, common,   Manganese, ferruginous oxid of,
"   earthy,   Silver, native, (very rare.)

APPENDIX.

Since a consideration of the minerals contained in the trap, will also involve a portion of those embraced in the conglomerate, the mixed rock, and red sandrock and shales, I will, before referring minutely to those of the trap rocks, lay before you a list of those which occur most frequently in the sedimentary rocks last mentioned. The fact that veins of mineral matter, traversing the trap, are frequently continued across the several sedimentary rocks, and that dykes are of frequent occurrence in these latter rocks, would lead to the inference that there would be a considerable degree of resemblance in the character of the minerals embraced in these dykes and veins, in both the trap and sedimentary rocks and to a certain extent, this inference would be true; but it should be borne in mind, as has already been stated, that the veins, in traversing the several upper rocks, undergo very great changes in mineral character.

Minerals of the Conglomerate, Mixed Rock and Red Sandrock.

Calcareous spar
Quartz, common,
" milky,
" drusy,
Chalcedony,*
Carnelian,*
Jaspar,*
Agate,*

Copper, native,†
" pyritous,†
" blue carb. of,†
" green carb. of,†
" earthy green carb. of,†
" black,†
Zinc, siliceous oxid of,
" carbonate of,
Iron, pyritous,
" black oxid of, (cemented iron sand,)
" red oxid of,
" hydrate of,
" silicate of.

---

*Occasionally occurring among the pebbles constituting the mass of the conglomerate.
†Chiefly in those portions of the veins traversing the conglomerate.

Mineral Veins of the Trap, Conglomerate, etc.

In order to render the subject of the mineral veins traversing the above rock so far intelligible as may be in my power, I have already been particular to define, as far as could be done without maps and sections, the relation which the trap rocks, together with the superincumbent conglomerate, mixed sand and conglomerate and red sandrock bear to each other, and it will be necessary in considering the mineral contents of these rocks and the veins traversing them to keep this relation constantly and clearly in view.

It will be recollected that the north-westerly range of hills, commencing at the extremity of Keweenaw Point and stretching from thence in a south-westerly direction into the interior, were referred to as being more clearly of trappose origin than either of the other ranges, and that the rock of the southerly portion of this range is either compact greenstone or altered syenite, while that of the northerly flank is almost invariably either an amygdaloid or a rock approaching to toadstone.

The several ranges of hills to the south of that last alluded to are either well formed, compact greenstones, altered syenite or, as we approach the primary range, imperfectly formed granites. So far as the several ranges of hills lying south from the northerly range are concerned, they would appear to be, as a whole, deficient in minerals, and the rocks are not apparently traversed by veins or dykes of any more recent date than that of the uplift of the northerly trap hills.

Veins clearly of a date posterior to the uplift of that portion of the trap rock last mentioned are of frequent occurrence, and these veins not only traverse a portion of the trap range, but also pass into the conglomerate, and sometimes completely across the three sedimentary rocks immediately above the trap, thus having an unbroken length of several miles. The class of veins to which I now allude, where they occur in a connected or continuous portion of the range rarely vary more than 12 to 15 deg. from a right angle to the line of bearing of the sedimentary rocks, and in pursuing this course they necessarily cut across the dykes of trap before alluded to as so frequently appearing between the strata, and conforming to the dip of the lower sedimentary rocks.

That the veins under consideration belong to a single epoch is inferred from the fact that none have been noticed with other veins crossing them, as also for the reason that none have ever been noticed with dislocations, heaves or disturbance of any kind, save what may be referred to causes connected with their immediate origin.

That these veins must be regarded in the strictest sense as true veins, cannot be doubted, and that their origin or source over the extended district alluded to has been the same is inferred from the perfect identity of their mineral contents, for a description of one of these true veins may be said to be essentially a description of the whole. Thus, while the mineral contents of the different portions of the same vein change as the rock traversed changes, the corresponding portions of different veins almost invariably bear a striking and close resemblance to each other.

These veins, as has already been stated, where they traverse connected ranges of the trap are regular in course and direction, but when they are connected with a single uplifted knob of that rock they are irregular and can scarcely be defined, appearing in the latter instance rather as matter injected into the fissures of a shattered mass of rock than as connected veins.

The importance of carefully studying the relation which these veins bear to the rocks which they traverse, as also the relation which they bear to the numerous trap dykes, together with the few cotemporaneous veins noticed in the trap, is very much increased by the circumstance that these veins are more or less connected with or rather contain metallic materials which, it may be fairly inferred, will hereafter become of very considerable practical importance. In fact, so far as we may be enabled to judge from the examinations already made in this district of country, it is confidently believed that most, if not all the metalliferous veins of the upper peninsula belong to veins of the epoch of those under consideration. It is true that native metals, more particularly copper, are sometimes found in place occupying the joints or natural septæ of the greenstone, but in these instances the amount of metal is always comparatively small, and, with one or two exceptions, I have invariably been able to establish some connection between the native metal occupying these joints and the termination of some metalliferous vein that traverses other portions of the rock not far distant, and it is believed that the metal filling these joints has invariably resulted from the action of causes precisely analagous to those which have placed similar metals in the veins to which I have alluded.

The earliest, as well as all travelers who have visited the district of country under consideration, have not failed to make frequent allusion to the loose masses of native copper that have been occasionally found scattered over it, nor has any one failed to allude to the large bowlder or loose mass of that metal upon the Ontonagon River. Almost invariably, the opinion has been expressed, from the frequent occurrence of these masses, that the metal must be abundant in the country. But, after all, the true sources from which these masses had their origin, or the relation which they held to the rocks of the district would appear never to have been understood; and all or nearly all that was known of their true relations was left to conjecture. The result of this has been, that while some have excessively magnified everything connected with the subject of which, in truth, nothing was known, another class, equally far from what is really true, have regarded these masses of native copper as bowlders transported from high northern latitudes.*

---

*The vast area of country over which the bowlders of native copper, from the district under consideration, together with its westerly prolongation, have been transported is worthy of remark. They are not of unfrequent occurrence in the sand and gravel of the southern peninsula of Michigan, and since the commencement of the geological survey many of these masses have been met, some of which weigh from seven to eight pounds. In the vicinity of Green Bay a mass was discovered some ten years ago which weighed 140 pounds, if my memory serves me correctly. Loose masses of a similar character have been met with in various other portions of Wisconsin, as also at various points in Illinois, Indiana and Ohio. In these cases the occurrence of these masses of native copper are no more indications of the existence of veins of the metal in the immediate vicinity, than are the immense numbers of primary bowlders scattered over the southern peninsula of Michigan indications of the existence of primary rock in place, in the district where they are found.

As far back as 1831 and 1832 I had occasion to pass no less than three times along the south coast of Lake Superior, as also to ascend several of the important tributaries of that lake, and during these years I passed by three different routes, widely separated from each other completely across to the Mississippi River. It is true that these journeys made through a complete wilderness, uninhabited except by savages, were necessarily made under circumstances that admitted of only very general observations; but the result of these previous examinations have proved of immense service to me in aiding the labors of the past season. I allude to these journeys and examinations at this time, in order to show you the difficulties by which a full understanding of the subject under consideration is surrounded, for I became satisfied at that time, not only that the subject was not understood by the mass of those who had traversed the country, but that even the natives of the country had no knowledge of the true sources from which the transported masses of copper had their origin.

During the time of the examinations referred to a bare glimmer of light was thrown upon the subject by an examination of some small masses of copper found occupying the joints of the greenstone; as also by the examination of a single vein in the conglomerate, containing the ores of copper, which has since been found to be the termination of a vein that is somewhat obscurely continued from the trap region.

While these examinations were sufficient to enable me to draw the inference that the masses of native copper came chiefly, if not wholly from the trap, and more rarely from those sedimentary rocks resting immediately upon it, it was supposed that this occurrence would follow the general law, and that it, together with the other ores of the metal, would occur in greatest abundance near the line of junction of this rock, with the overlaying sedimentary rocks. Nothing, or at least very little, was known of the true extent or range of the trap rocks, and the very great inaccuracies in the published maps of the country, rendered it almost impossible to apply even the data on hand to such purpose as to relieve the embarrasment.

With a full knowledge of these difficulties I determined during the past season to endeavor to surmount them by so far adding to our geographical knowledge of the coast of the lake and its immediate vicinity as to enable me to place whatever geological observations of importance might be made in such condition that the relation of the several parts might be understood. Having sufficiently accomplished this I proceeded to a very minute examination of the several rocks overlaying or resting against the trap, together with a determination of the thickness of the several members and their rate of decrease or wedging to the east. With these data I was enabled, by noting the dip of the rock upon the coast, to determine, with sufficient accuracy for the purposes to which the rule was to be applied, the line of junction between the trap and conglomerate rocks. This rule when put in practice enabled me to decide with a very considerable degree of certainty this line of junction, when the rocks were covered with a very considerable thickness of detrital matter, and when so covered I was enabled by traversing the country on the line of bearing of the upper rocks the more readily to gain access to such points as would admit of examination.

These observations soon showed me that this line of junction between the trap rock and the south edge of the conglomerate, instead of pursuing a course parallel to the coast, only continued its parallelism for a few miles westerly from the extremity of Keweenaw Point, after which for a long distance it recedes from the coast rapidly. These facts served to explain in part why the subject of the origin of the masses of copper had remained a mystery, for the country through which this line passes is hardly ever passed over even by the Indians, and probably large portions of it have never been passed over by whites, but in addition to this the obscure character of the metalliferous veins is such that they would scarcely attract the observation of the traveler whose attention was not called especially to the subject, for many of the richest ores are so far from having the appearance of the pure metal that they would be the last suspected to contain it in any form.

That the connection of these ores with the containing rocks was not understood by the English mining company whose attention was turned to this subject at an early day is to be inferred from the fact that they commenced their operations at Miners' River, where the rock is the upper or gray sandstone, which has never been observed to contain mineral veins; and also on Ontonagon River, near the mass of native copper, at which point a shaft was commenced and carried about 40 feet through a reddish clay, at which point the red sandrock was reached. Now, although the metalliferous veins sometimes pass from the trap across the red sandstone, these veins in the red sandrock have never been noticed to contain any other ores than those of zinc and iron, unless it be at the immediate point where the vein crossing comes in contact with a dyke of trap, which condition does not exist at the point alluded to on Ontonagon River. What indications could have induced those Quixotic trials at the points where they were commenced is more than I have been able to divine, and as might have been anticipated, the attempts resulted in a failure to find the object sought.

Having thus in a general manner set forth the obscurity by which the subject of the true source of the transported masses of native copper has been surrounded, together with some of the reasons which have served to prevent its being fairly understood, I will now proceed to a general sketch of the metalliferous veins of the district, so far as the same have been examined, premising that our knowledge of them is still deficient in very many important particulars which can only be supplied by a careful and continued examination of the subject, which, in fact, can only be said to be but just commenced.

I have had occasion to refer to the outer or northerly range of hills, or those from which the metalliferous veins may be said to spring as being composed of trap rock, and lest what has been said may not be fairly understood, I will repeat, that the more southerly part of the range is uniformly composed of compact greenstone, under which head I not only include true greenstone, but also those forms of altered granular gneiss and gneissoid granite, which sometimes are associated with it, while the outer or northerly portion of the same range is usually composed of an amygdaloid form of trap. The cells of the amygdaloid are usually filled with the different varieties of quartz, carnelian, chalcedony and agate, and sometimes, though more rarely, with native copper or with calcareous spar, though they are sometimes entirely empty, constituting a perfect toadstone.

The metalliferous veins cross this range or trap, usually very nearly at right angles to the prolongation of the hills, and are frequently continued in the same course across the upper or sedimentary rocks, thus crossing the latter at an angle varying but little from their line of bearing. While the continuity of course of the vein may remain perfect in its complete passage from the greenstone across the several members of the conglomerate, mixed and red sandstone rocks, the character and mineral contents of the vein undergoes essential change, and not only does the vein appear to be influenced in its mineral contents, but also in its width, for, as a general rule, the width of the vein increases as we proceed northerly, or from the greenstone. Thus, the vein which may appear only a few inches in width, or as a bare line in the southerly or greenstone portion of the range, increases in width rapidly as it approaches and passes across the amygdaloid, and at or near the line of junction between the amygdaloid and the sedimentary rocks it will frequently be found to have attained a thickness of several feet, while in its passage across the sedimentary rocks it is usually either still further increased in width, or becomes so blended with the rock itself, as to render it difficult to define it boundaries.

These metalliferous veins, like those which occur under similar circumstances in other portions of the globe, do not continue uninterruptedly of any given width for great distances, nor is their width increased regularly, for they frequently ramify or branch off in strings, that pursue a course generally somewhat parallel to the general direction of the main vein, and which eventually again unite with it. Sometimes these ramifications or branches destroy, as it were, for a considerable distance the whole vein; but they at length unite again, and the main vein is, after their junction, as perfectly developed as before.

While traversing the most compact southerly portions of the greenstone, the veins are most frequently made up of a very compact and finely granulated greenstone, sometimes associated with steatitic metals and silicate of iron, under which circumstances they usually are destitute of any other metallic mineral, but occasionally, instead of the materials above mentioned, their place is supplied by native copper, without vein stone or matrix, and usually free from nearly all earthly impurities, but almost invariably incrusted with oxid or carbonate of the metal. Those portions of the vein traversing the greenstone, in which native copper occurs, under the circumstances above mentioned, are invariably thin, rarely exceeding 3 to 4 inches in thickness and usually considerably less, and they are liable to very considerable variation in width from the divergence caused by the vein traversing the joints of the rock, where these joints produce the same character of change as is produced by the ordinary ramification of a vein.

As these metalliferous veins traverse the northerly portion of the range or approach the sedimentary rocks, they undergo a gradual change in width as well as in mineral character, and it has been noticed that where the amygdaloid is most largely developed, the vein, as a general rule, has not only a greater width, but also has its mineral contents more perfectly developed, a circumstance which might fairly have been inferred from the fact that those points where the amygdaloid occurs most largely may be regarded to have been so many centres of intensity of action at the time of the original uplift of the range, from which circumstance they would remain in a softened state, or in such condition as to admit of the more perfect formation of these cross veins for a longer space of time after that condition has been passed at other points.

In the outer or amygdaloid portion of the rock the vein is almost invariably accompanied by a veinstone of quartz, involving all the varieties before mentioned as associated with the trap rocks, which quartz, though occasionally it occurs massive, of several feet in width, usually appears in the shape of a series of irregularly ramifying and branching minor veins, that may be said to constitute the main vein. These subordinate veins of quartz, which may be stated as the true veinstone, vary from a mere line to several inches in thickness, and in the aggregate they may be said to constitute from one-third to one-half the total thickness of the vein. In their branches and ramifications, they sometimes include portions of the rock which they traverse, at other times they embrace imperfectly formed steatite, with silicate, carbonate and red oxyd of iron * and occasionally, though more rarely, it is associated with carbonate of lime, usually assuming the form of an opaque rhombic spar.

As the main vein traverses the conglomerate and overlaying rocks to, and including the red sandstone, these veins, as a general rule undergo still farther changes, for very soon after entering the conglomerate the veinstone changes from its quartzose character and is made up either wholly of calcareous matter, mostly rhomb spar, or of this mineral with occasional ramifications of quartz, the whole usually including and sometimes investing fragments of the conglomerate or the pebbles of that rock separated.

As the vein is continued still farther in the direction of and into the red sandstone, these changes are still noticed, and eventually the vein is found to be composed either entirely or mostly of calcareous spar, and eventually so completely is its metalliferous character lost that it would not if examined singly be suspected to be any portion of a metalliferous vein.

The metalliferous character of these veins is most largely developed almost directly at or near to|the line of junction of the trap and sedimentary rocks, and they rarely continue, without considerable change, for a greater distance than one-

---

*The latter closely resembling the Gossan of the Cornish miners.

fourth to one-third of a mile on either side of the line, though a few veins were noticed in which in the southerly or trap extension the character of the vein continued for a distance of over a mile nearly unchanged, while in its passage through the conglomerate for half that distance its character was also perfectly preserved.

The mineral character of the veins is somewhat varied in those having different degrees of thickness, though it is difficult, if not impossible, to lay down any rule which would characterize this change. The different veins vary very greatly in width, ranging from a mere line to 14 or 15 feet, the greatest observed width of any single vein.

In the descriptions of the veins given above I only intend to include those which are most perfectly developed, for in addition to these there are also many which are imperfectly formed and short, and in which many of the above characters are in part or entirely wanting. These latter are usually of little practical importance, and thus far have been comparatively little examined.

Of the metallic minerals occurring in those portions of the *true* veins which traverse the trap rocks, together with that portion of the conglomerate immediately resting upon or against the trap, by far the most important consist of the several ores of copper with which iron occurs disseminated in the forms before described, and occasionally, though very rarely, native silver has been detected associated in the same vein. After as minute an examination of the subject as circumstances will permit I am led to the conclusion that the only ores of the metallic minerals occurring in those portions of the veins which traverse the rocks last alluded to, which can reasonably be hoped to be turned to practical account, are those of copper.

In these portions of the veins, the metal referred to, occurs very frequently in the form of native copper, with which are associated the red oxyd, azure carbonate, green carbonate, and more rarely what may be denominated copper black, and still more rarely, pyritous copper. *None* of these have been noticed in a crystaline form.

It must not be imagined that these several minerals make up the whole or even any very considerable portion of the entire length and breadth of the veins in which they occur, for they are distributed in bunches, strings and comparatively narrow subveins, in a manner precisely analagous to that in which these ores are usually distributed in similar rocks in other portions of the globe. The quartz veinstone, before described, has always so much of the green tinge communicated by the carbonate of copper that it cannot fail to be detected; but the presence of disseminated native copper in this veinstone, would, at first, hardly be suspected, and it is not until a fresh fracture has been made and the mineral closely examined that the numerous dark points and minute threads are discovered to be copper in a native state. Large portions of this quartz veinstone, (when the included metal can scarcely be detected by the naked eye,) when examined with a glass are found to contain very delicate threads of native copper that traverse the quartz in every possible direction, and so completely is this latter mineral bound together that it is fractured with difficulty, and its toughness is very greatly increased.

The specific gravity of this veinstone is very considerably above that of ordinary quartz, and usually, the difference is so considerably, even in those masses where the copper can scarcely be detected by the naked eye, as to be apparent to even the most careless observer. But in addition to this finely disseminated condition of the native copper in the veinstone, it is also disseminated in a similar manner through the rocky matter embraced by the veinstone and in the amygdaloid and conglomerate portions of the rocks, it sometimes extends for a distance of from two to three feet into the rocky matter on either side of the veins, sometimes completely, or in part, filling the cells of the amygdaloid rock.

The conditions above described refer to the main portions of the veins only, while there are other portions in which the copper appears to be concentrated in larger masses, constituting bunches and strings, and in which places the sides or walls of the veins are sometimes wholly made up of thin plates of native copper. In these portions of the metalliferous veins where the metal appears, as it were, to be concentrated, it also occurs much in the form before described except that the masses of metal vary from the merest speck to that of several pounds weight. In opening one of these veins, at a concentrated point, the observer, unless he had previously examined other portions of the vein would be led to erroneous conclusions as to its richness, a source of error which cannot be too strongly guarded against ; for while the vein for a short distance may be found to be exceedingly rich in mineral, the mineral in another portion of the vein may either wholly or in part disappear, a condition which is similar to that observed in those veins of copper that have been extensively worked and found to be most productive on the continent of Europe and the island of Great Britain.

The excess of native copper (compared with the other ores) which occurs *in these portions* of the veins is a peculiar feature, for it may be said, in truth, that other ores are of rare occurrence. In those portions of the veins traversing the trap, and where other ores do occur, it is usually under such circumstances as to favor the presumption that their origin is chiefly from that which was previously in a native form ; for the carbonates and oxyds almost invariably appear either investing the native copper or intimately associated with it, though they sometimes appear in distinct sub-veins. Pyritous copper is so rare in connection with the trappean portions of the veins as scarcely to deserve notice.

I have already stated that native silver occasionally, though very rarely, occurs in the trappean portions of these veins, intimately associated with the copper, but it is in so minute quantities as to render it probable that it will not prove of any practical importance. Other mixed compounds of this metal occur so rarely as scarcely to deserve notice.

Leaving the trap rock, the character of these veins as they traverse the conglomerate undergoes important changes, for not only does the veinstone become gradually changed from quartz to calcareous spar, but the amount of native copper diminishes, and its place is either supplied wholly or in part by ores of zinc and calcareous spar, or wholly by this latter mineral. There are, however, occasional exceptions to this *general* rule, for occasionally the place of the native copper in the veins, in their passage through the conglomerate, is supplied by a variety of complex compounds of the same metal, which compounds are of exceeding interest; but this change would appear always to be intimately connected with or to bear some relation to the dykes of trap which traverse the conglomerate rock. Several instances of this kind were noticed upon the northerly side of Keweenaw Point, either directly upon or near to the coast, as also at several other places in the interior westerly from Keweenaw Point. A vein which may without doubt be referred to as one of this character (though in consequence of intervening bays and lakes between it and the ranges to the south, its connection with the main 'range has not been seen), will serve to illustrate the character referred to.

This vein, which reaches the immediate coast of the lake upon the easterly cape of the bay known to the voyageurs as the Grande Marrais of Keweenaw Point, terminates, so far as examinations can be made, in the coarse conglomerate rock. The coast of the lake for many miles on either side is made up of abrupt cliffs of a similar rock, the rock, as usual, being made up of coarse rolled pebbles of trap, chiefly cemented with calcareous matter, which is usually associated more or less with the red oxyd of iron. Immediately south of the coast a heavy dyke of trap traverses the conglomerate, which dyke corresponds in position with line of bearing and dip of the conglomerate rock.

The vein, which at its termination upon the immediate coast of the lake has an extreme width of about 10 feet, may be traced in the bed of the lake, in a direction north 5 deg. east, for a distance of several rods, after which, in consequence of the depth of water, it is completely lost. This vein at the point where it appears upon the coast, may be said to be in a concentrated state, or in a condition analagous to that before described, where the native copper occurs in the condition of bunches and strings, though the condition in which the metallic minerals occur is essentially different from that in the trap, for instead of native copper we have several mixed forms of the green and blue carbonates of copper and copper black, more or less intimately associated with calcareous spar, and in the adjoining rock and in small ramifying veins occasional small specks and masses of native copper, weighing from one to three ounces occur, but these are by no means abundant. No quartz occurs as a veinstone, and none of the ores have been noticed in a crystaline form.

It has already been stated that these true veins in traversing the conglomerate, frequently almost loose their character, and it becomes difficult to define their absolute width, or, in other words, it would appear as if at the time of the formation of the veins the conglomerate had not been perfectly cemented, the result of which would be that the mineral matter, which, under other circumstances, would constitute a perfect vein, would frequently appear in only an imperfect one, or the mineral which would, under other circumstances, make up the vein itself, may have been injected latterly through the interstices of the rolled masses constituting the conglomerate, in which case the mineral would, in fact, take the place of the ordinary cement, thus simply investing the pebbles of the conglomerate. Now, although at the point under consideration a wide and remarkably distinct vein is developed, the rock, for many feet on either side, has the interstices between the pebbles filled wholly or in part with various mixed and irregular forms of the ores, accompanied by calcareous matter, as before stated, and with occasional specks and small masses of native copper.

Those veins traversing the conglomerate take on a similar character to a greater or less extent rather frequently, but the place of the copper is more usually supplied by the siliceous oxyd, and more rarely by the carbonate of zinc, which compounds sometimes may be seen forming a perfect or partial cement to the rock for considerable distance on either side of the main vein. These ores of zinc, like those of copper,' are uniformly amorphous, and almost invariably more or less associated with some form of carbonate of lime, with which they may, under some circumstance unless closely examined be confounded.

Although these copper and zinc ores occasionally appear in considerable quantities in those portions of the veins traversing the conglomerate, they usually embrace or simply encrust portions of the rocky matter; or rather the rocky matter and those ores appear to be coarsely and mechanically mixed. These veins furnish beautiful cabinet specimens of the blue and green carbonates of copper, and more rarely of pyritous copper, together with the other varieties mentioned.

Having already devoted a larger space to the consideration of these veins than had been intended, I will simply add, that in pursuing their course northerly across the mixed rock and the red sandrock, their mineral character is nearly or quite lost, the veins as before stated, being made up either entirely of calcareous spar or of that material containing |very meagre ores or zinc.

The district of country to which these veins have been referred, thus far, only comprises the ranges of hills south of Lake Superior, but veins of a very similar character, and of similar mineral contents also occur upon Isle Royale. The order and changes in the character of the veins upon Isle Royale is necessarily reversed, or in other words, the southerly point of the vein corresponds to that of the north point in the district south of Lake Superior. The mineral veins of Isle Royale have not been examined with sufficient care to enable me to determine with much certainty their average width or value. Those examined were mostly narrow, the widest not exceeding 18 inches, but in these the mineral contents are essentially the same as in those upon the south side of the lake.

Native copper in very thin plates was occasionally noticed occupying irregularly the joints of the compact greenstone of Isle Royale, but invariably in comparatively small quantities.

It should, however, be noticed of Isle Royale, that the veins, so far as examined, are less perfectly developed in their passage across the conglomerate and that they very rarely contain any traces of zinc.

Upon the north shore of the lake, no attention was given to the subject of mineral veins, but from the character of the geology of that district it may be inferred that they will also be found in portions of it, and that, where they do occur, they will be uniformly either directly upon or not far from the coast of the lake.

In addition to the *regular* veins already described, irregular veins frequently occur traversing the whole or portions of the outliers of trap, or those knobs which appear to have been elevated singly; and although these veins may without doubt, be referred to the same epoch as the regular veins before described, they nevertheless frequently differ considerably in mineral contents.

The limits of the present report will not permit a separate description of these several distinct trap knobs. I will therefore confine my remarks to that already referred to, as occurring upon the south coast of Lake Superior, immediately northwest from Riviere Des Morts, and which forms the promontory known as Presque Isle.

In nearly all those portions of this knob where the trap, conglomerate and sandstone are exposed in such a manner as to permit examination, each of the rocks are seen to be traversed by innumerable irregular ramifying veins, which in the sandstones are made up of quartzose and calcareous matter; but many of which near the junction of the igneous and sedimentary rocks are metalliferous, and this metalliferous character is more fully developed as the veins are extended into the trap rocks.

The metalliferous portion of these veins rarely exceed three to four inches in width, and they ramify in such a manner that the mineral uniformly occupies situations similar to bunches or strings at the junction of the ramifications. The minerals contained in the metalliferous portions of the veins

FIRST GEOLOGICAL SURVEY OF MICHIGAN. 215

are sulphuret and carbonate of lead, earthy, green carbonate of copper, pyritous iron, and more rarely pyritous copper. Occasionally there is a quartzose, or mixed quartzose and calcareous veinstone, but more usually the several metallic minerals are blended in a base of rocky matter. The sulphuret of lead is distributed in the form of small cubic crystals, while the other metallic minerals are usually distributed either in irregular masses or investing portions of the rocky matter. These associations are referred to as showing the character which these irregular veins assume rather than from any supposed value which they may possess for practical purposes.

In addition to the minerals referred to, the trap of Presque Isle occasionally contains asbestus, common serpentine and imperfect agates, the two former minerals usually occupying the narrow joints of the rock.

Before referring to the economical considerations connected with the veins which have been described, I will briefly refer to another situation in which the ores of copper have been observed in intimate connection with the trap range of rocks.

The southerly side or greenstone portion of the trap range appears to have been elevated in such a manner as to have caused but little disturbance to the sandrock lying between that and the range of simply altered rocks lying still farther to the south, but near to the junction of the sandrock and greenstone there is usually a red slate resting against the trap, and which may be said to fill up, in a measure, the irregularities in the ranges of hills. This slate, which is sometimes seen of 100 to 200 feet in thickness, though usually it appears as a mere band, is traversed by irregular and imperfect veins of what may be denominated a ferruginous steatite, containing placentiform masses of greasy and milkish quartz, that sometimes contain more or less of the ores of copper. The earthy carbonates of copper are also sometimes so intimately connected with these veins of steatitac matter as at first to be scarcely recognized. More rarely, distinct, very thin veins of green carbonate of copper occurs, well characterized, in this red slate, though these veins are never of any great length. The red shale extends more or less perfectly along the whole length of the trap range, skirting that range of hills upon the south, but I have not yet been enabled to devote sufficient time to its examination to enable me to determine whether any portion of these veins can be regarded as of practical importance. The examinations which have been made would lead me to look unfavorably upon these veins, and I regard them as having an origin completely distinct from that of the veins which traverse the northerly escarpment of the trap rock.

Having thus considered all the general circumstances under which the several ores of copper, zinc, lead, iron, manganese and silver have been noticed in connection with the trap rock and the sedimentary rocks immediately resting upon it, it becomes important to consider how far inferences may be drawn from these examinations as to their occurrence in such quantities as to be of practical importance. I have already stated that so far as regards the ores of lead, iron, manganese and silver, I am led to conclude that at none of the points examined do they occur in veins or otherwise sufficiently developed to warrant favorable conclusions as to their existence in sufficient quantities to be made available, and from all that is now known of the country, I am led to infer that neither of these, unless it be iron, will be so found.*

The examinations which have thus far been made of those portions of the veins containing ores of zinc have not been extended sufficient to enable me to determine with much satisfaction their extent as a whole. At several points in the veins these ores are sufficiently abundant to admit of being profitably worked, but I would be unwilling, from an examination of a few points to attempt to determine the character of the whole.

In considering the practical value of the copper ores of the upper peninsula of Michigan, where we are as yet compelled

---

* These remarks are intended to apply directly to the trap region. Beds of bog iron ore occur east from Chocolate River, which probably may at some future day be profitably worked.

to judge from our examination, of what may be said to be the simply superficial portions of the veins, we can arrive at no safe conclusions, except by comparison of the district with those districts similarly situated, which have been extensively worked in other portions of the globe. Comparisons of this character, to be really useful, must necessarily be sufficiently minute to enable us to understand the relations which the ores in the district compared bear to each other in all respects, which circumstances renders it necessary that a degree of minute information should be at hand, that is not at all times to be obtained. As the information on hand with respect to the copper and tin veins of Cornwall, England, is more minute than that of any mineral district known, I propose, in order to avoid confusion, to confine my comparison to this district, simply, premising that however closely the two districts may resemble each other in character, it does not follow, as an axiom, that because the district with which we compare our own has been largely and profitably productive, that of Michigan must necessarily be so too, for it will be seen, as the subject is pursued, that there are not only several points in which it is impossible with our present knowledge of that of Michigan, to institute comparisons, but there are also some points on which there is a considerable degree of discrepancy.

The comparison instituted in the main is intended to refer rather to the character and contents of the mineral veins of the two districts than to the geology, although some general reference becomes necessary to the geology of the districts to render the comparison perfect. The topography of the Cornish district bears a close resemblance to that of Michigan, both districts being marked by their irregular and broken outline, and by the occurrence of more or less frequent, nearly insulated knobs, rising to a considerable height above the elevation of the general ranges.

Although the older rock of Cornwall, or that from which the metalliferous veins of the districts may be said to have their origin, is more distinctly granitic than that of the metalliferous region upon Lake Superior, the elements of which the rocks are composed may be regarded as essentially bearing a very close resemblance; a resemblance which, it is conceived, would have been still more perfect had the granitic rocks of Cornwall been subjected to the action of secondary causes similar to those of the region under consideration. The rocks resting upon or against the granitic rocks of Cornwall, consist of clay slates, hornblende rocks, etc., which bear little real analogy to the rocks resting directly upon the trap of Lake Superior, but it is conceived that the composition of these upper rocks has little bearing upon the origin of the metalliferous veins, and may be regarded as in a measure unimportant; and however much these rocks may differ they are traversed alike by the metalliferous veins o.' the lower rocks in such a manner that the close resemblance cannot be mistaken.

It is a matter of history that the ores of tin have been more or less extensively raised in the mineral district of Cornwall, from the earliest settlement of the island of Great Baitain, but the working of the veins of copper at an early day does not appear to have been carried o.i to any very considerable extent. The great importance to which the produce of copper from the Cornish veins, (in a district which compared with the mineral district of our own State is of very small dimensions) has arisen, will be shown from the accompanying table, which I have reduced from the official returns included in the several years, and which table, it will be seen, shows for a series of years the average annual amount of copper produced from the ore, the average amount for which it sold, together with the amount per cent. of copper contained in the ore, and the average value of the copper per pound at the smelting house. This table, which has been drawn with great care from data that can scarcely lead to incorrect results, will not only serve to show the large aggregate amount of the metal produced, but it also shows from the low average per cent. of metal contained in the ores, if we had no further knowledge upon the subject, that much capital must be required for, and a large amount of labor applied to the raising and smelting of these ores, a circumstance which should be carefully borne in mind in all that relates to the mineral district of Michigan.

Table showing the average annual produce of the copper mines of the county of Cornwall, England, from 1771 to 1822.

Years.	Average No. of tons of ore per year.	Av. No. tons cop- per pro- duc'd per year.	Average amount per year for which sold.	Av. per cent cop- per pro- duced from ore.	Av. val. of the copper per pound.
					c. m.
1771 to 1775—5 years,	28,749	3,449	$ 846,283	12	10 9
1776 to 1780—5 "	27,580	3,309	826,609	12	11 1
1781 to 1786—6 "	34,354	4,122	962,380	12	10 4
1796 to 1802—7 "	51,483	5,195	2,125,046	10	18 2
1803 to 1807—5 "	70,923	6,160	3,174,725	8	23
1808 to 1812—5 "	70,434	6,498	2,886,835	9	12 9
1813 to 1817—5 "	82,610	7,272	2,878,723	8 8	17 6
1818 to 1822—5 "	94,391	7,757	3,111,811	8 2	17 9

The general resemblance in the mineral contents of the copper veins of Cornwall and those of Michigan is for the most part very great, though in some respects there is a considerable discrepancy. It should, however, be remarked that some difficulty exists in comparing the mineral veins of Cornwall, where several of them have been worked to depths varying from 1,000 to 1,500 feet, with those of Michigan, where the examinations are nearly superficial.

In making these deep excavations, not only in the county of Cornwall, but also in the copper districts of Bohemia, Hungary, Silesia, Transylvania, Saxony, etc. (some of the veins in the latter district having been explored to a depth very considerably greater than those of Cornwall), an immense mass of facts has been accumulated, with respect to the general formation and mineral character of veins, or lodes of copper, which facts have led to an understanding of many of the contingencies connected with its associations so universal that when applied to this mineral they may be regarded as general laws that may fairly be inferred to govern with more or less certainty all those lodes or veins which have similar geological relations. Though a general consideration of those relations of the veins of other countries may perhaps be regarded as somewhat foreign to the present report, I deem it more advisable to refer to these general laws in such a manner as to leave the reader to judge by comparison the condition in which the ores of Michigan may be fairly inferred to occur, rather than to draw conclusions directly, and in so doing it will also become necessary to refer to some of the characters of mineral veins or lodes in general.

Veins are usually divided into two general orders, viz: "*cotemporaneous veins*, or those which are formed at the same time as the containing rock, and *true veins*, whose formation is supposed to be subsequent to that of the rocks which are contiguous to them." A *true* vein may be defined to be "the mineral contents of a vertical or inclined fissure, nearly straight, and of indefinite length and depth."* The contents of a true vein, as a general rule, differ widely from the character of the rocks which it intersects, though this does not invariably hold good, and the vein also, as a general rule, has well defined walls

The contents of contemporaneous veins bear a much closer resemblance to the rocks which embrace them, and as a general rule, they a shorter, more crooked, and less perfectly defined than true veins.

The metalliferous veins being contained under the head of true veins, it is to these that the whole of my remarks will be directed.

Metallic veins are the repositories of most of the metals excepting iron, manganese and chrome, which occur more frequently and abundantly in beds than in veins. The thickness of metallic veins varies from a few inches to many feet, and the same vein also varies in thickness in different parts of its course, sometimes contracting to a narrow string of ore and then expanding again to a width of many feet. The deposits of metal in the veins are as irregular as the widths of them, and so much so as to render the profits of mining proverbially uncertain. Ore is generally found to occupy certain portions of the veins only, differing constantly in extent, whether the

---

*Carne, on the mineral veins of Cornwall.

length or depth on the course of the vein be considered, or the portion of its width which is filled up by it. No veins occur which are regularly impregnated with metal to any great extent, and when ore is found, it is in what the miners aptly term bunches or shoots, or in interspersed grains and strings, which are more or less connected with or embraced in veinstone, that, according to the rock which the veins intersect will be fluor spar, calcareous spar, quartz, etc. The unproductive parts of veins, even in the most profitable mines, generally far exceed in extent the productive parts, but that mine is considered to be rich which has either frequent or extensive shoots of ore, and the great art of the miner consists in tracing and working the valuable accumulations of the metals, with as little waste of labor and expense on the poorer portions of the veins as possible. "In the mines of Cornwall the ores of copper and tin commonly occur in detached masses which are called bunches of ore, and the other parts of the vein being unproductive are called *deads.*"

The depth to which metallic veins descend is unknown, for we believe no instance has occurred of a *considerable vein being worked out in depth*, though it may sink too deep to render the operation of the minor profitable, or it may branch off in a number of strings which are too much intermixed with the rock to be worked to advantage.* Some veins appear to grow wider while others contract as they decend.

The superficial part of a vein generally contains the ore in a decomposing state, and it frequently happens that the ores in the upper and lower parts of the vein are different; thus, "in Cornwall, blende or sulphuret of zinc often occupies the *uppermost* part of the vein to which succeeds tinstone, and at a greater depth copper pyrites." When a metallic vein in its descent passes through different kinds of rock, it is frequently observed that the products of the vein vary in each bed, and when it passes through regularly stratified beds of the same rock there are particular strata in which the vein is always found most productive. This change in the productive-

*Koenig.

ness of mineral veins is more particularly noticed at or near to the transition from unstratified to stratified rocks; thus granite, syenite and those rocks which have a graniti-form structure are frequently noticed to contain metals at or near their junction with stratified formations. On the other hand, the veins which traverse stratified rocks are, as a general law, more metalliferous near such junctions than in other portions.*

Where a rock is crossed and penetrated by a great number of small veins in every direction, the whole mass is sometimes worked as an ore and is called by the Germans a "stockworke." Where the ore is disseminated in particles through the rock, such rocks are also worked for the ore when it exists in sufficient quantity.

As a general rule, those metals which are oxydable at ordinary temperatures, or which readily combine with sulphur *rarely occur in a metallic state*, but are usually found in combination either with sulphur, oxygen or acids. The chief ore of copper raised from the mines of Cornwall, is the yellow sulphuret, though the blue and green carbonates and arseniate are more or less distributed; native copper and the oxyds are also, though more rarely, found.

By a comparison of what has been said upon the character and mineral contents of metallic veins in general, I trust a just view of the real condition in which the ores of copper are invariable found, will have been conveyed, and that, by the aid of this we will be enabled to examine, without undue expectations, those mineral veins which occur within the limits of our own state. In the main, the resemblance between the character and contents of the copper veins of Cornwall and Michigan, so far as can be determined, is close; the veinstones (with the exception of fluor, which I have never observed in the latter,) are essentially the same; but in instituting this comparison, it should be borne in mind that the metallic veins of Cornwall have been in progress of exploration for centuries, and that shafts and galleries have been carried to great depths, while of those of Michigan, simply superficial examinations

---

*Lyell. Necker.

have as yet been made, and these in a wilderness country, under circumstances of the utmost embarrassment and attended with the most excessive labor, privation and suffering.

In respect to the character of the ores which occur in the two districts, there are important differences, for while pyritous copper is the most important workable ore not only in the Cornish mines, but also in those of other portions of our globe, it is comparatively a rare occurrence in the mineral district of Upper Michigan ; for, as I have already mentioned, the mineral of the trappean portions of the veins in the latter district is essentially made up of strings, specks and bunches of native copper, with which more or less of the oxyds and carbonates are associated ; while those portions of the veins traversing the conglomerate are characterized by the occurrence of the oxyds and carbonates, with occasional metallic and pyritous copper, or the places of all these are supplied by ores of zinc, associated with more or less calcareous matter. In the thin mineral veins of Presque Isle, pyritous copper is more abundant, where it is associated with sulphuret of lead, as before mentioned.

The occurrence of this native copper in the veins, and the manner in which it is associated with the veinstones, in all respects corresponds with the ordinary association of the other forms of ores in those veins that have been extensively worked in other portions of the globe ; but I confess that the preponderance of native to the other forms of copper was regarded as an unfavorable indication, at least until this had been found to be more or less universal with respect to all the veins. It should, however, be remarked, that in those portions of the veins where the quartz of the vein and the accompaning rock are very compact, the native form is much more common than in those portions where the veinstone and accompaning rock are more or less cellular and soft.

The worked copper veins of Cornwall are stated by Mr. Carne to average from three to four feet in width, and to have a length as yet undetermined. But few have been traced for a greater distance than one to one and a half miles, and but one has been traced for a distance of three miles.

The veins which I have examined in the mineral district of Michigan, exceed the average of those last mentioned, but the imperfect examinations which have been made render it difficult to determine this with certainty. I have traced no one vein for a further distance than one mile, and usually for distances considerably less. It was not, however, supposed that these veins terminated at the points where they were left, but the futher examinations were abandoned at these points in consequence of physical difficulties connected with the present condition of the conntry.

The native copper is frequently free from all foreign matter and is as completely malleable as the most perfectly refined copper, but it more usually contains disseminated particles of earthy minerals, chiefly quartz. I have not been able to detect the alloy of any other metal in a single instance.

The fatigues and exposures of the past season have so far impaired my health that as yet I have been unable to analyze as carefully as could have been wished the several ores furnished by the mineral veins of the upper peninsula, but sufficient has been done to show satisfactorily that the copper ores are not only of superior quality, but also that their associations are such as to render them easily reduced. Of those which have been examined, embracing nearly the whole (and not including the native copper), the per cent. of pure metal ranges from 9.5 to 51.72, and the average may be stated at 21.10. Associated with some of these ores I have detected a metal, the character of which remains as yet undetermined.

Were the analysis of the several ores of copper sufficiently perfected I should deem it unnecessary to lay them before you at this time, for with what is now known of the district, it is conceived the result would lead to erroneous rather than to correct conclusions. The analysis of separate masses of ore, no matter how much care may be taken to select the poor as well as the richer ores for the examinations, will usually be far from giving the average per cent. of what would be the product when reduced to practice. I have, in order to arrive at safe conclusions not only analyzed but also assayed many of them, but when we come to consider what constitutes the true value of a vein of copper ore we will perceive why it is unsafe to judge of the whole by the analysis of small portions.

By reference to the previous statistical table of the product of the copper mines of Cornwall it will be seen that the average produce of the ores since 1771 has never exceeded 12 per cent. of the metal, and that from 1818 to 1822 it was only 8.2. This shows the aggregate, and it is well known that while many of the productive veins are considerably below this, the largest average per cent. of any single vein in that district, it is believed, has never been over 20 per cent., and it should be borne in mind that this average is taken after the ores have been carefully freed from all the rocky and other impurities which can be separated by breaking and picking.

The value of a vein may be said to depend upon the abundance of the ore, and the case with which it can be raised and smelted, rather than upon its purity or richness. Upon this point, with respect to our own mineral region, public opinion would perhaps be more in error than upon any other, and most certainly we could hardly look for a mineral district where the character of the ores was more liable to disseminate and keep alive such errors. The occurrence of masses of native metal either transported or in place is liable to excite, with those who have not reflected upon the subject, expectations which can never be realized, for while in truth the former show nothing but their own bare existence, the latter may be, as is frequently the case, simply imbedded masses perfectly separated from all other minerals, or they may be associated in a vein where every comparison would lead to unfavorable conclusions as to the existence of copper in any considerable quantities. I have frequently noticed very considerable masses of native copper occupying the joints of compact greenstone, under such circumstances as I conceive might readily excite in many minds high expectations, but a little reflection would satisfy the most careless observer of the use-

(15)

lessness of exploring these joints under the expectation or hope of finding them a valuable repository of the metal. Again, not only native but also the other ores of copper occur in veins, either so narrow as to render it useless to pursue them, or so associated as to render it probable that exploration would not be attended with success.

While I am fully satisfied that the mineral district of our State will prove a source of eventual and steadily increasing wealth to our people, I cannot fail to have before me the fear that it may prove the ruin of hundreds of adventurers who will visit it with expectations never to be realized. The true resources have as yet been but little examined or developed, and even under the most favorable circumstances we cannot expect to see this done but by the most judicious and economical expenditure of capital at those points where the prospects of success are most favorable. It has been said of the Cornish district, in respect to the supposed large aggregate profits, that "a fair estimate of the expenditure and the return from all the mines that have been working for the last twenty or thirty years, if the necessary documents could be obtained from those who are interested in withholding them, would dispel the delusion which prevails on this subject, as well as check the ruinous spirit of gambling adventure which has been productive of so much misery."* And if these remarks will apply to a comparatively small district, which has been explored and extensively worked for centuries, with how much more force must they apply to the mineral district of our own state. I would by no means desire to throw obstacles in the way of those who might wish to engage in the business of mining this ore, at such time as our government may see fit to permit it, but I would simply caution those persons who would engage in this business in the hope of accumulating wealth suddenly and without patient industry and capital, to look closely before the step is taken, which will most certainly end in disappointment and ruin.

---

*Hawkins on the tin of Cornwall.

FIRST GEOLOGICAL SURVEY OF MICHIGAN. 227

The extreme length of what I have denominated the mineral district, (within the limits of Michigan) may be estimated at a fraction over 135 miles, and it has a width varying from one to six miles; but it must not be imagined that mineral veins occur equally through all portions of it, for sometimes, for many miles together none have been noticed, and the situation of the country is such as to render it probable they never will be. The range and course of the mineral district has been so far defined as to render it unnecessary to say more upon this subject, to enable such persons as may wish to examine, to pass directly along its complete length.

I have thus far omitted to allude particularly to the large mass of native copper which has been so long known to exist in the bed of Ontonagon River, less perhaps this isolated mass might be confounded with the products of the veins of the mineral district. That this mass has once occupied a place in some of these veins is quite certain, but it is now perfectly separated from its original connection, and appears simply as a loose transported bowlder.

The attention of the earliest travelers was called to this mass of metallic copper by the natives of the country, and it has been repeatedly described by those who have visited it. The mass now lies in the bed of the westerly fork of the Ontonagon River, at a distance which may be estimated at 26 miles by the stream from its mouth. The rugged character of the country is such that it is but rarely visited, in proof of which I may state that upon my visit to it during the last year I found broken chisels where I had left them on a previous visit nine years before, and even a mass of the copper which at that time had been partially detached, but which for the want of sufficient implements I was compelled to abandon, was found, after that interval, in precisely the same situation in which it had been left.

The copper in this bowlder is associated with rocky matter, which, in all respects, resembles that associated with that metal in some portions of the veins before described, the rocky matter being bound together by innumerable strings of metal;

but a very considerable proportion of the whole is copper in a state of purity. The weight of copper is estimated at from 3 to 4 tons.

While the mass of native copper upon Ontonagon River cannot fail to excite much interest, from its great size and purity, it must be borne in mind that it is a perfectly isolated mass, having no connection whatever with any other, nor does the character of the country lead to the inference that veins of the metal occur in the immediate vicinity, though, as before stated, the mineral district crosses the country at a distance of but a few miles.

The occurrence of carnelian, chalcedony, agate and amethystine quartz, in the amygdaloidal portion of the trap, has already been noticed, and these minerals are considerably abundant. They frequently possess very great beauty and perfection, and when ground and polished they may be used for all the purposes to which those minerals are usually applied.

Minerals of the Upper or Gray Sandstone.

Though the upper sandrock is largely exposed along that portion of the lake coast known as the Pictured Rocks, rising to a very considerable height in precipitous cliffs, there have, nevertheless, been no minerals noticed in connection with it except iron pyrites. Along a portion of the distance, however, the rock of the cliff is frequently colored by broad, vertical bands, having a variety of tints (which have given name to this portion of the coast), and these bands have been by some travelers supposed to indicate the existence of important minerals in the rock; but the coloring matter of these bands is merely superficial. It chiefly consists of the oxyd and carbonate of iron, with occasional faint traces of carbonate of copper, both having been deposited from waters while trickling down the cliffs, the same having previously percolated the rock.

No mineral veins have been noticed in connection with this rock.

Progress and Condition of the Survey, etc.

Notwithstanding the very many physical difficulties by which the geological survey of the upper peninsula of our state is surrounded, we have, nevertheless, been enabled to accomplish a much larger amount of the work than reasonably could have been hoped ; but there still remains much to be done before its geology and mineralogy can be fairly understood. Comparatively little has heretofore been known of the range and extent of the several rock formations, and, while the labor of the past season has shown the most interesting of these to have a much larger area than we had previously been led to infer, it has also shown that the amount of work required to enable us fairly to understand the geology and mineralogy of that interesting region was considerably more than we had reason to look for.

The reports of the several assistants will exhibit to you the progress that has been made during the past season in the surveys of the southern peninsula. Messrs. B. Hubbard and C. C. Douglass were engaged with me during the early part of the season in the upper peninsula; after which, they returned to carry forward the geological and topographical surveys of the lower peninsula. I was also accompanied, during a small portion of the season, by Mr. Frederick Hubbard, who acted as special assistant, and who has embodied a small part of his numerous observations in the form of a report, which is hereto appended.

The survey of the lower peninsula is mainly completed, but there are some few spaces, both in the geological and topographical portions of the work, which require to be filled up before the results can be fully laid before the public.

The drafting of the topographical portion of the survey has advanced steadily towards completion, and the several county maps are in progress of publication in conformity to your instructions.

While we had hoped to have been able to bring the survey to a close within the time originally contemplated, from the above statement of the progress and condition of the work, it will be seen, that some further time will be necessary for its final completion; but while this time will be essential to reach the object sought to be attained by our state, no further appropriation will be necessary for that purpose.

       DOUGLASS HOUGHTON,
          State Geologist.

Appended to the report of the State Geologist of 1841 is the following:

No. 1—Report of Frederick Hubbard, special assistant, Utica, N. Y., November 20, 1840. This report submits the results of a portion of the observations for the variation of compass, latitudes, surveys of harbors, etc., made by direction of the State Geologist during the recent expedition of the geological corps to the upper peninsula.

It sets forth that the subject of latitudes was made a matter of particular attention, no regular survey ever having been made by the general government of that part of the lake lying within the boundary of our State. A table of latitudes is given of principal points, also a table of magnetic variations, the angles being measured with a theodolite containing a needle of great delicacy. By platting these variations it appears that there is a constant increase in the amount of deflection in passing westward, and at the same time that the increment is not in proportion to the westing, but is in a decreasing ratio.

The line of no variation was found to pass through Ste. Marie River, crossing Drummond Island near its western, and St. Joseph through its central or eastern part.

Mr. F. Hubbard thus alludes to some interesting irregularities in the deviations:

"By marking upon the map the points 1, 2 and 3, etc., degrees of variation, and drawing through them lines parallel to the lines of no variation, it will be perceived that there are in a few cases important deviations from the general regularity in which the deflections are found to increase. These are by far too great to be attributed to errors in observation, to diurnal variation, or to the effect of atmospheric disturbing causes. It appears highly probable that something may be due to the outline of coast, to the unequal distribution of land and water, and to the influence of an open extent of sea on the one hand and of a mountain range upon the other. In all these cases there is a deflection of the needle towards the open lake, tending when the land lies to the west of the place of observation to increase the amount of easterly variations, and the contrary. Thus we find about the Riviere des Morts, where the trend of the shore is northerly, at the several points to the east of the Keweenaw Peninsula, and at the village of La Pointe, lying to the eastward of a high range of hills upon the main land, a too great deflection towards the east, as if the needle was actually affected by some repulsive influence existing in the land or a contrary principle in the waters."

Accompanying this report are maps of Grand Marais and Copper Harbor as fixed by triangulations, with soundings.

No. 2—Report of C. C. Douglass, assistant geologist, January 4th, 1841, states that the duties performed under the immediate direction of the State Geologist in the region of Lake Superior by the geological assistants necessarily delayed their work in the southern peninsula. The report is confined to remarks on the general character and geology of the northern portion of the lower peninsula.

This portion of the State, then new to settlement, was generally thought to be too far north, and too flat and wet to admit of successful agriculture. Mr. Douglass shows that this conclusion is wholly unwarranted as regards the greater part of the country, that the land continues to rise as we proceed into the interior, until it attains an elevation equal to if not exceeding any other part of the peninsula. That the upland is generally rolling, with a soil of sand and clay loams; is clad with evergreen timber interspersed with extensive tracts of beech and maple; that this character of country extends into the interior for many miles in the vicinity of Traverse Bay, bordering on a series of beautiful lakes varying in length from two to eighteen miles, and generally free from marsh and swamps. He alludes to the fact that the Ottawa Indians living on Grand and Little Traverse Bays and Manistee River have extensive cultivated fields which uniformly produce abundant crops, etc.

The general geology of the district he arranges in tabular form, and announces the fact that by "referring to the above locations of the rocks of Lakes Huron and Michigan it will be seen that the same rocks, with one or two exceptions, occur on both sides of the State, having the same geological position; also that they have very nearly parallel and uniform positions. And from their outcrops the rocks would appear to have a bearing nearly north 70 deg. west, and south 70 deg. east, which line of bearing corresponds with the outcrop of the black bituminious slate on the east side of Lake Huron and Upper Canada."

A general description is given of the rocks of Lakes Huron and Michigan within his district that contained fossils and minerals, and of their economical value and their want of it. Allusion is also made to ancient lake ridges, corresponding in character with the one determined by Mr. Hubbard in the reports of last year, as occurring in the southern part of the State. The elevations extended to 140 feet above the present water level; they were found most fully exhibited on the islands and on the main land bordering the straits of Mackinaw.

No. 3—Report of B. Hubbard, assistant geologist, January 24, 1841, states that upon the return from the portion of our State bordering on Lake Superior, where his services had been required during a large part of the season, he recommenced the detailed surveys in the organized counties of Michigan. These were conducted with a more especial view to the determination of the extent and value of the coal district of the peninsula. He adds: "A great mass of information both of practical and purely scientific character, and which could not be transferred to the maps nor be suitably embodied in the annual reports, has been compiled from my field notes, arranged for future reference and for such use as may be found advisable in the final report of the survey."

The report then proceeds to exhibit a comprehensive view of the rock formations throughout the organized counties of the State.

"The 'geological section' attached," he states, "will serve to exhibit at a glance the succession of the rock formations, from the universally superimposed sands and gravels down to the great lime rock formation of the southern portion of the State bordering on Lake Erie. This is intended to show the rocky basis which would be exhibited to view if the country could be cleft through in a line from Lake Erie to Maple River in Clinton county. The rocks in this section are grouped according to their distinguished characters and relative positions, and each group is distinguished by an alphabetical letter corresponding to the table. Subdivisions are given in the body of the report."

NOTE.—This "geological section," which is here reproduced from the field notes of Mr. Hubbard, was intended to accompany his report but had to be omitted because of the want of a capable engraver at Detroit. It is here published for the first time.

General Geology of the Organized Counties of Michigan.

In the "section" alluded to the rocks embraced within the district under consideration are divided into groups, as follows :

A. Erratic block group, or Diluviums.—a. Alluvions, ancient, recent.
B. Tertiary clays.
C. Coal measures. { Upper coal and shale. Lower coal and shale. Including sandstones. Limestone stratum.
D. Sub carboniferous sandstones.
E. Clay and kidney-ironstone formation.
F. Sandstones, of Point aux Barques.
G. Argillaceous slates and flags, of Lake Huron.
H. Soft, light colored, sandstones.
I. Black, aluminous slate.
K. Limerocks, of Lake Erie.

These will now be considered, as nearly as may be, in their consecutive order, beginning with the highest in the series.

GEOLOGICAL SECTION,

Exhibiting the order and comparative thickness of the Rocks of the Peninsula of Michigan, South of Saginaw Bay.

By B. HUBBARD.

(See Page 114, Report of Jan., '41.)

1840.

Forks of Maple and Grand Rivers.

Dip about 11 ft. to the mile.   Exaggerated in the above Section.

A—Erratic-block group, (Drift).   2. Au. Alluvion.
B—Clays of the Drift, or Diluviums (Tertiary.)
C—Coal Measures.
D—Sub-Carboniferous Sandstones.
E—Clay and Kidney Iron-Stone Formation.
F—Sandstones (of Pt. Aux Barques.)
G—Argill's Slates and Flags, (of L. Huron.)
H—Soft, light-colored Sandstones (lower salt rock.)
I—Black, Alums, Bitumin's, Slates.
K—Limerocks, of Lake Erie. (Helderberg group.)

} Waverly Group of Rominger.

ERRATIC BLOCK GROUP, OR DILUVIAL DEPOSITS.

These consists of sand, pebbles, and large water-worn masses of previously existing rocks, with occasional small local beds of clay. They have a thickness varying from one to upwards of one hundred feet; they form a universal mantle to the rocks and constitute the soils of all the interior counties.

As this whole deposit is one of transport by water, and is made up of the detritus and disruptured fragments of heterogeneous formations, its character depends upon that of the rocks from which it is derived. For instance, *sand* constitutes by far the greater proportion, and this circumstance may be in part accounted for, from the fact of the immense extent of sandstone rocks existing farther to the north; and in part, by the fact, further disclosed by the geological researches in the peninsula, that an immense thickness of rocks, mostly sandstone, which composed the upper series of the coal measures, has been broken up and removed from our geological series. *Fine gravel* constitutes the diluvium in the next proportion, and is the result of a similar abrasion of rocks of harder materials. Owing to the friable nature of the sandstones, as might be expected, few large boulders of that material occur. Limestone pebbles and boulders are abundant; a condition which also might be looked for, when we take into view the immense extent and thickness of the limerocks of our state, they being by far the most prominent formation above the primary.

These relations of the component parts of our diluviums give a character to the *soils* of the peninsula, which enables us to compare them most favorably with those of most other states in the union. Though being very generally what may be denominated sandy or gravelly, and often answering in appearance to a description of soils which, in the eastern states, are considered as absolutely barren, the variety and due intermixture of their components, and more particularly the large proportion of carbonate of lime which is combined with them, either in the form of pebbles, or in a very comminuted state, impart to them unusual strength and fertility. The latter circumstance is that which so admirably adapts them to the growth of wheat, and in this respect, most of the soils of the peninsula may fairly be pronounced unrivalled.

Whatever may have been the causes which swept these materials over the face of the rocks, whether oceanic currents or bodies of floating ice, the character of these *diluviums*, as well as numerous accompanying facts, plainly imply that they came in a direction northerly from their present beds, and often from great distances. Consequently we find intermingled, as well as scattered upon the surface, numerous rounded fragments of those primary rocks which are known to exist in the peninsula of northern Michigan and in Canada, from the size of the largest "hard-heads" down to fine gravel. In proceeding from our state southerly, these deposits are found gradually to thin out, evincing a diminution of the sustaining power with the increased distance from the original bed of the transported materials. So that, while the peninsula of Michigan has been most liberally supplied with an uncommonly deep and arable soil, made up of a variety of materials, the states of Ohio and Indiana, on the south, are in great parts destitute; its place being supplied by the clays of the next lower formation.

The deposition of these materials took place with or without apparent order and uniformity, according to the character of the existing surface, and other circumstances which may have governed the transporting forces. From this cause considerable variations are to be found in the depth, nature and composition of the diluviums, and hence, also, material differences are occasioned in the soils and other characteristics of the country. In many places a uniform stratification has taken place, as if the result of quiet deposition. This is more particularly apparent on the east and south side of the main ridge of the peninsula, and may be considered as a natural consequence of so considerable an obstacle as this partial barrier must have interposed to the force of northerly currents. Here, wells have been carried to the depth of 90 feet, through beds of stratified gravel.

Throughout all the diluviums, thin local beds of clay are of frequent occurrence, and occasional strata of hard pan or cemented pebbles. These clays, unlike those of the tertiary, contain little or no lime.

Most of the country thus covered by the diluvial deposits exhibits the action of strong currents and eddies in a very striking manner. Districts of many miles extent frequently present a continued and close succession of rolling knobs or cones of gravel, with deep intervening basins. The more ordinary character of surface is a gentle roll or slight undulation, occasionally subsiding to a perfect plain.

Except where a deposit of clay underlies, the growth of timber is almost invariably scanty, constituting what are denominated "oak openings." The character of their timber changes with the varying conditions of the soil, from white and black oak to burr oak or hickory, and the plains are frequently altogether destitute of timber. A dense growth of the usual hard wood timber sometimes occurs over isolated tracts, in swales, or along banks of streams. Of the character of country described are found the three most southerly ranges of counties, with the exception of those which immediately border the peninsula on the great lakes, together with parts of the adjoining counties, and the counties of Ingham and Eaton. All the latter have a sub-stratum of clay belonging to the great deposit to be presently described, and in consequence differ very materially in surface, soil and timber.

To this extreme thickness and comparatively loose texture of the diluviums, may be ascribed the great abundance of springs, and consequently of the small streams which irrigate the whole surface of the state, affording abundance of that element so desirable to the farmer. An undulating surface gives to most of these a sufficiently rapid flow to preserve a healthy current and to furnish a sufficiency of mill power From the same cause, also, little difficulty is experienced in obtaining pure water by sinking of wells, and it may safely be said that Michigan is better supplied with living water, uniformly distributed, than any other state in the Union.

The vast numbers of small lakes for which Michigan is so remarkable, are due to the same causes. They occupy generally deep hollows, seemingly scooped out of the mass of diluvium, and are fed by the living springs that percolate through it. The number of these peninsular lakes is stated by the state topographer at not less than 3,000; being in proportion of one acre of water to every thirty-nine of dry land.

Another striking feature in the peninsula landscape is the number and extent of wet prairies or marsh. Of these the proportion is much larger than of the lakes, and they often cover many miles of surface. These have their origin also from springs issuing from the diluvium, aided often by the artifical dams of the beaver, and from being originally mere pools or shallow lakes, in time they become receptacles for beds of marl and peat. From the very tolerable hay which these prairies afford, and the very early supply of tender "feeding" for cattle, in the spring, the apparently waste places have been an invaluable aid to the settlement of the country. The primitive settler came hither, not to a desert waste or a "howling wilderness," but to lands cleared without aid from the woodman's axe, and verdant with unsown crops. He did not wait to provide pasture, but brought his herds and flocks with him, and the marshes furnished them ample sustenance throughout the year. And we hazard nothing in saying that these marshes, waste as many of them are now suffered to be, are destined to become still more valuable in sustaining the failing vigor of the country whose youthful prosperity they promoted. Their successful drainage is no longer a matter of experiment. Scarcely a marsh of much extent exists, which is not capable of thorough drainage, with comparatively small expense, and, when thus subdued, of furnishing a soil rich almost beyond comparison. The literally exhaustless beds of marl and peat with which these marshes abound, constitute another item of value no less important. But the consideration of these may more properly be referred to the head of *Recent Alluvions*.

But though affording a medium for the absorption of rain waters and their percolation through strata of gravel or quicksand, the diluviums are rendered sufficiently retentive, by the alumina contained in them, and by seams of cemented gravel and sand. Were it not for this, the moisture absorbed by our light, sandy soils, would soon be drained off and lost to the crops. A sub-stratum of cemented gravel, retentive of water, is common to many if not all the prairies, and to this circumstance may no doubt, in great measure, be ascribed their accumulation of rich loam and consequent fertility.

Much curious inquiry has been excited on the question of the causes which produced the peculiar varied and open character of so large a portion of our peninsula. After the view which we have just taken of our diluviums, it may seem less a matter of surprise, that portions of the state should be adapted to the production of a dense growth of hard timber, and others only to the several species of oaks or to hickory, according to the continually varying conditions of the soil and its substrata. The existing analogies of the vegetable world, which exhibit similar results elsewhere, might lead us to infer these changes, and we may, without doubt, attribute to the peculiar characteristics of our diluvial envelop, and its varying conditions, the accompanying peculiarities in the features of the country and the growth and character of its timber.

How far the impervious character of the "hard pan," which so generally, if not universally, forms the sub-stratum to the prairies and plains, may account for the destitution or sparse growth of large trees, we are not altogether prepared to decide, and, therefore, avoid for the present, considerations which at best may be considered somewhat theoretical. Nor will we assume to decide, with confidence, upon the extent of the effects produced by the ravages of the annual fires which formerly swept over these tracts. It is but reasonable to conclude that all these, and perhaps other concomitant causes have operated together in producing the results we witness, while, according to peculiar circumstances, one of these several causes may have operated more or less powerfully than others.

ANCIENT ALLUVION.

As the consideration of that immense mass of materials to which has been applied the name of *diluviums* or *erratic block group*, was necessary, in order to a correct appreciation of those lesser deposits now to be considered, (which are associated with, and in fact compose a part of the former,) that important group claimed our first attention. We come now to the consideration of a class of deposits which may be called *alluvial*.

Some interesting facts in relation to the assumption that the waters of the great lakes were formerly at a much higher level than at present, covering a large part of the border portions of the peninsula, were noticed in my report of last year. During the past season a continuation of the "ridge," which is supposed to coincide with the beach of the ancient lake, has been traced through Macomb into St. Clair county, and further facts confirmatory of the positions assumed last year were observed in other more northerly districts. In the county of Macomb this ridge has been much broken up by crossing streams, and is very irregular, showing frequently the existence of large entering bays and curvatures of the coast. This was the more particularly noticed from the fact that elsewhere, so far as observed, the course of the ridge is very remarkably continuous and well defined. In this county also a number of inferior ridges of evidently similar origin were observed between the main one and the present lake shore, leading to the supposition that the subsidence of the waters did not take place gradually and constantly, but that sudden lapses occurred and the water line had been stationary at intervals.

The soil and detrital matter superficially covering that portion of the peninsula which is embraced between this ancient lake ridge and the present shores of the lakes, I have denominated *ancient alluvion*, to distinguish them as well from alluvions now in process of formation as from the immense mass of *diluviums* which overspreads the whole interior of the State beyond this separating ridge.

The portion thus distinguished by alluvial deposits embraces a broad belt of border country, varying in width from about 25 to 50 miles. It is, with small local exceptions heavily timbered and very level. But on passing the bounding ridge there is in general an almost immediate change to a soil of coarser character and a more undulating surface. This ancient alluvion is a deposit from a quiescent condition of the waters, and similar to that which is now taking place in the beds of the present lakes. It forms in general but a thin mantle to the underlying formations, consisting often of mere ridges of sand, and owing to the deprivation of its lime, has in general less fertility than the diluviums.

The heavily timbered district is not altogether coincident with the extent of this alluvion, but is dependent chiefly upon the following cause. Throughout their whole extent the alluvions are underlaid by the tertiary clays. These are a formation anterior to both the dilluviums and alluvions, and are frequently found extending far beyond the old lake ridge. The country thus underlaid is that which is almost wholly clothed with a dense growth of timber. This formation will be found described under the head of tertiary clays.

RECENT ALLUVIONS.

Under this head I shall here allude only to local beds of marl, bog ores and peat.

Marl occurs in the greatest abundance, universally distributed throughout the diluvial district, and consists of local deposits which originate solely from the lime so profusely contained in the diluviums. Such beds are in constant process of formation and increase wherever that ingredient exists. As it is present in a much less degree in the ancient alluvion no extensive beds are consequently found throughout the district occupied by the latter.

Bog iron ores are deposits originating in a similar manner from the iron contained in the soil, which is dissolved out by the rain waters and collects in low grounds.

Peat beds are exclusively of vegetable origin, and are common both to the alluvial and diluvial districts.

The character, abundance, and value of the marl, peat and bog ore beds of our State having been fully dwelt upon in the reports of last year, I shall make no further remarks upon their practical applications. I cannot avoid, nevertheless, once again directing the attention of the farmer of Michigan to the fact of the unexampled abundance in which the two former occur, conveniently distributed for universal use *as a manure*, and urging the use of them, as the cheapest and in most cases the best of mineral manures, and which will be found a very important means of improvement in his agricultural economy.

Organic Remains.

Bones of the mastodon were last year discovered in the ancient alluvion, in the western part of Macomb county. They were mostly so much decayed as not to bear exposure to the atmosphere, and a molar tooth only has been preserved. Similar relics were several years ago disinterred on the Paw Paw River in Berrien county. There is now in possession of a gentleman in this city a vertebral bone of enormous size said to have been found many years ago upon the St. Joseph River, and which is pronounced by the State zoologist, Dr. Sager, to be the caudal vertebra of a whale. It measures in vertical diameter, including spinous process, 18 inches; transverse diameter, including lateral processes, 2 feet; diameter of body, 11 inches; length of body, 10½ inches; length of spinous process, 9 inches. Its weight is 21 lbs., which is probably less than one-half its original weight, as the bone is partially decayed.

TERTIARY CLAYS.

These extensive deposits belong to an era subsequent to the removal of the upper coal bearing rocks. They cover all the border counties on the east and west slopes of the peninsula, and in some instances stretch far inland. These clays extend over more than two-thirds of that part of the State which lies south of Saginaw, Maple and Grand Rivers, embracing nearly the whole of the counties of Ottawa, Allegan, Van Buren, Berrien, Monroe, Wayne, Macomb, St. Clair, Sanilac, Huron, Tuscola, Saginaw, Lapeer, Clinton and Eaton, and a large portion of Ingham, Genesee, Shiawassee, Ionia, Kent, St. Joseph, Branch, Hillsdale and Lenawee. The remaining portions of the counties last named, and very nearly the whole of Oakland, Livingstone, Washtenaw, Jackson, Calhoun, Kalamazoo and Cass, are destitute of this sub-clay formation, and their diluviums rest immediately upon the rocks.

A dense growth of timber almost invariably accompanies this formation, whatever may be the immediate soil. We find this observation applicable to large portions of Eaton, Ingham, Clinton, Shiawassee and Genesee counties, though these counties are based in part on the sandstone rocks of the coal series, and have sandy, diluvial soils, while the sandstone country south of them presents little else than oak openings and plains.

These clays are an extension of the same formation which covers the western and northern part of Ohio, and the east and north of Indiana, and which constitutes the soil of a large proportion of those districts.

The upper portion is a gravelly, yellowish clay, varying in thickness from one to fifteen feet, and having an average probably not exceeding 5 feet. Beneath this is a similar clay of a blue color, and which in some places has been found to exceed in thickness one hundred and twenty feet. Both clays contain at least 20 per cent., by weight, of carbonate of lime, and this marly character injures them materially for the manufacture of bricks or pottery.

On the western slope of the peninsula the place of the yellow and blue clays is sometimes supplied by clay of a reddish color of great thickness. No fossils have yet been discovered in any of the clays of this formation.

APPENDIX.

Coal Measures.

The rocks which include the coal beds of our State occupy, comparatively, but a small portion of that part of the State under consideration, and are embraced within the counties of Jackson, Calhoun, Ingham, Eaton, Kent, Ionia, Clinton, Shiawassee and Genesee. They consist of strata of sandstone, shale, coal and limestone. Covered as these rocks are with thick deposits of diluviums and clays, they make out crops at but few points, and the determination of their order and extent has been a matter of no small difficulty. From the dip of the rocks composing these measures there can be little doubt that the coal basin extends northerly beyond the counties named, perhaps as far as to the head branches of the Tittabawassee and Maskego Rivers. But that country is as yet almost wholly unsettled, and though partial explorations have been made through it since the commencement of the geological surveys, the thick mass of overlying materials has hitherto prevented a determination of the northerly extent of these rocks

Limestone Stratum.

As this stratum, from its position, (being the lowest in the series) determines the extent of the rocks considered as composing our coal basin, I shall, for the sake of greater precision give to it the first consideration.

A gray limestone, in irregular, detached beds, is found along the extreme border of the coal bearing sandstones. They are evidently relics, in place, of a thin but extensive stratum, and as no coal has been found below this rock, I have assumed it as the terminating rock of the "coal measures" proper of our state. Following this rock, as it makes its occasional appearance, the southerly limits of the coal basin may be traced by a line drawn from the Shiawassee River, at Corunna, through the easterly parts of Ingham and Jackson, between ranges one and two east to near Napoleon in the latter county. It then turns westerly through town three south, ranges one and two west; from whence, taking a direction north-westerly it pursues an irregular line, passing through Bellevue in the south-west corner of Eaton county to Grand Rapids, in Kent county. Here the lime rock is more extended and a thickness has been determined to it of fourteen feet. The rock is characterized by the fossils Nucula and Cyathophyllum vermiculare. This stratum affords the only limestone for the kiln or other purposes, except occasional boulders, to be found in the interior of the state, and its value is the more to be appreciated as the formation is itself of very limited extent.

Lower Coal.

But two continuous beds of workable coal are ascertained to exist in the state. The lowest of these lies at a small distance only above the limestone stratum, and is associated with a very thick bed of shale, which is also sufficiently bituminous to answer the purpose of an inferior coal.

Coal of Jackson County.—That portion of the lower coal bed which underlies a portion of this county makes an outcrop in the valley of Sandstone Creek, town of Spring Arbor, and has there been penetrated to the depth of three feet. The thick bed of shale opened at Jackson undoubtedly is associated with and belongs to this coal stratum.

Coal of Ingham County.—Passing down the easterly side of the basin the coal is again met with in the north-east corner town of Ingham county, where it is embraced in a succession of shales and friable sandstone, cropping out in the bank sand bed of the Red Cedar River. The coal has here been penetrated two and a half feet. But neither here nor in Jackson county is the entire thickness of the bed determined. "The coal at this point," as is observed in the report of Mr. Douglass, of last year, "is very accessible, and must, ere long, prove of great importance. It is situated on a stream that may be made navigable for flat bottomed boats and perogues, with comparatively small expense, for a considerable portion of the year, and opening a direct communication with Lake Michigan."

It may here be observed that the coal of this lower bed, universally, has more than usual compactness and purity, and is equal to the best bituminous coal of Pennsylvania.

Coal of Shiawassee County.—The coal again makes its appearance at the border of the basin near the county seat of Shiawassee county, where it crops out between thick and extensive layers of sandstone in the banks of the small creek entering Shiawassee River. The coal has here a thickness of from three and a half to four feet, and is accompanied by shale the entire thickness of which is not ascertained. This coal is very eligibly situated for mining. It is of excellent quality, and the dip is so slight that but little depth of excavation will be required. This is the only locality in the state where coal, to much extent, has been raised for economical use. Both the coal and associated shale are constantly employed to great advantage at the steam mill of Mr. McArthur, in Corunna, as well as by neighboring smiths.

From an area of eight by nine feet Mr. McA. raised four hundred and sixty bushels of coal and shale, and he informs me it can be sold at the county seat for ten cents per bushel.

The underlying limerock stratum makes an out crop about a mile south-west from this point, in a bed of probably many acres in extent.

Shales of Flint River.—The coal bed and its accompaning shale may be traced still further east, to the Flint River, in Genesee county. Here the former probably has nearly thinned out, as only loose masses are found in |the bed of the river. The associated black shale and slate may be observed in the river banks, (town eight north, five west,) where it attains a thickness of sixteen feet, and is underlaid by the sandrock.

The coal of the Shiawassee and Flint Rivers appears to occupy the extreme edge of the coal basin, which here thins out into a wedge form, narrowing gradually until it terminates in a mere point, probably as far easterly as Lapeer county. The inclination of the strata is north-westerly, to an amount which would soon carry the coal beneath the surface; but appearances seem to warrant the conclusion that at this point a large part of the rocks of the coal measures continued northerly have been entirely removed.

Upper Coal.

The outcrops of this coal, within that part of the state under consideration are of small extent. It is found at the surface on or near Grand River, in the northern part of Eaton county, and with its associated shales and sandstones, occupies the central part of the coal basin, probably including the whole of Clinton and Gratiot counties. Except in the extreme southwest corner of the former county it lies too deep for examination.

Most of this coal is inferior in quality and thickness to the lower coal. It composes several layers not exceeding in thickness from one to two feet each, and is embraced in alternating strata of dark gray shales, blue clay, sandstones and thin beds of argillaceous iron ore, exceeding in the whole 20 feet.

Coal of Eaton County.—Sections of the alternating strata of coal and accompanying rocks, taken on Coal and Grindstone Creeks, were given by Mr. Douglass in his report of last year.

As that report contained full local details of all the coal-bearing rocks of Jackson, Ingham and Eaton counties, I shall here allude to the rocks of that portion of the state only in such a general manner as will be necessary in order to afford a comprehensive view of the extent and value of the coal measures of our state. By reference to the document alluded to, it will be seen that, though inferior in thickness to the lower coal bed, the several strata of coal exposed on the creeks above mentioned, have an aggregate thickness of from two to three feet, and will, no doubt, prove of importance under a more settled condition of that portion of the state.

INCLUDED SANDSTONES OF THE COAL MEASURES.

Gray and Yellow Sandstones.—The sandrocks included between the upper and lower coal are mostly of a coarse quartzose character, and of a light gray or yellow color. Most of the strata are friable, but harden on exposure. They are distinguished from the quartzose sandstone below the lower coal, by containing impressions of the coal plants. These are referable chiefly to the genera Lipidodendron, Stigmaria and Calamities.

These rocks are found outcropping at numerous points through the northern part of Jackson county, the western part of Ingham and eastern part of Eaton counties, and portions of Calhoun, Clinton, Shiawassee and Genesee. In all of the above named counties they occur in situations which admit of being economically quarried, and may often be obtained in firm blocks of any dimensions required. From this series of sandrocks was furnished the material for the construction of the State penitentiary at Jackson, and at several places, as at Napoleon, excellent grindstones are manufactured from it.

Red or variegated sandstone.—This rock immediately underlies the upper coal and shales. Its outcropping edge is found in the valley of Grand River in the northern part of Eaton county, and in the banks of the Lookingglass River, in the adjoining towns of Clinton county, and in township seven north, six west, Ionia county. No fossil plant was discovered in this rock. It has been employed with advantage as a building material. The entire thickness of the included sandstones must be several hundred feet.

The following general section will exhibit at one view, the relative order and thickness of all the rocks of our coal measures, above described, so far as a subdivision of them has been found practicable.

General Section, Applicable to the Coal Basin of Michigan.

	Thickness.
	Feet.
Diluviums and tertiary clays...............................	1 to 100
Brown or gray sandstone*....................................	20
Argillaceous iron ore, in thin included beds*...........	1
Coal strata, alternating with friable slaty sandstone and thick beds of black shales and slate,* in the whole probably..	30
Red or variegated sandstone (Clinton and Ionia counties)...	Undetermined.
Light gray, coarse, quartzose, micaceous sandstones. Generally in thick layers and forming ledges, mostly friable and easily quarried (seen at intervals along Grand River from Jackson to Grindstone Creek, Eaton county)..	
Coal and black bituminous shale (Jackson, Ingham, Shiawassee and Genesee).....................................	20
Blue, compact, slaty sandstone (Shiawassee co)........	
Gray limestone, found in local beds, being relics in place of a once continuous stratum (encircles the coal basin from Grand Rapids to Shiawassee River)	14

The rocks in the above section embrace all those which are included in the division marked C in the "geological section" prefixed to this report.

SANDSTONES IMMEDIATELY BELOW THE COAL.

These sandstones (marked D. in the plate), as well as most of the formations below the coal, were fully described in my

---

*Counties of Clinton and Eaton.

report of last year. I shall, therefore, now notice them only so far as to exhibit their relative position in the series, viewed as a whole, and the extent of country occupied by them.

These sandstones, which in the report alluded to are described under the name of *fossiliferous, ferruginous sandstones*, excepting in some of the uppermost strata, are generally fine grained and of a yellow color. Some strata of the latter abound in marine fossil shells, among which the genus Nucula is very abundant, and there were observed species of Atrypa, Bellerophon, Euomphalis and Pterinea.

Though here classed as beneath the coal rocks, these sandstones are associated with that series of rocks which are usually regarded as belonging to the carboniferous era. They occupy nearly the whole of Calhoun county, the lower half of Jackson and the northern half of Hillsdale county; through which counties their outcrops may be observed at numerous points, or they are reached in almost all the deep wells. It is probable, also, that these rocks occupy most of the eastern portions of Jackson and Shiawassee counties east of the limestone stratum above described; and they make their appearance at its eastern edge on Lake Huron, near the entrance of Saginaw Bay.

The aggregate thickness of these sandstones may be estimated at upwards of 300 feet.

CLAY, CONTAINING KIDNEY ORE OF IRON.

This very valuable formation immediately succeeds to the sandstones above described, underlying them and cropping out at the extreme southerly bend of the basin. It occupies a part of the south-western portion of Calhoun county, the whole north-eastern portion of Branch county, or nearly so, and part of the western and central portions of Hillsdale.

It consists of an indurated, grayish brown clay, having much the appearance of a shaly limestone or dark gypsum, regularly stratified, in which are imbedded nodular masses of kidney ironstone. This is a rich and valuable ore and occurs at several points conveniently for working.

This formation is the lowest that is discoverable in this portion of the state, and is not certainly known to make an outcrop elsewhere.

For further description of this clay and its contained ore, I refer you to the annual report of the State Geologist of 1840, and to my own appended thereto, for many practical considerations relative to the value of the ore and its imbedding clay. This formation is marked E, in the plate.

SANDSTONES OF POINT AUX BARQUES.

These are mostly of coarse, greenish gray or rusty yellow rock, in some of the layers approaching a conglomerate. They form cliffs along the shore of Lake Huron in Huron county, rising at Point aux Barques to twenty feet. Fossils are rare, but Atrypa and Calymene were obtained. These sandstones occupy the coast north of town seventeen, being visible in ledges for about twenty miles. The upper portion of the series contains numerous small imbedded pebbles of quartz, so as to resemble a conglomerate of puddingstone, but no great thickness is observable of rock possessing this character.

An extension of the outcropping edge of these sandstones, it is probable, gives rise to that swell of land which forms the summit level of the peninsula, stretching in a south-westerly direction from Point aux Barques to Hillsdale county, where the green and yellow fossiliferous sandstones, above described, overlie it. But throughout this whole extent no outcrop of the rock is visible owing to the thickness of the diluviums.

These sandrocks, taken in connection with the formation next described, hold a place in the geological series, corresponding to the "waverly sandstones," and "conglomerate," of Ohio, but the deposition seems to have been made under somewhat differing circumstances. No well defined series is apparent in our state answering fully to the Ohio conglomerate; though the upper portion of the sandstones of Point aux Barques approach that character.

The whole thickness of these sandstones probably exceeds 250 feet. This group is marked F, in the plate.

CLAY SLATES AND FLAGS OF LAKE HURON.

Alternating with the lower portions of the sandstones of Point aux Barques, are strata of slaty sandstone, approaching the character of slate ; to which succeeds a compact micaceous clay slate of a blue color. This latter rock continues to occupy the coast for about thirty miles, or from township twelve to township eighteen north, and rises in ledges of from five to fifteen feet.

The slaty sandstones intervening between these clay slates and the overlying coarser sandstones are of a flaggy structure in some of the layers, and from these were obtained those fine flagging stones which have been extensively used for three years past for pavements in the city of Detroit. Some of these strata are distinguished by *ripple marks*. No fossils have been discovered in this formation.

These slates and alternating sandstones may be considered as the upper salt rock of our state. They have been passed through in boring for salt at Grand Rapids, and found to yield strong supplies of brine. At this point they are found also to alternate with beds of gypsum and gypserous marls, as will appear by reference to the table of the strata passed through, given on a subsequent page. The thickness ascertained to these slates, at that point is about 170 feet.

SOFT, COARSE GRAINED SANDSTONE.

A series of sandrocks answering to this description, and generally of a dark color, succeeds to the clay slates and shales last above described, and has been penetrated at the borings at Grand Rapids 230 feet. There are, as yet, no data for ascertaining the entire thickness of this series, since it does not make its appearance at any point on the coast of the peninsula, this rock evidently forming the bed of Lake Huron near its foot, and lying too deep for observation. In relative position and perhaps in character, this rock, or a portion of the series corresponds with the lower salt rock of Ohio and Virginia, and is the rock from which, in these states, the strongest supplies of brine are obtained. The result of the borings in our own state, thus far, would seem to confirm the opinion that this rock is the equivalent of the lower salt rocks of those states.

BLACK, BITUMINOUS, ALUMINOUS SLATE.

Underlying the sandstones above noticed, though, also, nowhere observed to make an outcrop within the portion of the state now under consideration, there is a well characterized black bituminous slate. Is rock makes an outcrop much further to the north, and is described by Mr. Douglass in his accompanying report, to which I refer you. This slate contains much sulphuret of iron; it will burn readily, and in general character and position it agrees with the black shale stratum of Ohio and Indiana, but its thickness is probably not nearly so great.

LIMESTONES OF LAKE ERIE.

This formation, which immediately underlies the black slate, is by far the most continuous and extensive rock formation in the western states. It is found outcropping in several district ranges throughout Monroe county, forms a considerable part of the lake coast and serves as a basis to the islands at the mouth of Detroit River, and is an extension of the rock formation which occupies the whole western part of Ohio and the northern and eastern portions of Indiana. It is found forming the bed of Lake Michigan at its head, and undoubtedly is the underlying rock of a considerable portion of the extreme south-western part of our state. The overlying tertiary clays conceal a great part of this formation.

The character and economical adaption of these limestones have been sufficintly set forth in former reports, to which, accordingly, I refer you for detailed information.

Among the fossils contained in the limerock I distinguish the following genera : Calymene and Asaphus, Cyathophyllum, Productus, Terebratula, Spirifer and Dethlyrus, Bellerophon, Atrypa, Strophomena, Orthocera, Encrinus, Retepora and Madrepora.

In proceeding southerly from the outcrops of the slates of Lake Huron a limerock is met with, which may be seen in the bed of a small stream near the lake coast, town nine, north, sixteen east. In character and fossil contents it bears a resemblance to that of Monguagon, Monroe county, but its position would seem to indicate it rather as an included stratum in the series of sandrocks and shale, which are higher in the geological series.

The following general section will exhibit the order of succession and approximate thickness of the rocks above described, *lying below the coal basin*, and is a continuation of the table given on page 249 of the successive rock formations of the settled portions of our peninsula:

FIRST GEOLOGICAL SURVEY OF MICHIGAN. 255

General section, applicable to all the rocks below the coal beds of Michigan, in that portion of the peninsula included in this report.

		Mean thickness in feet
D.	Sandstones of Jackson, Calhoun and Hillsdale. { Coarse quartzose, grayish sandrocks. Fine grained, ash colored and dingy green, interstratified with slaty sandstone and clay shales. Yellow sandrocks, colored by iron, and abounding in fossils	300
E.	Dark gray and blue indurated clay, containing kidney iron (counties of Hillsdale, Branch and Calhoun)............................	45
F.	Coarse sandstone, or partial conglomerate, Yellow and greenish sandstones (coast of Lake Huron, at Point aux Barques).....................	250
G.	Slaty, argillaceous sandstone, alternating with sandstone and clay slates, Blue clay slates and flays, with alternating gypsum beds and gypseous marls (Lake Huron coast, below Point aux Barques).....................	180
H.	Soft, coarse grained sandstones (occupies bed of Lake Huron at its foot), exceeds.................,...........	230
I.	Black aluminous slate, containing pyrites (coast of Lake Huron at Thunder Bay)...................	
K.	Gray limerock, fossils abundant (west end of Lake Erie)...	

The rocks in the above section embrace all those which are included in the divisions marked D, E, F, G, H, I, and K, in the GEOLOGICAL SECTION prefixed to this report.

Dip of the Rocks.

Great irregularities of dip are observable in all of our rocks, which circumstance has increased the difficulty of determining the precise relative position, extent and thickness of the several strata. Many of the sandstones belonging to and immediately underlying the coal, are much shattered, as if by a quick vibratory motion, and a similar cause has occasioned contortions of dip in most of the still older rocks. I have, therefore, refrained from noting the amount and direction of dip at the various localities mentioned. All the rocks on the eastern slope of the peninsula south of Saginaw Bay have a general dip north-westerly, while the dip along the southerly and westerly border of the basin of the coal bearing rocks is such as to indicate the counties of Clinton and Gratiot as occupying nearly the central part of the coal basin. This being the case, the carboniferous sandstones, with their included coal beds, may be considered as extending far to the north of the Saginaw and Grand Rivers, possibly as far as town 23 north, or to the head waters of the Maskego and Tittabawassee Rivers. This supposition, the character of that region, as well as the dip of the rocks would seem to warrant. But the country alluded to, is, at present, in an uninhabited condition; the surface, moreover, is very generally level, and so completely overspread by the deposits of diluviums and tertiary clays as totally to conceal the rock formations. Surveys have, however, been extended into that region so far as was practicable with the means afforded, and much valuable information is collected.

If I am correct in the above conclusion, the coal bearing sandstones, or, strictly speaking, the *coal basin* occupy an extent of surface, nearly oval in form, whose centre very nearly corresponds with the true centre of the peninsula. The tract thus embraced is 150 miles in length, north and south, and upwards of 100 in extreme breadth; covering an area of about 11,000 square miles, or one-fourth of the entire area of the lower peninsula.

It may be added, that the average dip of all the rocks described, does not probably exceed 15 feet in the mile; though the dip may be said to vary, at different points, from 10 to 20 feet per mile.

Borings at the Salt Well, Grand Rapids.

The borings for salt at the village of Grand Rapids, Kent county, commenced in the limerock stratum mentioned above, page 244, as constituting the terminating rock of the coal basin. At this point, several of the next succeeding series of sandrocks appear to have thinned out, and their place is here occupied by alternating strata of clay slates and sandstones with gypseous marls and beds of gypsum. These continued to a depth of 190 feet, and below this the borings have been carried mostly through series of sandrocks to the depth of 415 feet.

Two beds of beautiful crystalized gypsum were passed through at a depth of about 60 feet, and were found to be from 4 to 6 feet in thickness. This gypsum, it will be recollected, from the notice of it in former reports, appears at the surface at Gypsum Creek, three miles distant; showing an inclination to the rocks, at this point, of about 20 feet in the mile.

By reference to a map of the state, it will be apparent that the strongest brine springs, (among which are included those in the vicinity of these borings,) make their appearance along a line which will be found to correspond with the "synclinal axis," or axis of the dip of the rocks composing the great peninsula basin; a circumstance which would be looked for from the fact that the ordinary law of gravitation would conduct the strong brines to the lowest levels of the rock strata. While, therefore, the depth to which the boring must be carried, in order to reach the lower salt bearing strata, will be greater than would be the case in some other portions of the state, the comparative strength of the brine obtained may be expected to be proportionably increased.

Through the politeness of the Hon. Lucius Lyon, I am enabled to subjoin a section of the strata passed through at the boring above mentioned.

(17)

Diagram of Strata passed through at salt well of Hon. L. Lyon, Grand Rapids.

		Thickness in feet.	Total depth feet
1	Hard gray limerock, irregularly stratified, and in portions cavernous..	14	14
2	Yellow Sandrock, producing fresh water..............	6	20
3	Blue clay..	2	22
4	Coarse, reddish sandrock.......................................	5	27
5	Blue clay...	3	30
6	Clay slate, with thin layers of gypsum interstratified..	11	41
7	Clay slate...	18	59
8	Gypsum...	4	63
9	Clay slate	2	65
10	Gypsum...	6	71
11	Clay slate...	3	74
12	Bluish sandrock, very hard, with sharp grit...........	3	82
13	Bluish clay rock, intermixed with particles of reddish rock, compact. This rock is strongly impregnated with saline particles.......................	18	100
14	Sand and clay rock, alternating.............................	7	107
15	Carbonate of lime and gypsum combined, very compact..	10	117
16	Gypsum...	7	124
17	Clay slate...	9	133
18	Gray sandrock of very sharp grit and hard...........	5	138
19	Clay rock...	2½	140½
20	Gypsum, with vein of salt water.........................	6½	147
21	Clay rock...	6	153
22	Gypsum and clay slate, or gypseous marls, alternating..	19	172
23	Gypsum...	3	175
24	Clay rock...	3	178
25	Gypsum...	1	179
26	Hard sandrock, producing fresh water..................	1½	180½
27	Clay rock, free from saline matter.......................	10½	191
28	Hard sandrock, very compact and of dark color.....	7	198
29	Soft sandrock, nearly colorless.............................	18	216
30	Soft sandrock, of dark blue color.........................	32	248
31	Loose, coarse grained sandrock, of reddish color, opening a very copious spring of fresh water.....	17	265

Below the strata last noted in the above table, the borings have continued through a further depth of 150 feet, but the data received are not sufficiently minute to enable me to extend the table. From the information obtained, they would seem to have passed through mostly soft, light colored sandrocks of a coarse grain and with a sharp grit, and in the lower portions containing cavities into which the drill sometimes falls several inches. Particles of salt were brought up, and the rock yields a very strong brine.

All the strata from the depth of 81 to 179 feet, or until the sandrock was reached, were strongly impregnated with saline particles, and yielded brine one-fifth saturated. These clay slates and marls may be regarded as the "upper salt rock," and they are thus shown to furnish a brine superior in strength to that of many of the salt wells of Ohio, and which, even could no stronger brine be obtained, is capable of sustaining a profitable manufacture.

The brine now obtained at a depth below the above of about 230 feet, may be supposed to proceed by veins from the "lower salt rock," lying at still greater depth, and from which the strongest and best supplies of brine in our State may be expected to be obtained.

The immense quantity of fresh or slightly brackish water which is discharged through the orifice, equal to a hogshead per minute, in the present state of the operations, renders it impossible to decide with absolute certainty what will be the full strength as well as supply of the strong brine, but from that which can be obtained it is estimated that of the brine which the well is now capable of furnishing from fifty to sixty gallons only will be required to produce a bushel of salt. This, it will be seen, is equal in point of strength to that obtained from the salt wells on the Kenawha River of the Ohio, where the borings are carried to about the same depth, and at which are manufactured annually from one to two millions of bushels of salt. Next to those of the State of New York the Kenawha salt wells are considered the best in the Union.

In addition to the quality of the brine obtained, the advantages for the manufacture of salt at the point under consideration are not exceeded at those places in our country where the manufacture is conducted to the largest extent. The supply of wood for fuel and other necessary purposes is abundant, and will tend greatly to reduce the price for which the manufacturers will be enabled to furnish this article.

And, though the whole matter may be said to be still in an incipient state, there is every reason to feel satisfied with the prospect which so fair a beginning holds out to the State, for obtaining a result so very desirable as that of supplying her citizens with this important article from the product of her own manufacture.

SUMMARY,

Comprising General Observations on the Economical Results of the Survey.

From the view we have now taken of the rock strata which compose the lower half of the southern peninsula of Michigan, it will be seen that the geology is of an exceedingly simple character, while it is at the same time richest in the mineral wealth most important to an agricultural community.

Michigan occupies a portion of the great valley of the Mississippi—the richest in the world—and which is wholly occupied by a broad extent of the rocks classed by geologists in the transition and secondary formations. Of these the great limestone formation (of which that of the west end of Lake Erie is a portion, and which concluded our view of the several geological groups which make up the organized portion of the State) occupies the lowest place, and is the lowest and oldest of the rocks found on the lower peninsula of Michigan. The upper peninsula of our State, as will be seen by the report of the State Geologist, is constituted of lower and still older rocks, and presents in consequence a very different aspect as well as a different mineral character from the lower peninsula.

The most important of the minerals usually associated with the rocks of those formations which compose lower or Michigan proper are iron and lead ores, coal, salt, gypsum and marls. There are no indications which would warrant the supposition that lead, in any valuable quantity, exists on the lower peninsula. At least it may be positively assumed that no ores of lead will be found throughout any of the present organized counties of the State. All the other minerals mentioned exist, and some of them, as has been shown, in great abundance. The results of the examinations into the economical geology of the State, as regards the most important of its minerals, I shall here briefly recapitulate.

IRON.—An ore of this mineral, under the form of kidney iron-stone, exists chiefly in the counties of Branch and Hillsdale. It is sufficiently extensive to be of much value, and will give an average yield of about 30 per cent. of metal. This ore is embraced in the clay formation described on page 250 of this report, and a more extended notice will be found in the geological report of 1840.

Iron, under the form of bog ores, is found in various parts of the State. The most extensive deposits, and those alone which it may be safe to assert will yield a rich profit, are at the county seat of Kalamazoo, near Concord, in Jackson county, in the county of Oakland, and perhaps Wayne. No furnaces for the reduction of these ores have yet been erected. It is shown by the late census, that there are 15 furnaces in the State for the casting of pig iron, requiring 614 tons, and the whole amount of iron imported, under various forms, is much greater. The cost of this importation, which in so heavy an article as iron is very considerable, might and ought to be saved to the State by a domestic manufacture from our own material. For more detailed observations, and an account of the localities in which this ore occurs, see geological report of 1840.

BITUMINOUS COAL will be found in abundance for all the wants of the State. The only locality where mining operations have been commenced is at Corunna, Shiawassee county, where this mineral has been already used to considerable extent, and though in the midst of a heavily timbered country is for many purposes preferred to wood or other combustible. Other points also, eligibly situated for the mining of coal, have been made known in Ingham, Eaton and Jackson counties, and it may be fairly inferred from the facts already determined of the range of coal bearing rocks, that outcrops of the coal beds will be found at numerous other points than those now known in these counties, and that coal will also be discovered in several counties where it is not now known to exist, as through parts of Kent, Ionia and Genesee counties. (See further, as to the lower coal beds, page 245 of this Report.)

SALT.—There no longer exists any doubt that this mineral may be obtained at a cheap rate and in any required quantity, for supplying the great and increasing demand in our State. The operations commenced at the State salt wells near Grand Rapids, Kent county, and on the Tittabawassee, Midland county, are not sufficiently advanced to determine the extent of the anticipated profit of the manufacture. The strongest brine obtained up to this time at the salt well of Mr. Lyon, at Grand Rapids, will, without doubt, prove as productive as that of the best wells of Ohio and Virginia. So that the present results may be considered as certainly indicative of the success that was formerly supposed would attend the boring for salt if properly conducted within our State.

Michigan *imports* salt probably to the amount of $300,000 annually, which large amount of money might, as it soon will, be saved to the State, by the supplies furnished from her own resources. The average price of salt at the ports of entry has been about three dollars per barrel for the last four years. But when the works now in progress shall have been brought into successful operation, supposing no stronger brine to be obtained than that above stated, the article of salt can be furnished at a much less price than it now costs the consumer.

GYPSUM.—An extensive deposit of this very valuable mineral occurs in the vicinity of Grand Rapids. The bed is here very extensive, is about six feet in thickness, and in quality is equal to the best gypsum of Nova Scotia. The same mineral is found elsewhere in our State, but this is by far the most important locality at present known, and one that affords every facility for quarrying and distributing the mineral over the State. A mill was erected during the past summer, and the ground plaster, for manure, is already manufactured in considerable quantities.

Though the above locality is the only one known at which gypsum occurs, in the interior of our State, yet from the ascertained geological character and dip of our rocks, and the associations of this mineral it may be presumed that gypsum and its associated marls will be hereafter disclosed at other points in the vicinity of the above bed, and that it will be found also to occur at other localities in the interior which are concealed from present observation.

SHELL MARL occurs in the greatest abundance throughout the State, but more especially among the marshes and lakes of the openings. It forms deposits, varying in extent from 1 acre to 100, and these are pretty widely distributed. Its exceeding great value and cheapness as a manure is far from being truly appreciated by our citizens. But the time is rapidly approaching when this invaluable mineral will be no longer despised because it is abundant, simple and cheap, and our State will then find in her numerous marl beds one of the richest treasures of which she is possessed. For a full account of the nature and uses of this mineral, the reader is referred to page 94 of the report of 1840, and to previous reports.

The character, applications and value of the rocks with which the above mentioned minerals are associated, together with other matters of practical interest connected with the geological structure of our State, are so fully detailed in the preceding pages and in previous reports, that further allusion to them in this place is deemed unnecessary.

From the foregoing facts it cannot fail to be seen that while the soils of our State are admirably adapted to the various purposes of agriculture, and for the production of wheat—the most important product of the soil—superior to those of any known portion of the Union, Michigan possesses also within herself all the mineral treasures that are really requisite for sustaining and renovating her soil, for supplying the wants of her homesteads, and for maintaining those branches of domestic industry which are of the most importance to her people. Thus science discloses those treasures buried in the earth which art and industry may appropriate to increase the profits of labor. And though the objects of science are general in their nature, and not confined by the limits of districts or states, the legislator feels a peculiar interest in having those resources developed by its aid, which may be turned to the advantage of his rising commonwealth; commerce, agriculture and the arts receive a stimulus by the new sources of wealth and supply which it opens to the wants of each. In this view the study of geology becomes one of the most universally useful that can occupy the attention of practical men.

In comparing the extent of our resources thus obtained with the little that was known concerning them a few years ago, we have reason to feel satisfied with the prospect of future wealth and importance which it has opened to us. If during the stirring times of an early settlement so rapid as has been that of our State for the past five years, less interest was excited by the development of our mineral resources than their importance might demand, a satisfactory cause may be found in the imperfect state of the knowledge hitherto obtained, and in the pressure of the more immediate wants of a new, somewhat fluctuating and unsettled community. During the period mentioned, however, the population of southern Michigan has advanced from a less number probably than 60,000 to 212,000, a rate of increase unexampled even in the annals of a series of settlements, to the progress of which the world affords no parallel. Meanwhile the liberal course of our State policy has been steadily unfolding her resources, and at this moment, notwithstanding the burden of a heavy debt, and the accumulated pressure of more widely felt financial difficulties, we are rapidly advancing in wealth, and are becoming awakened to the means of which we find ourselves possessed for successfully competing with older States, in the departments of agriculture, commerce and manufactures. With lands among the richest in the world, well watered and advantageously situated for market, with water power abundant, and with an extent of coast and facilities for water transportation unequalled by any other inland State, and added to this a population possessed of a large share of that character for enterprise which distinguishes their countrymen, nothing will tend more to give full efficacy and permanency to these advantages than to make more perfectly known the value of our mineral resources. Our State is now sufficiently advanced to be able to avail herself properly and with certainty of the advantages alluded to, and there is every reason to believe that these will not longer fail to command attention, and that the results will equal the most sanguine anticipations.

BELA HUBBARD,
Assistant Geologist.

No. 4—Report of S. W. Higgins, topographer of geological survey, Jan. 24, 1841, states that the topographer has in his present report brought together such observations relating to the magnetic variation in this State as will, he trusts, assist hereafter in affixing data to important facts:

The general law regulating the forces of magnetism with its direction and intensity has been untiringly studied, until by certain tests it has at last been discovered that palpable effects are produced by the magnet on all substances whether organic or inorganic, and there seem to be only two ways of accounting for the phenomena: "either that all substances in nature are susceptible of magnetism, or all possess particles of iron or some other magnetic metal from which this property is derived."

The obvious perturbations of the needle as seen in all situations at times arise from many small causes combined, and which, so far as they exert their force, influence the greater power of terrestrial magnetism, whereby it becomes proportionably feeble, as these combinations are multiplied. Atmospheric changes operate still further and in a more sudden manner to affect the needle, but the first causes mentioned are the most perplexing, and surveyors have attributed to local causes that which is found to be inherent in all substances.

The following single experiment will evince how far local causes are concerned in general. If a small needle be constructed of any substance and suspended between two magnets it will be found to fix itself in a line in the direction of the poles of the magnets, and the number of oscillations in a given time will usually determine in different needles the quantity of matter susceptible of magnetism in each; thus an important discovery has been made by means of this active principle, whereby is detected the least insensible traces of iron, when all other tests have failed.*

The opinion then is an erroneous one that mineral must always be present in masses to cause the aberrations of the needle. This is not necessary, nor is it the fact, for those minerals which are deeply buried can have no influence, inasmuch as their influence decreases inversely as the squares of the distance, and it may be said that the needle is wholly indeterminate in their neighborhood in respect to them, "since the resultant of magnetic forces being then vertical," or nearly so, or nothing, "the horizontal element would be nothing."

If it is true, as has already been abundantly proved, that magnetism, electricity and gravitation are governed by the same laws, and that they decrease in the ratio of the squares of their distances from attracting bodies, it becomes difficult to define what is meant by "local attraction," in the common

---

*Professor Farrer.

acceptation of the term, unless it be granted that the regions where it has been met with so commonly abound in ores or metallic substances to a great extent, or that it has been the misfortune of the surveyor to come so nearly in contact with mineral masses, above or near the surface of the earth, as to occasion the utter temporary loss of the polarity of the needle.

It may be laid down as a rule applicable hereafter in explanation of most of the deviations of the needle which occur in the central and western portions of the State (there being but few rocks in *situ* that appear on the surface, and those lime, slate and sand rock, and the geological structure of the peninsula being such as to preclude all opinion of there being ores or metals, or any kind of minerals, except bituminous coal, marl and the like, further than what is found in all alluvial and mountainless countries and there being an utter impossibility of any masses other than what may be eratic, capable of producing any great effect), that as the direction of the needle is the effect of a principal terrestrial force, its deviations arise only from those smaller secondary forces which we have said are inherent in all substances.

Many facts might be adduced in verification of the above supposition from the thousands of observations which have been made during the course of the surveys of the public lands in the State. Entire lines have been measured from the southern to the northern boundary of the peninsula across its whole breadth on true meridians, and these lines have again been intersected by others running east and west at right angles, each line having the magnetic variation recorded at intervals of every six miles, the points of intersection. Within the limits of these lines is included the whole area of the lower peninsula of Michigan (and by an exact enumeration of the meanders of the coast in the intervals between the terminations of these lines is obtained with the greatest accuracy the number of square miles it contains), now from the collected observations, after rejecting those east of the principal meridian, mentioned in my report of last year as erroneous—and a few others that might be specified which are made to correspond to the measurement of fractional lines— an area of 41,304 square miles is laid out with the accuracy of a map, and the magnetic meridians traced with the same facility as any other known and prominent feature; in fact we have a magnetic chart indicating the declination of the needle over this extensive region on parallels of equal distances of six miles.

Let us pause here a moment to satisfy the inquirer who may have doubted even the ordinary correctness of the observations generally obtained by the men whose duty it has been to establish the standard and other exterior lines in the survey of our State. To this end the two examples mentioned in another part of this report will be sufficient, though, as I have stated, others might with equal propriety be adduced. One of the examples consists of forty-nine townships, and the other of fifty townships.

These examples are all verified by actual measurement, and as it was to be expected, one of them falls a little short and the other has an excess, only of five links in a mile, above the convergence which all meridian lines have when run north. Now, if an error, the gross of which should amount to 15', had been made in their observations, the result would be a departure from parallelism in the lines of thirty-five links to a mile, whereas the result exhibits an error of less than 2' to a mile.

Now, it is obvious from the foregoing that there must be one of two conditions, which have given precision to the examples we have adduced; either the magnetic parallels have become greatly diminished in intensity and accommodated themselves to the plane of astronomical longitude, or care and skill have been exercised to modify the effects produced by them.

The latter condition is the true one, as we shall shortly demonstrate. We begin, then, at a point where the line of no variation passes out of Lake Huron, and first touches the south side of Drummond Island. This island is one of the northwesternmost of the chain of the Manitous, which divide the waters of the Straits of Ste. Marie. It first touches the island near the meander post on the shore, between ranges 7 and 8 east, in township 41 north, and is the tangent point to a curve of 4½ miles radius which it then makes on the island, the western extremity of the curve touching again the south shore of the island in the middle of the next township, in range 6 east, whence a reversed curve of 3¼ miles radius approaches closely to the corners and one-fifth of a mile south of fractional township 41 and 42, ranges 5 and 6 east, thence on a course south 85° west, 6 miles, intersecting township line 41 between ranges 4 and 5, near the meander post south shore of the island, which is another tangent point to a curve whose radius is 3¼ miles. Along this curve, at the distance of one mile, is the western end of the island, and at the meander post for fractional township 41 and 42, range 4 east; thence crossing the channel to the opposite side nearly, the curve terminates between Round Island and the main land of the upper peninsula, one-fourth of a mile from the shore; thence another reverse curve of 2¼ miles radius just sweeps along the edge of the shore northward of Pointe de Tour, the western termination of the curve being in a lake on the southwest corner of township 42 north, range 3 east; thence again the curve is reversed, whose radius is 2½ miles, crossing the south boundary of the same township 1¾ miles from its wes'ern boundary; whence the curve is again reversed, with a radius of 2¼ miles, passing off the coast into Lake Huron again, passing over one of the small islands near Massacre Island; thence ascending, it re-crosses the south boundary of township 41 north, in range 2 east, between sections 33 and 34; thence curving north-westerly with a radius of 6¼ miles it crosses the town line between ranges one and two east, 1¾ miles from south boundary; still slightly curving northwardly, on a course of 12 miles, it crosses north boundary line of township 43, range 1 east; thence two miles it intersects Monusco Bay, and curving westerly leaves the water and crosses the southeast corner of town 45, range 1 east, ¾ of a mile from corner post, into town 45, range 2 east; thence curving with a radius of 6½ miles, enters at the mouth of the Miscota Sawgee River the Canoe Channel of the Straits of Ste. Marie, and crosses it about one mile above the Nebish Rapids in that channel, touching the most westerly point of Great Sailor's Encampment Island, and keeping the western and northern shore with a curve whose radius is 8 miles; here its course is again reversed, and beyond this we have no sufficient data to pursue it farther.

It is believed, however, to pass directly on to the southwest point of Sugar Island, keeping along its westerly side, and crossing again the Straits of Ste. Marie on to the main land, at the forks of the Montreal Channel and Great Hay Lake, five miles east of the Saut de Ste. Marie; thence irregularly over the granite formations, and in conformity to the littoral features of Goulais and Batcheewauanung Bays, touching Michipicoten Harbor; thence, leaving the eastern end of Lake Superior, it has been said that it becomes forked, taking the circumference of Hudson's Bay, or that the variation is the same on the eastern and western sides of the bay.

We have now followed it from Drummond to Sugar Island through its actual and determined course, leaving nothing to conjecture; and we remark that for that distance it is as well determined as any other ascertained line.*

This line, before touching Drummond Island, where we first commenced with it, may with almost equal certainty be traced down along its southern course in and to the foot of Lake Huron, although for the reason that it is confined to the lake we may not always ascertain its distance from the shore.

The course it would now take in the diminished part of the lake, approaching the Straits of Mackinac would be somewhat analagous, it is presumed, to that in the Straits of Ste. Marie. This fact is proved from observation, first on the Island of Mackinac on the west, and along the north-east and east shore of the peninsula south of and opposite Drummond Island. It makes a large curve, which approaches the end of

---

*The hour should be noted as 10 o'clock a. m. for observations on this line.

the lake, without touching Mackinac, and receding from it descends south-easterly to the termination on the coast, of the town line between ranges 4 and 5 east, in town 36 north, where the variation is 1° 55' east. The same variation is found at the termination of town line 34 north, ranges 6 and 7 east; thence east eight miles, at Presque Isle, it is imperceptible. On Thunder Bay Point it is 45' east, the line of no variation passing between the light-house on the outermost Thunder Bay island, four miles from the shore, and this point; its course thence is to the outlet of the lake, near Fort Gratiot, where it crosses into Upper Canada..

From the fact that the line of no variation passes through a part of our State, we are in some measure better able to determine the *rationale* of another system of curves found elsewhere on the peninsula, particularly on its western side, at the Great and Little Pointe aux Sable, where a greater intensity is observable on approaching Lake Michigan from the east.

Under the ordinary ideas of magnetism it would not have been believed that a line so curved as we have described could have existed, without ascribing its irregularity to some corresponding cause of local force.

Although the upper peninsula of Michigan differs from the lower in regard to its geological features, the conclusion might be drawn that at the line of junction of the rocks of the Riviere Ste. Marie, as described in your third annual report, where it is well defined as at and through the outlet of the lake, the magnetic lines would be deflected somewhat with the line of bearing of these rocks in a distance of thirty miles, but its course on the contrary appears to be independent of them, crossing them at right angles, and without regard to their character.

Another peculiarity is that corresponding curves exterior to the line of no variation on either side bear no comparison. At the head of Great Sailor's Encampment Island, at the distance of two miles west, the variation is 1° 10' east; and opposite the middle of the same island, at one mile east of the line, it is 40' west; at five miles, 1° west, and at six miles, 1° 10' west; one mile south of Monusco Bay, the distance of one and a quarter miles east of it, the variation is 1° west; five miles west, 2° 35' east only, and the curve mentioned as again entering the lake between towns 2 and 3, as well as the curve which passes around the edge of the shore above Pointe de Tour, have no variation at their centres, but on approaching either way, east or west, variation increases to 30', and then again decreases to 0, on touching the line of the curve.

The same peculiarities are observed on the western side of the lower peninsula, particularly at Great and Little Pointe aux Sable, where the intensity increases, and the curves, though larger, exhibit as little conformity. It is evident that the needle "hauls to the land," to use a nautical phrase, for at these points the increase of variation amounts to 3° in thirty miles, exceeding 6° at the points, while the increase is but 1° for the whole breadth of Lake Michigan, the variation being but 7° in Wisconsin on the opposite shore.

The instrument used in ascertaining the particulars we have been stating, is one totally different in its principles and construction from the common compass, and is not even dependent for its accuracy on the needle. It was invented by Judge Burt, of Macomb county, and the Messrs Burt have given me the results of observations made by them with this instrument during most of the last summer. The needle is used with this compass only when the sun is obscured by clouds; when the sun shines the needle is screwed fast, and the time then consumed in obtaining the true meridian is not longer than that ordinarily taken by a needle to settle, while it is infinitely more correct.

I had intended to have given a description of this valuable invention, but to do this clearly without an accompanying drawing was found impracticable. It is called the "solar compass," and consists chiefly of three arcs, one of which is graduated to the ecliptic, the other to the complement of latitude, and the third to the sun's declination, whereby, if the latitude be known, the others are known, viz., the sun's

FIRST GEOLOGICAL SURVEY OF MICHIGAN. 273

declination and the apparent time, and consequently the magnetic variation; or if the sun's declination only be known, then the latitude and the others are known; or if the time be known the others can be ascertained by an almost instant adjustment.

We have not only now been enabled to adduce facts confirmatory of the general principles of terrestrial magnetism, but to enter considerably into detail on the subject of magnetic variation. A variety of reasons seemed to require this, the principal of which was the definite course obtained of the line of no variation, and the consequent illustration of other lines on either side of it being also irregular, demonstrating a system of curves, and a series of distinct and separate centres of attraction. This has been effected over no very limited space, and is free from all that might be considered empirical.

It is believed that in accuracy and fullness of detail these observations exceed all that has been hitherto attained, nor am I aware that the line of no variation was ever before traced continuously for any great distance, or that other observations have been taken than at those points where it has been crossed by the surveyor or mariner.

It has been pretty well determined by Professor Loomis, of Western Reserve College, Ohio, that the "present annual changes of variation, caused by the retrograde motion of the needle, which commenced everywhere as early as 1819, and in some places as early as 1793, is about 2' for the southern States, 4' for the middle and western States, and 6' for the New England States." This is true in general of the magnetic lines in this State where they are at a distance from the line of no variation, as at Detroit. Here the decrease or amount of retrograde motion is $4\frac{4}{10}'$ annually; the line of no variation has been quite stationary, at least for the last eight years, at points where it was known at that period. While, therefore, we observe a greater intensity as we approach nearer to the line of no variation, we likewise observe the distance to increase between the lines of equal variation, and while the first is stationary the latter is retrograding.

(18)

While the parallelism which takes place in needles proves that the magnetic force of the terrestrial globe may, like that of gravitation, act in parallel lines, we see also an exception. The lines of gravitation are always perpendicular to the surface of the sphere, while the lines of magnetism, which like gravitation, never cross each other, are composed of every variety of curve.

Though the diffusion of magnetism be general it is by no means equal. It is found at the equator and at the poles, an interposed space equal to the earth's radii, and for this space no loss is apparently felt in its force, and it is not more difficult to conceive an exerting force through this or a greater interposed space than that the hand should communicate motion to a stone with which it is demonstrably not in contact.

If then magnetism be a real power, at what distance does it terminate? Can we give it an inferior level, and determine its final bounds, connected with solar light and heat? Does it not emanate from, and is it not governed by that great central source, the sun, which controls the more palpable and grosser materials of which the planetary system is composed, which effects every change either in the interior or exterior of this globe, and to which every element is subject, and by which are conducted in silent processes all changes and revolutions since time began?

ELEVATION AND DEPRESSION OF THE WATER IN THE GREAT LAKES.—The last year is the second since the unusual elevation of the waters of the lakes; since which time there has been yearly a remarkable coincidence in the ratio of their subsidence, the more unlooked for, when taken in connection with the causes which tend to equalize the amount of falling water, in the form of rain, snow, and dew, with the constant action of evaporation.

In bodies of water like these lakes, slight changes in the seasons produce visible effects, in as much as they have no equalizing under-currents.

The quantity of rain must have been much less, and the evaporation more, than for many years past, to have produced the decrease mentioned below. This decrease amounts in the first year to one-quarter of the total rise, and in the second to one-half, making the proportion each year as thirty-three to forty-four nearly.

The maximum of August, 1838, was five feet three inches above that of 1819; that of 1839, three feet eleven inches; and that of 1840, two feet seven and one-half inches. The ratio of decrease, therefore, between the highest water in 1838 and 1839, is one foot four inches; and between the highest water in 1839 and 1840, one foot three and one-half inches.

Its rate of decrease is much more rapid than that of its increase from 1819 to 1838. In 1830 it was only two feet above the level of 1819; in 1836, three feet eight inches; having risen one foot eight inches in six years. In 1837, it was four feet three inches; increase, seven inches; in June, 1838, five feet; increase, nine inches; and, in August of the same year, five feet three inches. Having been nineteen years in attaining the maximum of five feet three inches, and only two years in reducing that height one-half, or to the average year of 1833. Thus the rapidity of its decrease in two years, equals the increase of five years.

I have not been able to ascertain whether the decrease of former years was thus sudden, or whether the period of the minimum, or lowest stage of water, continues for any great length of time; it is quite probable, however, that it does, and that the overflowing of the lands caused by the maximum rise, is but temporary, and only for one year, whence immediately commencing its decrease, it arrives very soon at its former standard, and remains there with little variation. Indeed, this is the more probable, from the example of the last three years, and from the appearance of long and undisturbed processes in the growth of trees and vegetation, with the formation of permanent channels in the interim, as well as the security felt by those who have erected buildings and planted orchards formerly, upon those lands which were inundated.

The diminution in a given quantity of water, exceeds by evaporation, all the supplies which it receives from rain, that is, the average amount of falling water is equal per year to 33 inches; evaporation will reduce it to 44 inches, when fully exposed to the sun and air. One season of extreme drouth would, upon the expanse of these lakes, produce an extreme depression, while the contrary would have the effect of producing a corresponding rise. It cannot be a matter of so much astonishment that such expanded areas of water, subject to such influences, should be greatly affected; the wonder is, that they do not oftener present greater fluctuations than they do, the equal and almost unvarying stage at which we find them is due to the uniformity of the seasons, and the systematic order in which nature is conducted in all her works.

The semi-annual alternations observable in summer and winter, arise from other and well known causes. In summer, the supply is unchecked, and the consequence is, an increase to the height of 30 inches, or thereabouts; when in winter, these supplies are again checked, a consequent depression follows. Measurements to ascertain exactly these semi-annual fluctuations, have never been thought necessary. Besides, it is not uncommon for ice, in large bodies, to collect at the outlets of the lakes, and, for the time, prevent the usual discharge, and a lower stage of water is the consequence, than otherwise would be. When this occurs in the chain of lakes, as it frequently does at the outlet of Lake Huron, in connection with a west wind, as in 1824 and 1831, it diminished the depth of the Detroit river, opposite the city, to over ten feet, widening the beach more than twenty rods, and making it practicable, (except in the immediate channel,) to cross without danger, on foot, from the American side, to Isle au Cochons or Hog Island; and a further proportional decrease took place in Lakes Erie and Ontario, while the pent up water flowed back into Lakes Huron and Michigan. For these reasons, and the want of uniformity in the temperature of the winter months, the minimum height is not to be depended upon.

Besides all this, the effect of winds sometimes acts in favor, as well as against, the other irregularities. The geographical position of the lakes is such, that, allowing them to prevail from the same point, at the same time over them all, (which is, by no means, always the case,) they produce a variety of results. A west wind forces the water of Lake Erie into the Niagara River, at the same time the waters from the foot of Lakes Huron and Michigan are forced into the Straits of Mackinac, and these again are met by the waters of Lake Superior through the Straits of Ste. Marie. Hence the straits which connect Lakes Huron and Erie have all the indications of a tide, though irregular as to time as well as to the amount of its elevation and depression, and it has often both risen and fallen in about the same proportion, and sometimes in the same period, as the lunar tides in those rivers which empty into the ocean. But whenever these tides take place either in the lakes themselves or in the straits connecting them, they are fortuitous and are the results of accidental disorder, common throughout the lake region.

Another feature may be observed of the lakes, different in nothing from the ground swell of the ocean—the reaction of the water—after having been pressed by the wind for a few days or hours in one direction.

The most favorable points for noticing this reaction is at an inlet or bay; Lake Superior which has the largest surface, presents the most marked traits. Here, while the explorations by the geological corps were in progress the past season at the mouth of the Grand Marais River, which empties into a bay one mile wide and two miles long, having an outlet of a quarter of a mile wide into the lake, was observed the returning waters from the west, in wide undulations. The effect upon the smooth surface of the bay was a gentle elevation, which arose to one foot or more for a period of fifteen minutes, then subsiding, again returned at equal intervals of time, until the lake, after a lapse of a few hours, resumed its natural level.

Table of Elevation and Depression in the Waters of the Lakes, Compared with that of June 1, 1819.

			–	Feet.	Inches	Feet.	Inches
1838.	August	21	Highest stage of water			5	3
1839.	January	1	Decrease	3	8	1	7
	July	31	Highest stage			3	11
1840.	January	30	Decrease	3	2		9
	July	4	Highest stage			2	7½
1841.	January	1	Decrease	2	1		6½

DETAIL OF THF ELEVATION AND DEPRESSION FOR 1840.

				Feet.	Inches	Feet.	Inches	Feet.	Inches
1840.	January	30	Height of water						9
	April	25	Increase	1	5	2	2		
	May	9	" Rain and wind from N.E., fluctuations from 15 to 18 in		1½	2	3½		
	"	19	" Same		1½	2	1½		
	June	8	" Wind west, season dry and hot		1	2	4½		
	July	4	" Light showers, weather same as last observation		3	2	7½	2	7½
	"	22	Decrease, much rain in June and July, on Lake Superior		3½	2	4		
	September	1	" Season dry, little rain		2	2	2		
	"	13	"		½	2	½		
	"	20	" Wind west, river fell suddenly		4½	1	9		
	October	1	Increase, heavy rain last 24 hours		4	2	1		
	"	12	Decrease		3½	1	9½		
	"	29	" Moderate		½	1	9		
	November	10	Increase, do		1½	1	10½		
	"	24	Decrease, freezing, wind moderate from west		4½	1	6		
	December	10	Increase, ice made in river in considerable quantities		½	1	6½		
	"	21	Decrease, river blocked up by ice, no wind		2	1	4½		
1841.	January	1	" River nearly closed, wind moderate from west		10		6½		6½

January 5, 1842, the State Geologist sent to the legislature a report relative to the State salt springs (six pages).

In this he states that the work which for more than eighteen months had been arrested had been again commenced, and up to a very recent day has been continued according to the provisions of the contracts; that it will be indispensable to continue the borings until the shafts shall have passed very nearly through the lower salt rocks, before brine of the maximum strength can be looked for. At the point selected for the State well, on Grand River, it is estimated that the shaft should be sunk to the depth of 700 feet, and at Tittebawasse River to a depth in round numbers of 600 feet.

That at the State salt springs on Grand River the upper salt rock had been perforated, followed by an abundant supply of salt water, but that no attempt had yet been made to separate the salt water from admixture of fresh. That at 300 feet the amount of salt water flowing from the nine inch tube was by actual measurement found to be 130 gallons per minute, an amount almost incredibly large, and unequalled by any rock boring in any other portion of the United States. Analysis of this mixed water shows that $110\frac{1}{2}$ gallons contains a bushel of salt. These facts sustain the original position assumed relative to the salt deposits of our State.

After comparing the strength of the brine at the State wells with the best salt wells of New York, Virginia and elsewhere, the Geologist adds: "The improvement of our State salines has now progressed so far as to satisfy the most sceptical of actual success. And it is hardly necessary to call your attention to the great importance or the necessity of speedy completion."

280   APPENDIX.

FIFTH ANNUAL REPORT.

On January 27, 1842, was sent to the legislature the fifth annual report of the State Geologist (six pages).

It states that the communication will be confined almost exclusively to the condition and wants of the department. That the field work of the geological and topographical surveys upon the plan originally contemplated is mainly completed, but that in consequence of the small amount of funds applicable the amount of work accomplished has been less than that of the preceding year. That the labor so applied has been chiefly devoted to the westerly portion or mountainous district of the upper peninsula.

That in connection with duties assigned him relative to the boundary line between Michigan and Wisconsin, he has been enabled to complete a very perfect geological section of nearly 180 miles in length, crossing from the mouth of Montreal River to the mouth of Menominee River of Green Bay.

"In addition to several geological sections completed, all the rivers entering Lake Superior have been carefully examined to their very sources, and the Porcupine Mountains have been traced out through almost the entire range. The results of these surveys have served to add confidence to our previously expressed opinion respecting the value of that part of our State. The copper ores associated with the altered conglomerate and sandstone rocks in *this* portion of the range have been found to be more extensive than has been originally supposed."

In speaking of the limits of the southerly range, within which falls the lead district of Wisconsin and Iowa, the report says: "It should be recollected that the outer or northern range of mountains of Lake Superior constitute what has been called the true copper district, and that in this district no lead and none of the ores of which sulphur is a constituent have been noticed, while in the southern range in Michigan the ores are almost entirely sulphates, and lead occurs more abundantly than copper. Thus far I have been unable to trace any portion of the great limestone formation of the upper peninsula to any near proximity to this range, where the same traverses that portion of Michigan, and in tracing the range westwardly no considerable deposits of lead have been found until the lower rocks are covered by heavy deposits of limestone, which would lead to the inference that these upper deposits have performed an important part in arresting and fixing the minerals referred to (minerals associated with the lead ores), and which minerals may fairly be inferred to have had their origin from the lower rocks to which reference has been made."

The report alludes to the very great assistance derived from the Honorable William A. Burt, who during the last two years has been engaged in surveying the United States Township lines.

Of the drafting from the field notes, Dr. Houghton states, that since in the topographical department there has been only a single assistant, the amount of drafting has continued to accumulate upon his hands, and there yet remains an amount to be done which can scarcely be accomplished in an entire year. The fund applicable to these objects being absorbed there will be required a small appropriation. He enumerates six counties of which maps have been engraved, and says that had not the state of the Treasury made it impossible, these with thirteen others would have been published before this date.

On January 27th, 1843, the Geologist makes a report relative to the State salt springs, (6 pages.) (In conformity with an Act approved February 1st, 1842, which appropriated $15,000 for the improvement of the State salt springs.)

At the State salt springs on Grand River, Kent Co., the work has been nearly completed. The depth obtained is something over 800 feet, and is on the lower salt rock. Since the date of last report the quantity of water discharged has very considerably increased, and now exceeds 200 gallons per minute. As the water now flows from the iron tube it is mixed with all the fresh water entering the well above the upper salt rock, a difficulty which will be overcome by proper tubing. In continuing the work it is of the utmost importance that the borings be carried entirely through the lower salt rocks, and then, and not until then, can the capacity of the well be fully determined. He adds, that it is now satisfactorily shown that the place of the salt water in the subcarboniferous rocks is as originally set forth, and that the supply of water is abundant, and further that the character of the brine is such as will admit of the manufacture of salt at such rates as will enable our citizens to compete with that manufacture abroad.

At the State salt well on Tittabawassee River, no further progress has been made, the reasons for which suspension are contained in section 708 of an Act relative to the State salt springs, approved Feb. 16, 1842.

THE SIXTH ANNUAL REPORT

of the State Geologist bears date February 10, 1843 (five pages). It sets forth the condition and progress of the geological survey of the State towards completion.

"Since the date of my last report I have been chiefly engaged in arranging and putting in shape the immense amount of details, both geological and topographical, which have accumulated; in analyzing and studying the immense collection of specimens illustrating the geology and mineralogy of our State, and in the chemical analysis of our soils, minerals and rock specimens." He announces the field work for the entire survey as now completed, with the exception of a few points where the work still wants connecting.

In the topographical office during a portion of the year the work was suspended in consequence of the absence of the topographer, who was engaged several months in locating lands for the State. Notwithstanding the work of drafting is so far advanced that a large portion is ready for the hands of the engraver.

"The publication of State and county maps as directed by the Legislature was long ago commenced, and the engraving of several of these maps had been completed before the date of my last report, but the inability to procure such funds as would purchase the paper has caused delay and in fact has for a time virtually suspended all action upon the subject." He adds—"This series of State and county maps, it is hoped and believed, will be more full and perfect than any which have heretofore been published of any equal portion of our United States, and there can be no doubt but when once placed before the public they will do much to disseminate a knowledge of the immense capabilities of our State and the advantages which she offers to the emigrant; and that they will in that way afford sufficient aid towards increasing her population. When the maps already engraved shall have been thrown before the public, it is hoped and believed that a sufficient amount will be received from their sale to enable us to proceed with the engraving and publishing of the balance without further embarrassment, and that they will more than pay the expenses incident to their publication.

"The engraved plates of these maps will remain nearly as perfect after the proposed edition shall have been worked off as they were at first, and as other editions may from time to time be wanted, the names of newly organized towns, new roads, etc., may be added without difficulty, at a mere nominal expense, and without interfering with the method adopted for exhibiting on them the soils and timber, and the geological and topographical features of the country."

The report thus concludes: "The geological and topographical surveys of our State, which have been carried forward by a corps few in number compared with that furnished by any other State, and extending over an area greater than that claimed by any of them, has been a work of immense labor. To accomplish the end desired the most constant and untiring industry has been required, added to which it has been necessary during protracted periods in the wilderness country to dispense with the ordinary comforts of life, but the labor has been rendered light with the hope that in aiding to develop the resources of our State, in placing upon maps her geology, topography, and the character of her timber and soils, her settlements might be increased and something added to her prosperity and wealth."

THE SEVENTH ANNUAL REPORT

of the State Geologist was sent to the legislature February 15, 1844. It states that "a portion of the season has been devoted to connecting the work on the upper peninsula and completing the skeleton of the surveys of that part of the State, but by far the greater amount of work has been performed in the office, in compiling and arranging the materials for the final report, and in the completion of the maps, together with the figuring of sections and fossils illustrative of the several groups of rocks of our State.

"The drafting of the county maps according to the plan directed has mainly been performed, and excepting some slight addition, these are now ready for the engraver. Of the county maps four have been struck off and are now in the market. Ten additional counties are to be placed in the engraver's hands, and I hope to be able to lay the maps of these fourteen counties, together with the State map, before the public at an early day in the ensuing spring.

"An appropriation of $1,000 to $1,500 will cover all that will be required to be paid out of the treasury before a sufficient amount will be realized from the sales to enable the work to progress without further demand upon the treasury, and I confidently believe that the proceeds of the sales of these maps will fully refund to the State the cost of their publication.*

---

*Regarding thes maps it is proper to say that none of the county and State maps since published on private speculation at all compare in accuracy and amount and value of detail with those prepared and ready for publication under Dr. Houghton· such civil features as the progress of improvement have since added of course excepted. It is greatly to be regretted that lack of interest, or parsimony on the part of officials, should have rendered useless to the public materials and work obtained at such great cost and with such commendable enterprise.

"In addition to the ordinary duties of the survey, the extra duty required at your last session of furnishing the State land office with township maps, has been performed so far as calls have been made by the State commissioners.

"The engraving of the geological sections, fossils, etc., will occupy some time, and it is desirable in order to prevent delay that this portion of the work of the final report should be commenced at the earliest day possible. In order to hasten this the Geologist adds: "I have made a temporary arrangement for the wood cuts with a wood engraver who is fully competent, and who is now engaged in this duty, but in order to continue this work some provision will be necessary."

Dr. Houghton thus refers to the results which he hoped to accomplish by means of the connected geological and linear surveying which he had projected.

"While in the survey of the upper peninsula it is very desirable that the grand outlines should be filled up with more minuteness than has hitherto been done, to develop its topography, geology and mineralogy, in such a manner as its great importance and the intrinsic value of its mineral treasures make desirable, it would require a larger amount of expenditure than our State is well able to appropriate to that object. The United States linear surveys afford a fine opportunity for accomplishing this in a way which will render the work exceedingly perfect, and at the same time will be attended with little expense. I hope to perfect such an arrangement (the connecting of the United States surveys with the geological surveys of Michigan) through the co-operation of the commissioners of the general land office, as will enable me to provide more perfect geological and topographical maps of the upper peninsula than have ever been constructed of the same extent of territory in our United States. In addition to such provisions as you may see fit to make for the engraving of the several county maps, the wood engraving and publication, there will be required for current expenses of the survey during the ensuing year an amount not exceeding $400."

DOUGLASS HOUGHTON,
State Geologist.

In his "Outlines of the Political History of Michigan," page 489, Judge Campbell says, relative to the materials for the final report:

"The general financial depression prevented any extensive work after 1841, and in the careless management of some of the State property after Dr. Houghton's death, all of his engravings, which were numerous and very beautiful, and many of his collections which had been left in the State offices before their removal to Lansing, disappeared.

"Dr. Houghton had, before his death, secured the services of Mr. Beneworth, a wood engraver whose marvellous skill had obtained him honorable testimonials in Holland, London and Germany, and who executed some of those minute gems of engraving which beautify Harper's Bible. This artist had become desirous of seeing the New World, and was disposed to set out for the undefined West, of which he had very vague notions, when Dr. Houghton found him in New York, and being mutually interested he was induced to enter upon the work of engraving the illustrations which would be needed for the final report. The blocks were engraved and left with uncut margins to prevent abrasions, and in this condition deposited for safe keeping with one of the State officers. Besides these, Mr. Higgins had drawn carefully on stone a large number of fossils and other specimens, and several maps were engraved; all have been lost. Their money value was not less than many thousands of dollars; their artistic as well as scientific value cannot be reckoned."

PART VI.

A Connected History of Geological Explorations in Michigan Since the First Organized Survey.

A brief but connected statement of the progress of geological investigation in our State since the death of Dr. Houghton cannot but interest the reader and serve to render our Summary complete.

A Connected History of Geological Explorations and Publications Regarding Michigan, Following Those of the First State Survey.

PAMPHLET BY JACOB HOUGHTON.

In 1846 appeared a bound pamphlet entitled "The Mineral Region of Lake Superior," by Jacob Houghton, Jr., and F. W. Bristol. It contained reports of Mr. Wm. A. Burt and Bela Hubbard on the geography, topography and geology of the United States Surveys of the mineral region of the south shore of Lake Superior, for 1845.

(19)

It was accompanied by a list of organized mining companies and of mineral locations, and a *correct map of the mineral region;* also a chart of Lake Superior.

The appearance of the above mentioned reports of Burt and Hubbard is explained by the following communication:

DETROIT, Feb. 16, 1846.

TO THE HON. LUCIUS LYON,
    Surveyor General, etc:

SIR,—By contract with the commissioners of the general land office, under date of June 25, 1844, the late Dr. Douglass Houghton was required to make both a linear and a geological survey of a section of country bordering on the south shore of Lake Superior. He was engaged in this work at the time of his lamented death. As administrators of his estate we have caused the field notes and papers connected with the survey as far as completed to be carefully examined, and the accompanying reports of Messrs. William A. Burt and Bela Hubbard to be prepared. Mr. Burt, who was the principal assistant of Dr. Houghton in the field, reports in full as to that portion of the country surveyed by him, and Mr. Hubbard, assistant State geologist, has prepared a like full report upon the remainder of the surveyed territory, from the field notes of the survey and the specimens collected. It would not be expected that the information contained in these reports would be as complete and as accurate in detail as it would have been could they have been prepared by Dr. Houghton himself. Enough, however, will appear to enable the Government to appreciate both the advantages and the perfect feasibility of the plan of connecting geological with the linear surveys of government lands, as originally proposed and zealously advocated by Dr. Houghton.

    (Signed)   Respectfully yours,
                               HENRY A. WALKER,
                               SAMUEL P. DOUGLASS.

The report of William A. Burt embraces Keweenaw Point and the tract of country bordering the coast from Chocolate to Carp Rivers, and extending a length of 120 miles, being the district over which he had run the township lines. He gives the highest elevations as 900 feet above Lake Superior, describes the courses of the mountain ranges, the harbors, rivers, soil and timber, and the general geology.

The report of Bela Hubbard embraces 37 townships, namely, eight at and west of Chocolate River, three at head of Keweenaw Bay, and the remainder include Keweenaw Point north of Portage River, being the district sub-divided in 1845 under the direction of Dr. Houghton, deputy surveyor.

It includes a description of the granite and metamorphic rocks, dividing the latter into quartzite and trappose portions.

The first named or more southerly portion is composed of white and brown quartz rocks, talcose, volitic and clay slates, slaty hornblende, and specular and micaceous oxides of iron. These rocks are throughout pervaded by the argillaceous red and micaceous oxides of iron, sometimes intimately disseminated, and sometimes in beds or veins. The two largest beds noticed are in town 47, north, range 26 west, and made up almost entirely of granulated, magnetic and specular iron.

The most northerly of these hills of ore extend nearly east and west at least one-fourth of a mile, with a breadth little less than 1,000 feet, the whole of which forms a single mass of ore, with occasional thin strata of imperfect chert and jaspar, and dips north ten degrees east, about thirty degrees. "This bed of iron," the report states, "will compare favorably both for extent and quality with any known in our country."

This report contains the first published account of the iron ore beds of Michigan. The clay slates of the red sand rock, which is considered as the equivalent of the Potsdam of New York, are described, and the general character of the geology of the Keweenaw Point district, its traps, conglomerates and sandrocks and mineral veins. In regard to the latter, the report states that the courses of many veins have been fixed with accuracy, and the veins themselves traced in some instances for several miles across the conglomerate and sandrocks, and into and across some portions of the trap. The observations thus made are confirmatory of the fact, first noticed by Dr. Houghton, that the true veins of the district referred to pursue a course nearly at right angles to the line of bearing of the trap range.

The report closes with appropriate observations upon the advantages resulting from the new system as devised and prosecuted by Dr. Houghton, of the union of geological with the lineal surveys, of which the first experimental results are now returned. And it calls attention to the unwonted accuracy with which the lines have been run. This is due to the exclusive use of Burt's solar compass. Nearly the whole region subdivided abounds with mineral attractive to the magnet, and a variation fluctuating from six to twenty degrees on either side of the true meridian was not uncommon through the length of an entire township.

Professor A. Winchell, State Geologist of 1861, referring to these reports of Messrs. Burt and Hubbard says: "These two reports unfold in an admirable manner the geological structure of the trap and metamorphic regions of Lake

Superior, and anticipate results which were subsequently worked out by the United States Geologists."

The pamphlet above mentioned was followed in July of the same year, 1846, by a somewhat larger and more extended edition by Jacob Houghton, Jr. It comprised, in addition to the matters contained in the previous volume, a brief sketch of the early history of the mineral regions, and the report of the State Geologist of 1841 in full.

May 15, 1846, the legislature of Michigan passed a joint resolution authorizing and empowering the Governor of the State to select and appoint some competent person to collect, collate and arrange all the geological notes, memoranda, specimens, maps, engravings and drawings, including geological surveys, kept, made, collected and preserved for and in behalf of the State by the late Dr. Houghton, State Geologist, and designed and intended by him to be used in making a final report for the benefit of the people of said State, and from the materials thus collected, and the requisite additional information derived from other sources, to prepare a final report upon the geology of Michigan.

No appropriation seems to have accompanied the above resolutions, and it may have been for that reason and for some objection or inability to apply to the purpose intended any portion of the contingent fund, that. Gov. Felch failed to give effect to the Act of the legislature embodying the wishes of the people of Michigan. No person was appointed by the Governor under this resolution, nor were any steps taken to carry out its provisions.

Fifteen years exactly after the last official act of Dr. Houghton as State Geologist of Michigan, an Act was passed by the legislature, approved Feb. 18, 1859, entitled, "An Act to Finish the Geological Survey of the State."

This Act authorized and directed the Governor to appoint some suitable person to finish the geological survey of the State, with maps and diagrams, and a full scientific description of its rocks, soils and its botanical and natural productions. The Governor was also authorized to appoint competent assistants. It appropriated the sum of $2,000 for the year 1860, and requires the geologist in charge to report to the legislature that should be in session.

Under this Act Prof. Alex. Winchell, of the State University, received the appointment of State Geologist, and his first biennial report of the progress of the geological survey, embracing observations on the geology, zoology and botany of the lower peninsula, was made Dec. 31, 1860, and was published by the State, Lansing, 1861.

FIRST BIENNIAL REPORT OF PROF. WINCHELL, 1860.

In the introduction of the report the Geologist recounts the action theretofore taken by the State in relation to a geological survey, and does full justice to the labors of Dr. Houghton, and his assistants, of whose reports a complete *resume* is given.

In addition to the 190 pages devoted to the geology, are reports of Dr. M. Miles, State Geologist (part 2 zoology), accompanied by a catalogue of mammals, birds, reptiles and Molusks of Michigan. This catalogue contains about one-third more species than those enumerated by Dr. Sager in his report of 1838. Part 3, botany, contains a valuable list of plants of the State, occupying 84 pages, compiled from all the sources within reach.

In his introduction Prof. Winchell thus alludes to the explorations conducted by the United States government in the Lake Superior region of Michigan.

Little more than a year after the suspension of the survey under Dr. Houghton, congress passed an Act, approved March 1, 1847, embracing provisions for the geological exploration of Lake Superior land district, organized by the same Act. Under this Act, Dr. C. T. Jackson was appointed by the Secretary of the Treasury to execute the required survey.

After having spent two seasons in the prosecution of this work, he presented a report of 800 pages and resigned his commission.

In the meantime the survey was continued and subsequently completed by Messrs. Foster and Whitney, United States Geologists. Their report of 224 pages on the "copper lands" was submitted as "Part No. 1, April 15, 1850." Part 2, on the iron region and general geology, was submitted Nov. 12, 1851, and forms a volume of 406 pages, with 25 plates. The fossiliferous region was passed upon by Prof. James Hall, the veteran paleontologist, of New York, whose observations and conclusions are embodied in the report, together with papers on the geology of Wisconsin, by Dr. J. A. Lapham and Col. Charles Whittlesey. The latter also communicated important chapters on the "observed fluctuations" of the surface of the lakes.

"The examinations reported in part 2 extended around the entire lake shores of the upper peninsula, as far as the head of Green Bay, and embrace the islands at the head of Lake Huron.

Parallelism was established between the geology of this lake region and that of New York.".

Previous to the passage of the Act, March, 1847, by congress, the United States Surveyor General, anxious to continue the plan of the union of the geological with the linear surveys, first suggested and afterwards successfully begun by Dr. Houghton in 1846, commissioned Mr. Bela Hubbard to receive the reports and specimens and continue the geological investigations over the region on Lake Superior then being subdivided in the progress of the United States linear surveys.

Mr. Hubbard's report upon the geology of the district thus surveyed in 1846, was returned to the general land office, together with the regular returns of the linear surveys, but no official publication was known to have been given.

INAUGURATION OF NEW STATE GEOLOGICAL SURVEY.

Ten years after the Act of February, 1859, of the legislature of Michigan, re-establishing the State geological survey, under which Act only a single year's report of progress was made, a new survey was inaugurated by Act of March 26, 1869. This Act established a board of geological survey, consisting of the Governor, the president of the board of education, and superintendent of public instruction, to control and complete the geological surveys of the State, the board to appoint a suitable person as director, salaries of the director and his assistants to be fixed by the board; a report to be made to the board as often as possible, and on completion a complete memoir to be published. One-half of all appropriations to be expended in the upper peninsula. The Act appropriates $8,000 for each year of the survey. To this the board afterwards added $1,000 for chemical work.

Prof. A. Winchell was made director, but resigned in 1871, and the further prosecution of the work was done under the direction of the board.

Vol. I. and II. of this survey were published by authority of the legislature of Michigan, with an atlas of maps, and is confined to the upper peninsula. Twenty thousand dollars was appropriated for 2,000 copies in 1873. It consists of three parts, viz.:

Vol. I. Part 1—The Iron bearing Rocks, by T. B. Brooks (320 pages).

Part 2—Copper-bearing Rocks (economic), by Raphael Pompelly (140 pages).

Part 3—Palaeozoic Rocks, by Dr. Romminger (102 pages).

Vol. II consists of Appendices to part 1, Vol. I (292 pages).

These volumes, in addition to observations upon the age, structure and lithology of the rocks, contain a large amount of details connected with the development of the iron mines.

Mr. Brooks prefaces his report with an historical sketch of geological discovery and development. Alluding to the material which had been accumulated by the first State Geologist, he says: "Any one familiar with the geology of the upper peninsula who will peruse the manuscript notes left by Dr. Houghton will be convinced that his views regarding the geology of the older rocks were far in advance of his time, and such only as geologists years after he recorded them universally accepted."

Vol. III of this survey was published by the legislature in 1876. It is confined to the lower peninsula of Michigan.

This is by C. Romminger, and consists of 155 pages of text and 55 plates of fossils.

Part 1—Geology.

Part 2—Palaeontology.

It is accompanied by geological maps.

Vol. IV contains the geology of the upper peninsula, and was published in 1881. It is by C. Romminger.

Part 1—Marquette Iron Region.

Part 2—Menominee Iron Region.

The following correspondence, cut from a Detroit Journal of 1867, is here inserted, as indicating the interest early taken by citizens of Michigan in the subject out of which these "memorials" have grown. The list of names will revive the memory of many well known friends of Dr. Houghton.

LECTURE BY PROF. BRADISH.

By the accompanying correspondence it will be seen that Prof. Bradish will lecture at Young Men's Hall on Monday evening next, his subject being "A Biographical Sketch of the Late Dr. Douglass Houghton":

Professor A. BRADISH:

DEAR SIR:—Having understood that you have prepared a biographical sketch of the late Dr. Douglass Houghton, we would respectfully request you to give a public reading of it before the Young Men's Society of our city. Dr. Houghton's name is so closely connected with the interests of our state and city, which he did so much to further and advance, that his memory will always be honored among us. And it will give especially to his numerous personal friends in the society of which he was a principal founder, and in the community where he displayed so much public spirit, very great pleasure to have their recollections refreshed by a recital of his life and character. Your own position as his near connection, and an old fellow-citizen of our own, will add to the interest of the subject. We therefore beg leave to urge upon you a compliance with our request.

S. A. McCoskry,
Geo. Duffield,
Jno. S. Newberry,
James V Campbell,
Hovey K. Clarke,
Jacob M. Howard,
Sylvester Larned,
Elon Farnsworth,
D. C. Holbrook,
Henry B. Brown,
A. H. Redfield,
B. B. Noyes,
Jacob S. Farrand,
A. Sheley,
Fred. C. Wetmore,
Theo. H. Eaton,
Geo. E. Hand,
J. Owen,
W. Ingersoll,
F. Buhl,
D. Bethune Duffield,
Geo. V. N. Lothrop,
A. H. Adams,
Wm. A. Butler,
George Taylor,

Daniel J. Campau,
Henry Chaney,
Ross Wilkins,
Alfred Russell,
Wm. D. Wilkins,
Moses W. Field,
Samuel Lewis,
Alex Lewis,
Samuel Pitts,
E. C. Walker,
C. H. Buhl,
W. A. Moore,
R. McClelland,
Robt. E. Roberts,
S. T. Douglass,
H. N. Walker,
F. Norvell,
Francis Raymond,
D. Goodwin,
Jacob Houghton,
J. L. Whiting,
W. N. Carpenter,
P. E. DeMill,
C. C. Trowbridge,
T. H. Hinchman,

E. N. WILLCOX, H. T. STRINGHAM,
A. G. BOYNTON, Z. PITCHER,
SIDNEY D. MILLER, BELA HUBBARD.

DETROIT, Dec. 12, 1867.

To S. A. McCoskry, Geo. Duffield, Z. Pitcher, Ross Wilkins, and others:

GENTLEMEN :—Your letter of this date, in which you do me the honor to ask me to read a biographical sketch of the late Dr. Douglass Houghton, before the Young Men's Association of this city, I have just received. The expressions of your invitation are so kind and earnest, that I am again impressed with the universal esteem felt in this community for the memory of that distinguished citizen.

In reply, I beg to thank you for these expressions, and to say that it will give me great satisfaction to comply with your request.

I am, gentlemen, with much respect, your obedient servant,

ALVAH BRADISH.

FULL LENGTH PORTRAIT OF DR. HOUGHTON—DESCRIPTION.

(See Frontispiece.)

The artist has represented the Geologist as standing on the rocky shore of Lake Superior. Much of his severe and perilous labors had been made in that region, and it was there that he closed his brilliant career. It is suitable, therefore that this able explorer should be represented in the midst of scenes that he had long been familiar with, and which his disastrous death has surrounded with a mournful interest. His dress as seen in this historical portrait is that of an outdoor geologist, a loose summer coat without vest, leather suspenders, pants of a lighter color, with high-top boots, suitable for wading in swamps and crossing deep streams. He is resting, as it were, from severe labor; his attitude is easy but emphatic; his looks are eager and penetrating; the expressions of his countenance are serene, but his brow and eyes indicate the anxious thoughts of a mind deeply moved by questions of science that press for solution. One arm is stretched out, the hand resting on the symbol of his profession, the geological hammer. The other holds to his side the well-remembered, crushed, rusty hat that had seen some rough service. The rocks are broken and shelve down to the water at his feet. These ledges are hardly concealed by wild vines and lichens, that spring from crevices and drape the rugged wall.

Back of this figure are seen the famous Pictured Rocks of Lake Superior, sacred to Indian song and tradition, and made classical by the pen of Gov. Cass. These rocky ledges form the main portion of the background of this historical portrait. A cloudy perturbed sky may prefigure that fatal storm that overwhelmed the Doctor in its fury, and the expanse of water leads the observer's eyes to the distant, lurid horizon.

An arched rock that would admit steamers under its lofty dome, headlands, deep rock cuttings, cascades and chasms diversify the scenery of this carefully studied portrait of the pioneer Geologist of Michigan. At his feet, looking over the water, stands his famous dog, "Meeme," a devoted friend that always accompanied Dr. Houghton in boat or on land, in storm or in sunshine. This faithful companion was with him in the boat on the night that proved fatal to his master, but was washed ashore.

It may not be unsuitable to say that the little favorite water-spaniel reached his home, Fredonia, N. Y., at last, survived several years, and is buried near the spot that his master had rendered memorable as the scene of his boyhood's struggles for supremacy, and his first inspirations in the cause of science.

www.ingramcontent.com/pod-product-compliance
Lightning Source LLC
Chambersburg PA
CBHW022043230426
43672CB00008B/1054